NICKELODEON

降世神通

AVATAR
THE LAST AIRBENDER

Created By
Michael Dante DiMartino &
Bryan Konietzko

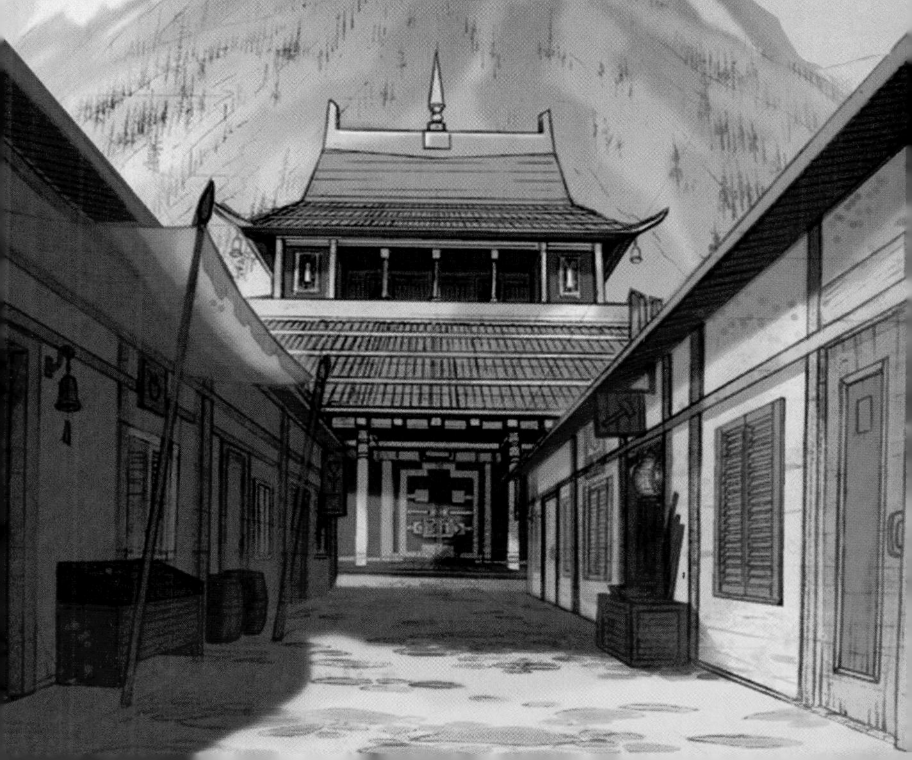

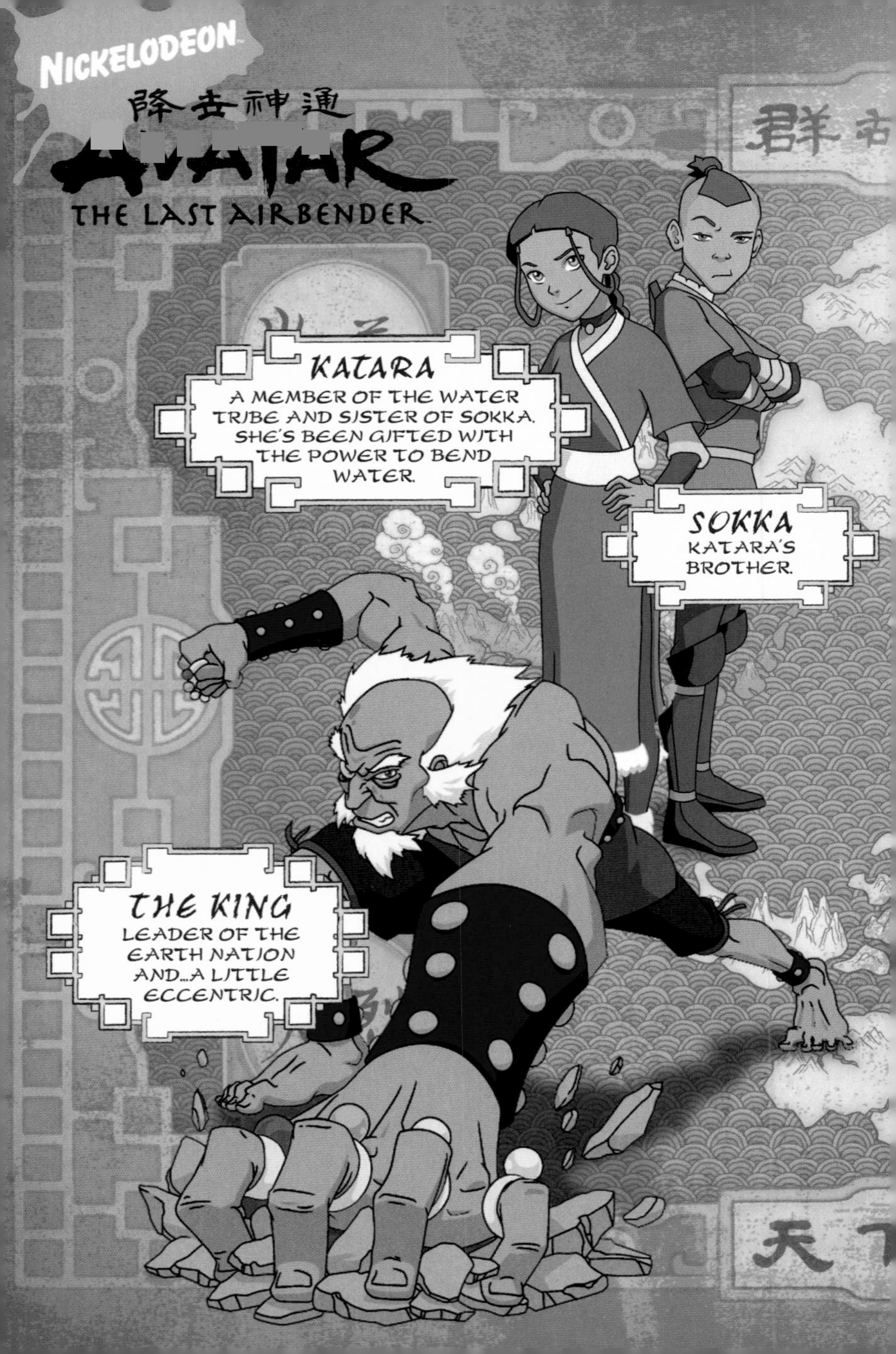
NICKELODEON
THE LAST AIRBENDER
KATARA
A MEMBER OF THE WATER TRIBE AND SISTER OF SOKKA. SHE'S BEEN GIFTED WITH THE POWER TO BEND WATER.
SOKKA
KATARA'S BROTHER.
THE KING
LEADER OF THE EARTH NATION AND...A LITTLE ECCENTRIC.

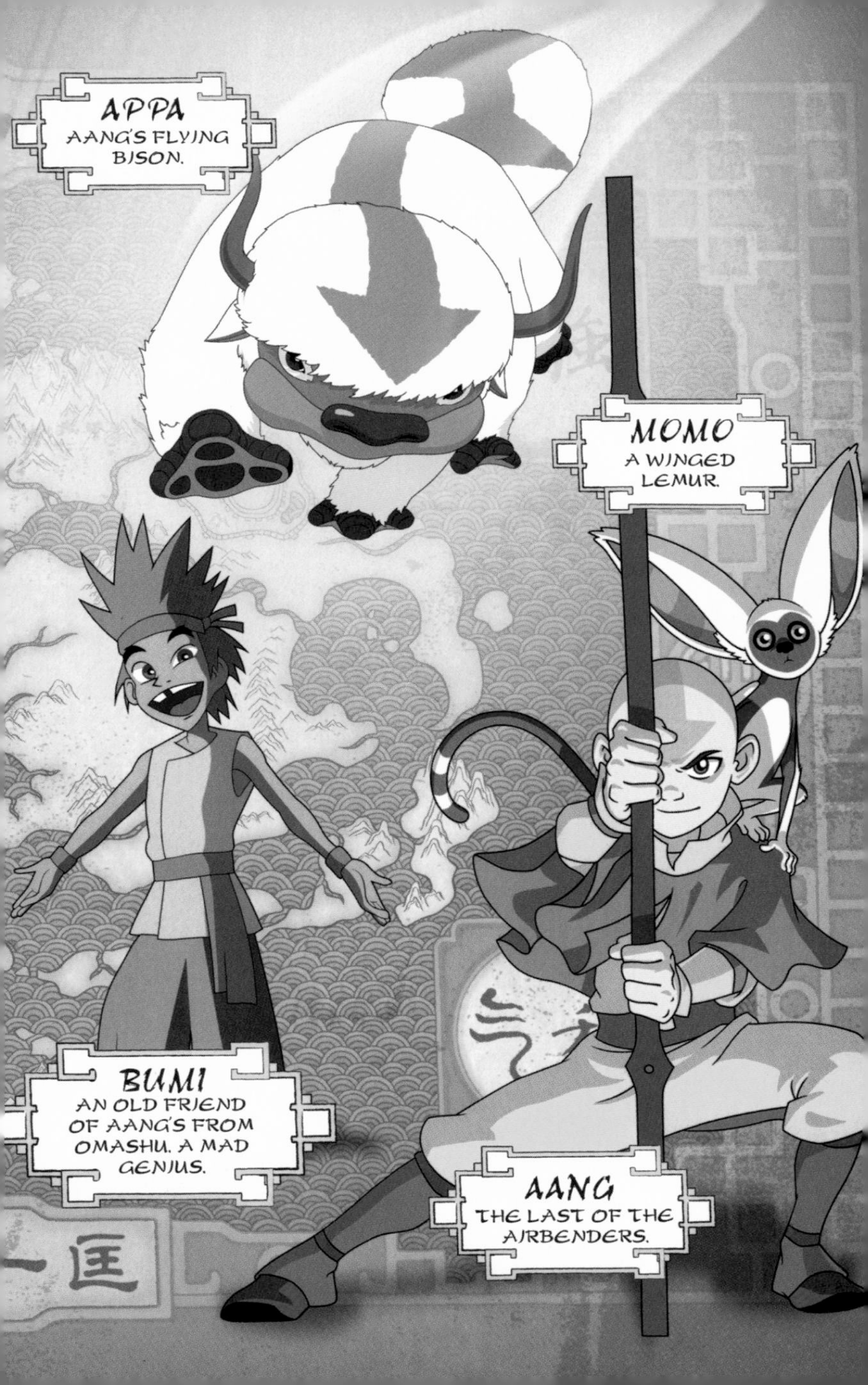
APPA
AANG'S FLYING BISON.
MOMO
A WINGED LEMUR.
BUMI
AN OLD FRIEND OF AANG'S FROM OMASHU. A MAD GENIUS.
AANG
THE LAST OF THE AIRBENDERS.

NICKELODEON

降世神通
AVATAR
THE LAST AIRBENDER

CHAPTER 5:
CONTENTS

THE STORY SO FAR...

THE VISIT TO KYOSHI VILLAGE TAUGHT AANG AND HIS FRIENDS MUCH ABOUT FRIENDSHIP, RESPECT, AND COURAGE. AFTER RESCUING THE VILLAGE FROM A FIRENATION ATTACK AND LEAVING THEIR NEW FRIENDS BEHIND, THE TEAM CONTINUES THEIR JOURNEY TO THE NORTH POLE. BUT FIRST, THEY NEED TO MAKE A QUICK DETOUR TO THE GREAT EARTH KINGDOM CITY OF OMASHU! AANG WILL WITNESS, FOR THE FIRST TIME, THE AWESOME POWER OF EARTHBENDERS, AND HOPEFULLY FIND A LONG LOST FRIEND HE HASN'T SEEN IN A HUNDRED YEARS!

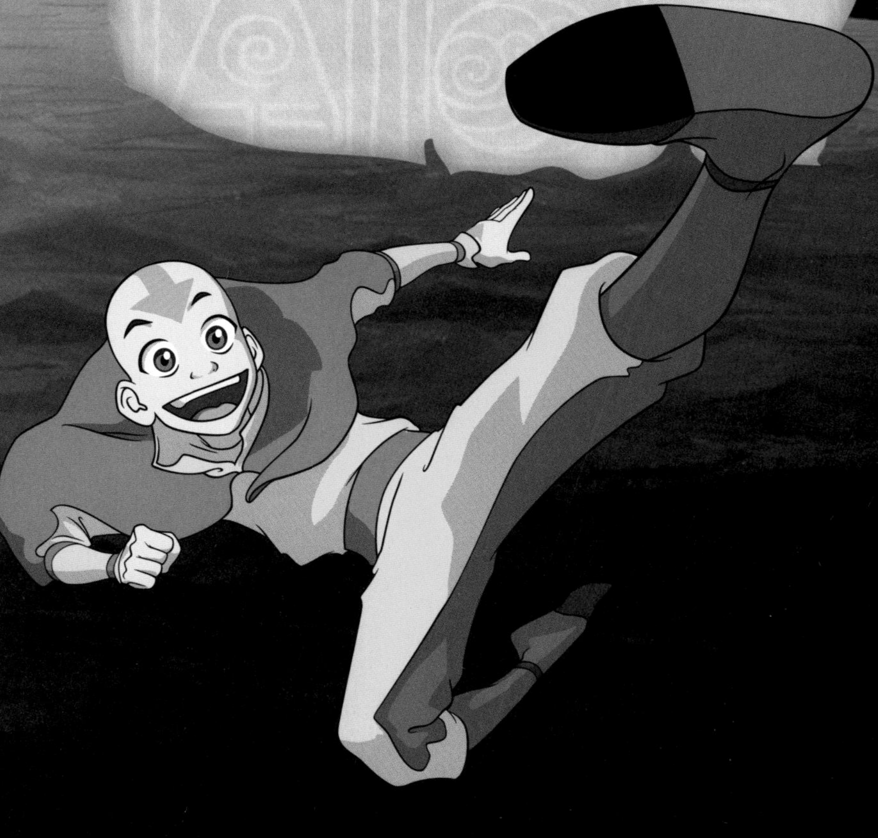

BOOK ONE: WINTER

CHAPTER FIVE: THE KING OF OMASHU

WRITTEN BY

JOHN O'BRYAN

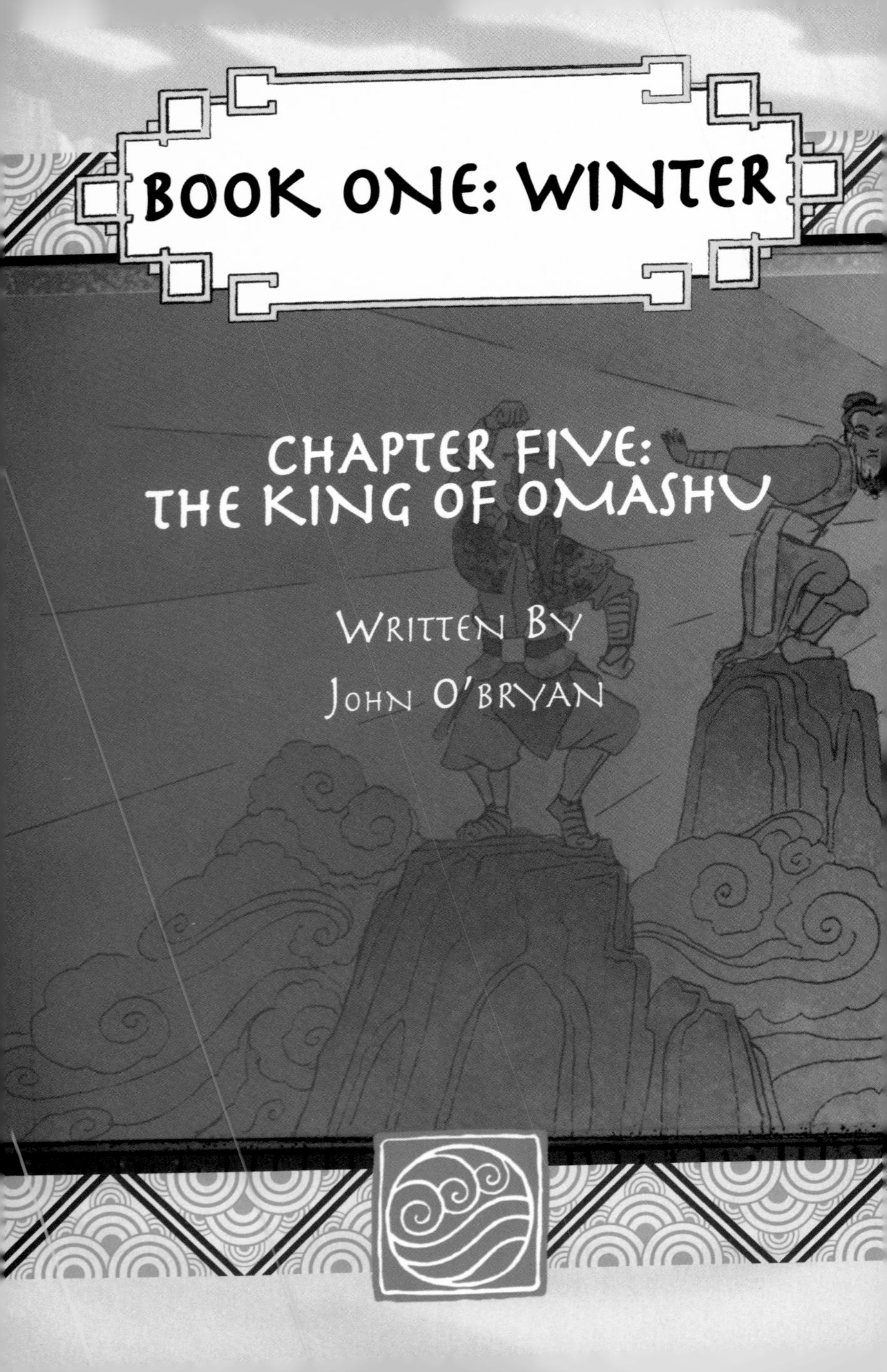

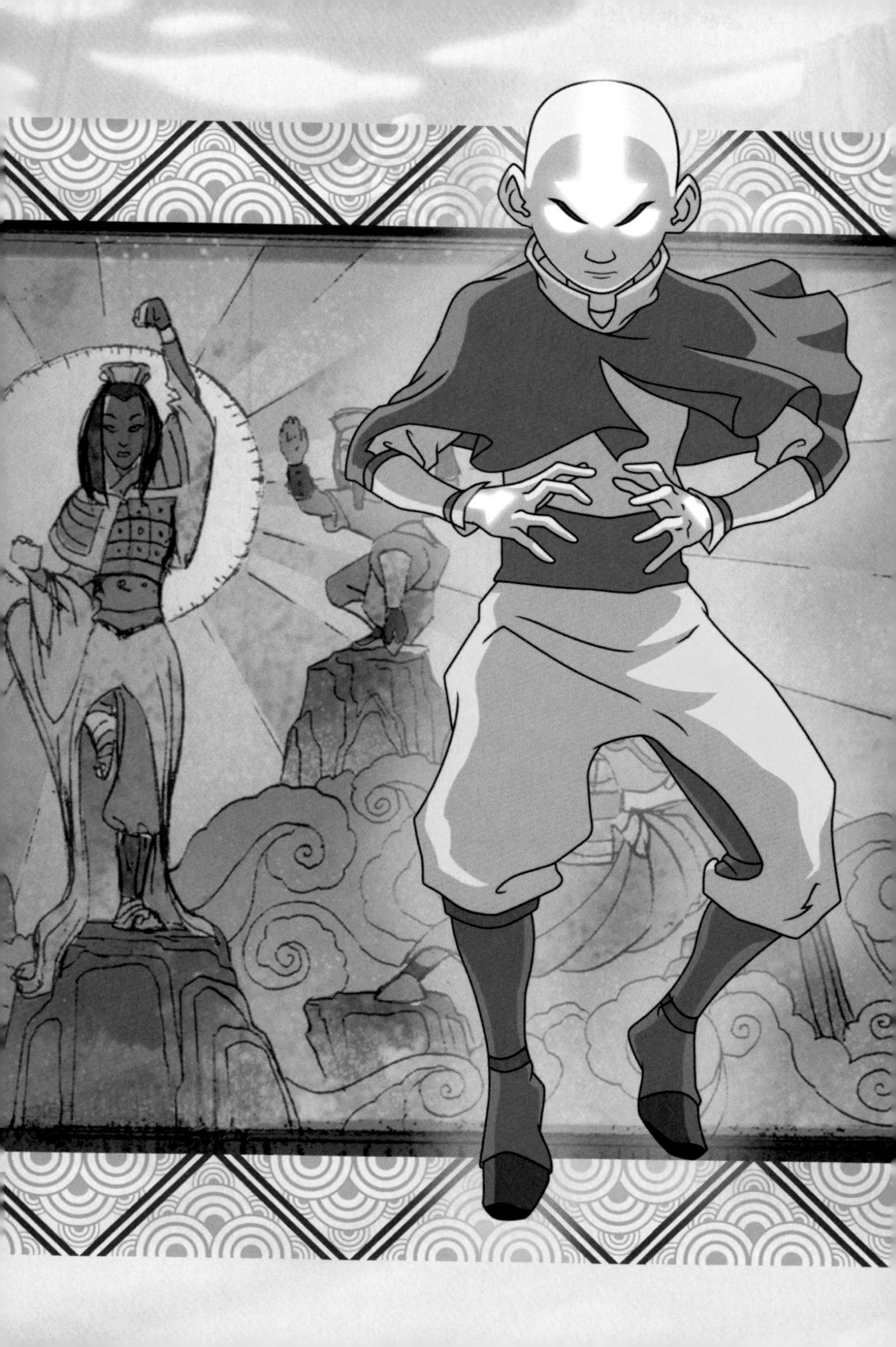

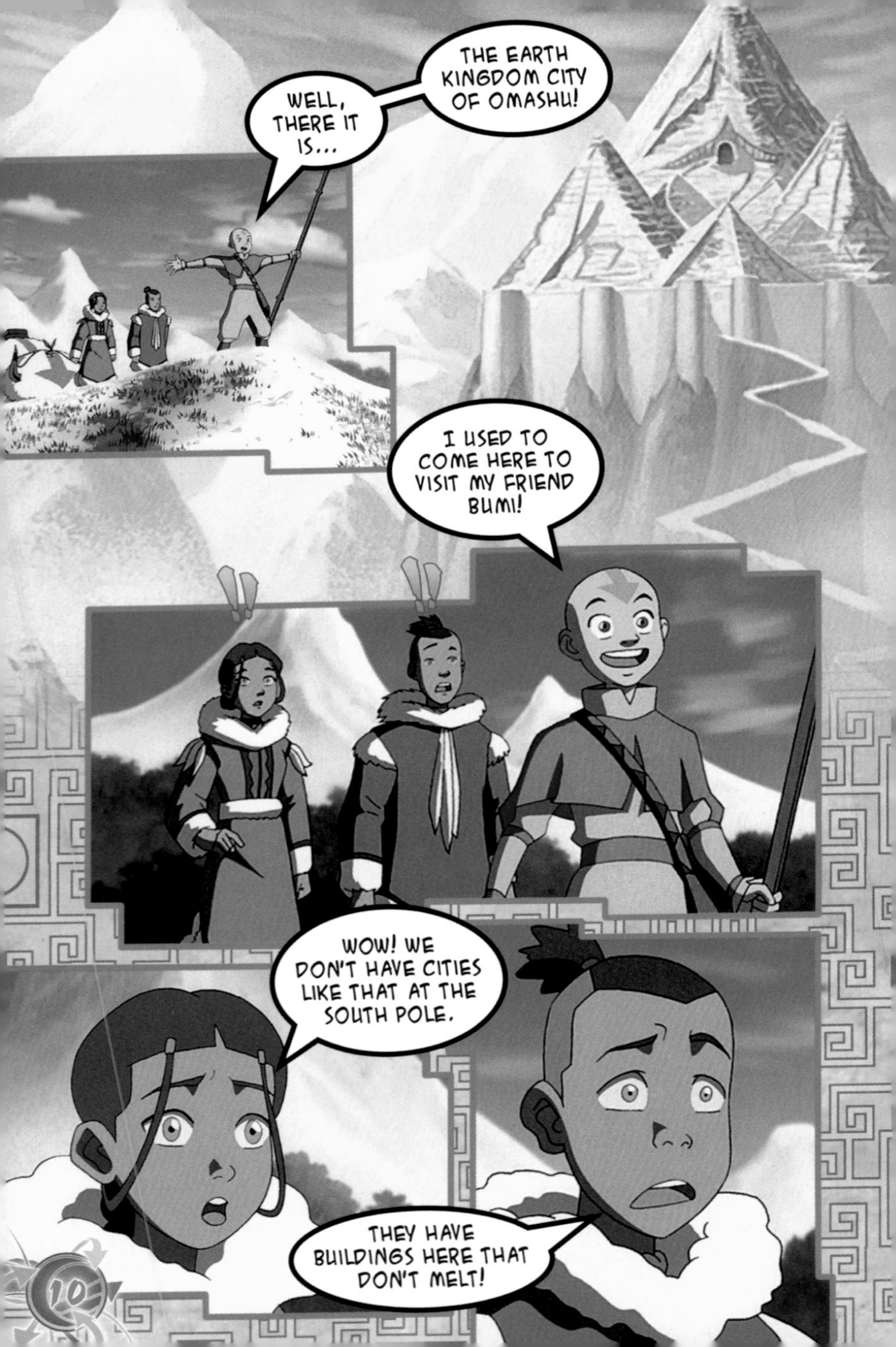
WELL, THERE IT IS...
THE EARTH KINGDOM CITY OF OMASHU!
I USED TO COME HERE TO VISIT MY FRIEND BUMI!
WOW! WE DON'T HAVE CITIES LIKE THAT AT THE SOUTH POLE.
THEY HAVE BUILDINGS HERE THAT DON'T MELT!

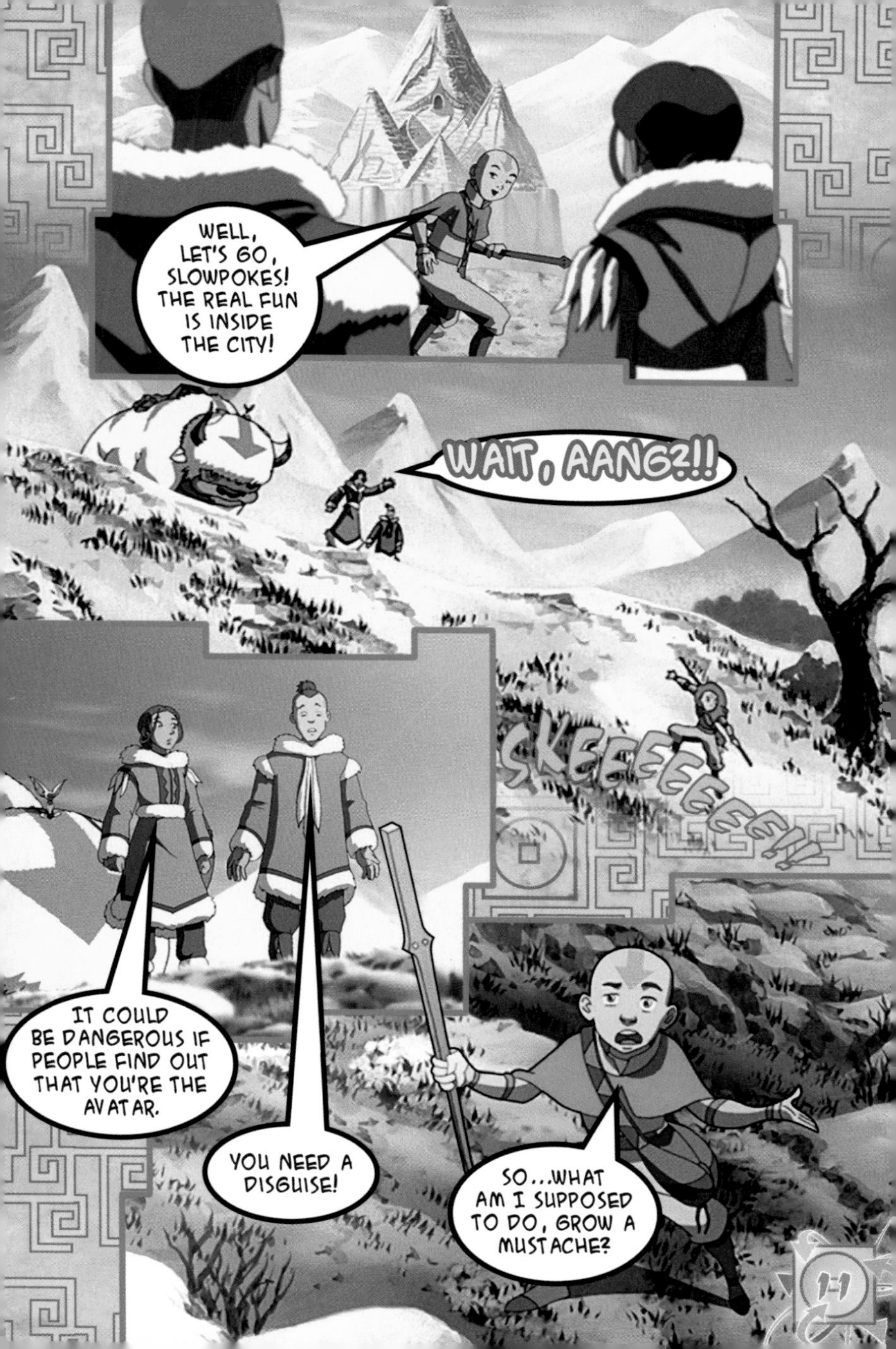
WELL, LET'S GO, SLOWPOKES! THE REAL FUN IS INSIDE THE CITY!
WAIT, AANG?!!
SKEEEEEEE!!!
IT COULD BE DANGEROUS IF PEOPLE FIND OUT THAT YOU'RE THE AVATAR.
YOU NEED A DISGUISE!
SO...WHAT AM I SUPPOSED TO DO, GROW A MUSTACHE?

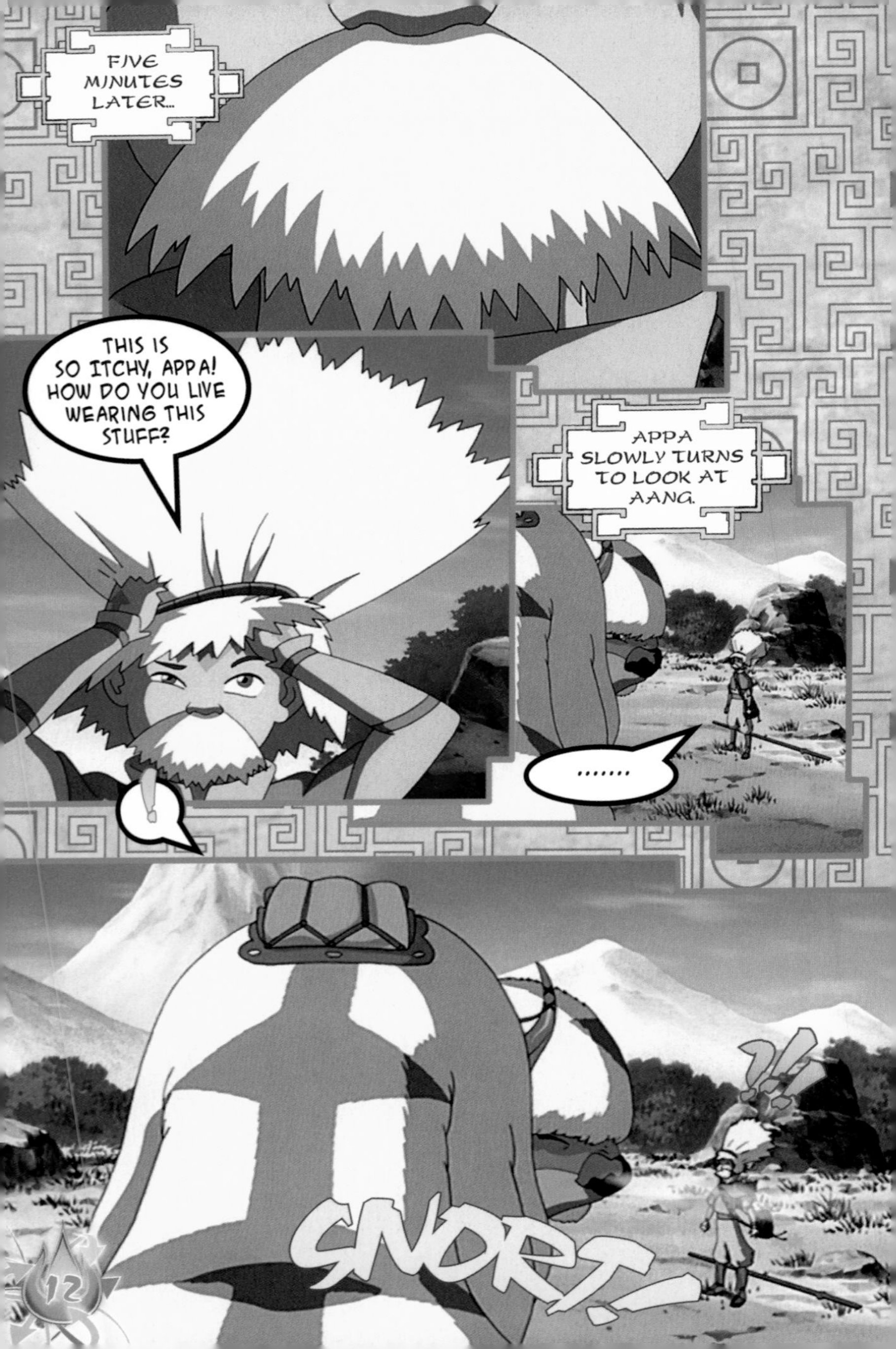

FIVE MINUTES LATER...
THIS IS SO ITCHY, APPA! HOW DO YOU LIVE WEARING THIS STUFF?
!
APPA SLOWLY TURNS TO LOOK AT AANG.
....
!!
SNORT!

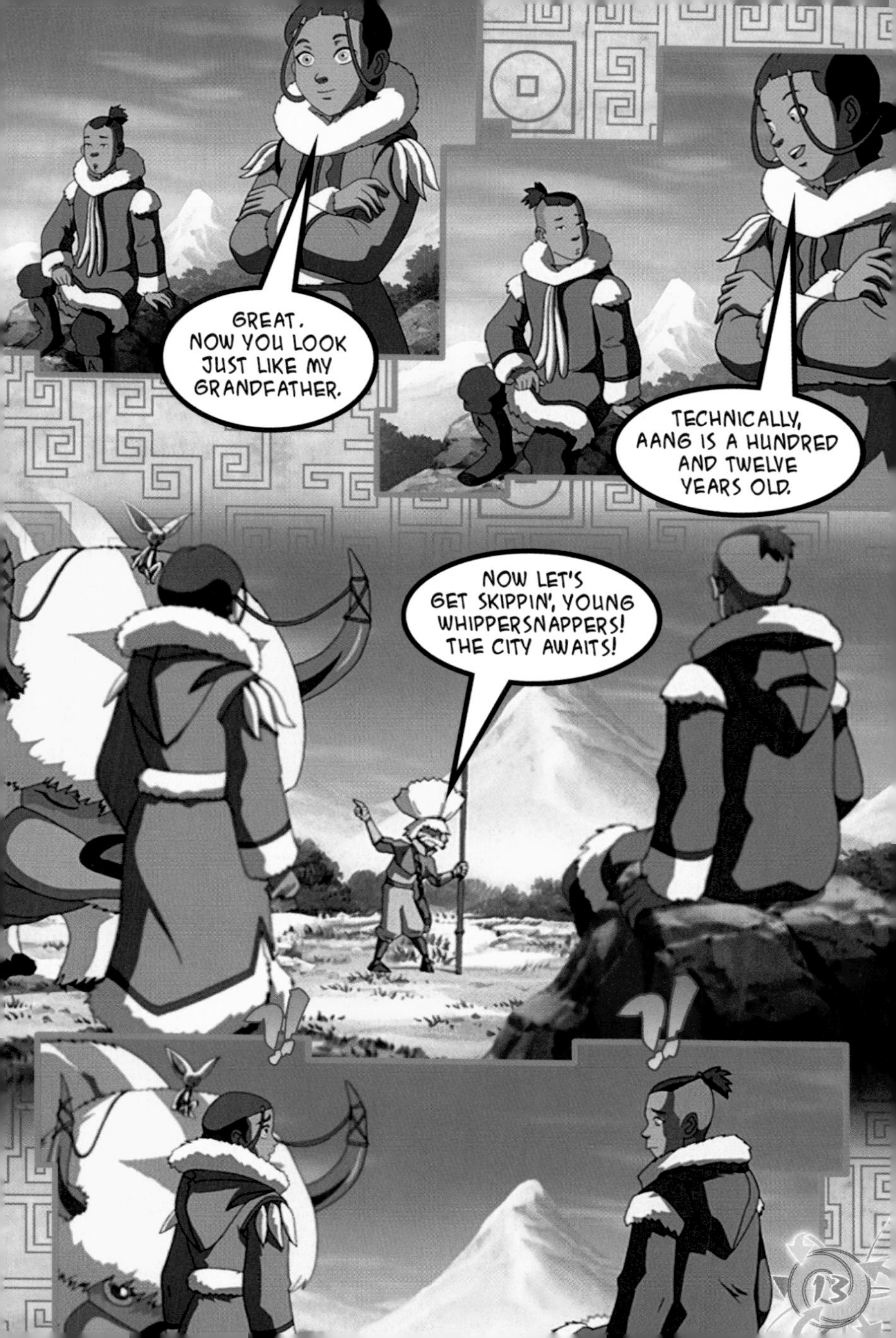
GREAT. NOW YOU LOOK JUST LIKE MY GRANDFATHER.
TECHNICALLY, AANG IS A HUNDRED AND TWELVE YEARS OLD.
NOW LET'S GET SKIPPIN', YOUNG WHIPPERSNAPPERS! THE CITY AWAITS!
13

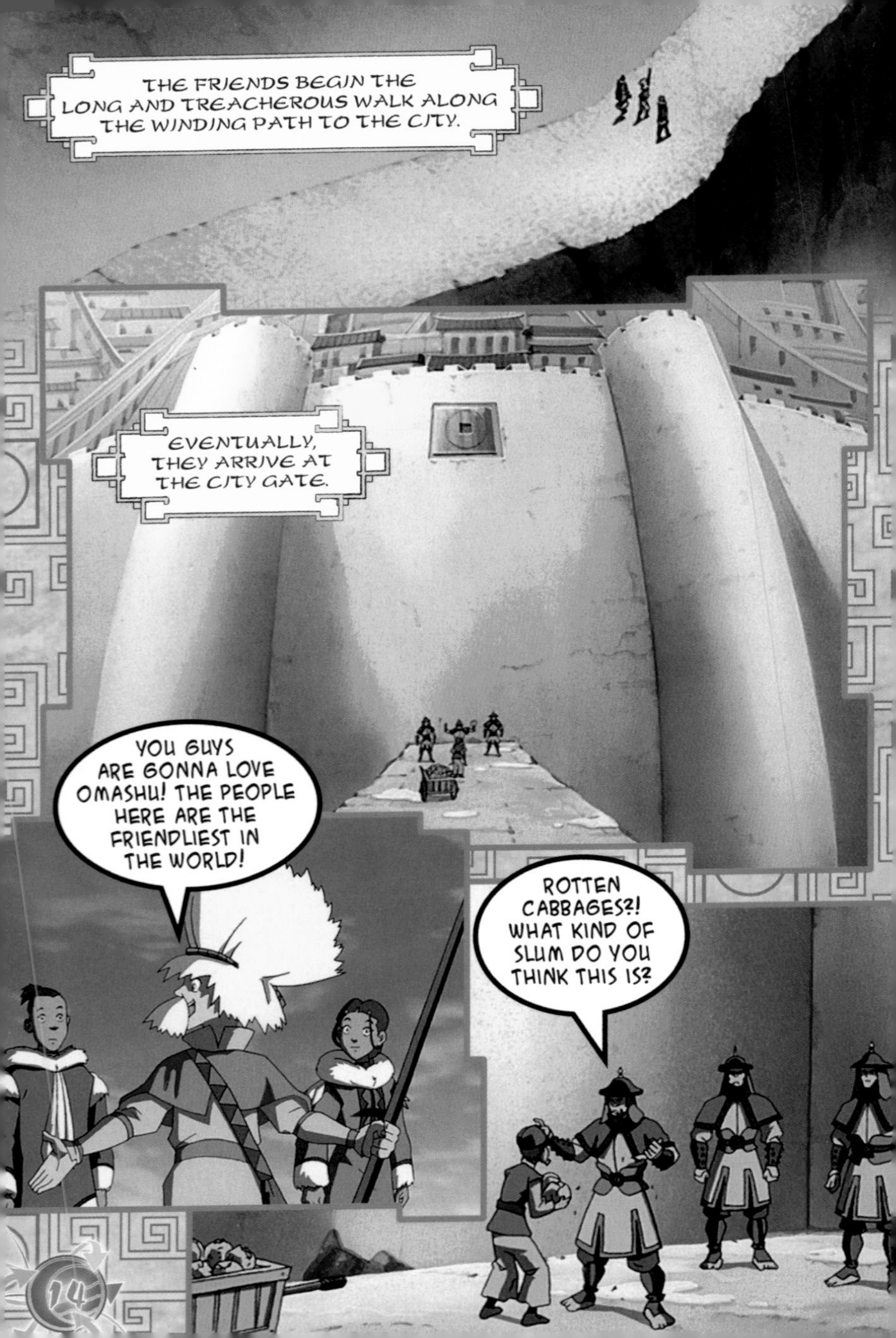
THE FRIENDS BEGIN THE LONG AND TREACHEROUS WALK ALONG THE WINDING PATH TO THE CITY.
EVENTUALLY, THEY ARRIVE AT THE CITY GATE.
YOU GUYS ARE GONNA LOVE OMASHU! THE PEOPLE HERE ARE THE FRIENDLIEST IN THE WORLD!
ROTTEN CABBAGES?! WHAT KIND OF SLUM DO YOU THINK THIS IS?
14

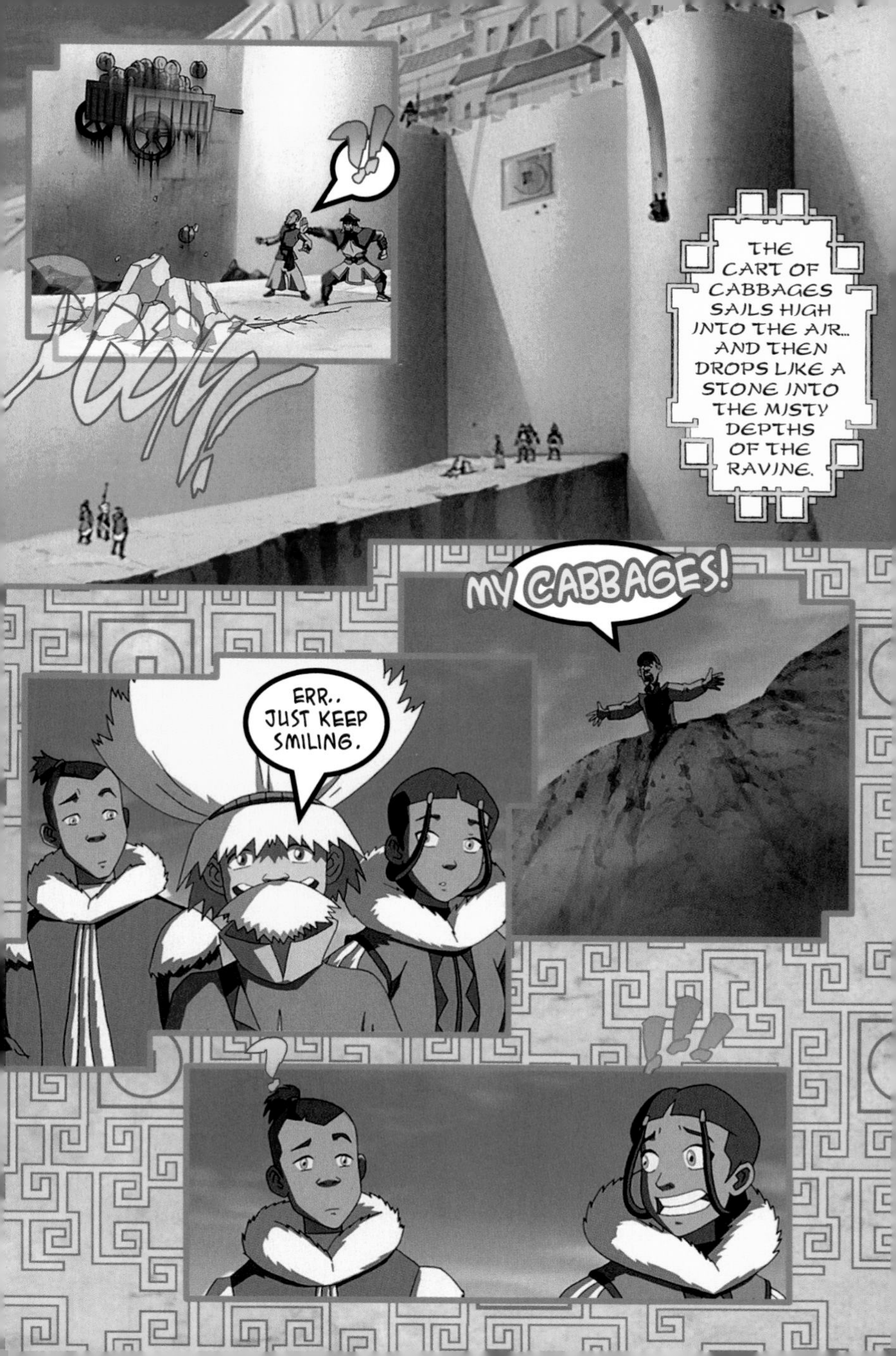
THE CART OF CABBAGES SAILS HIGH INTO THE AIR... AND THEN DROPS LIKE A STONE INTO THE MISTY DEPTHS OF THE RAVINE.
ERR.. JUST KEEP SMILING.
MY CABBAGES!

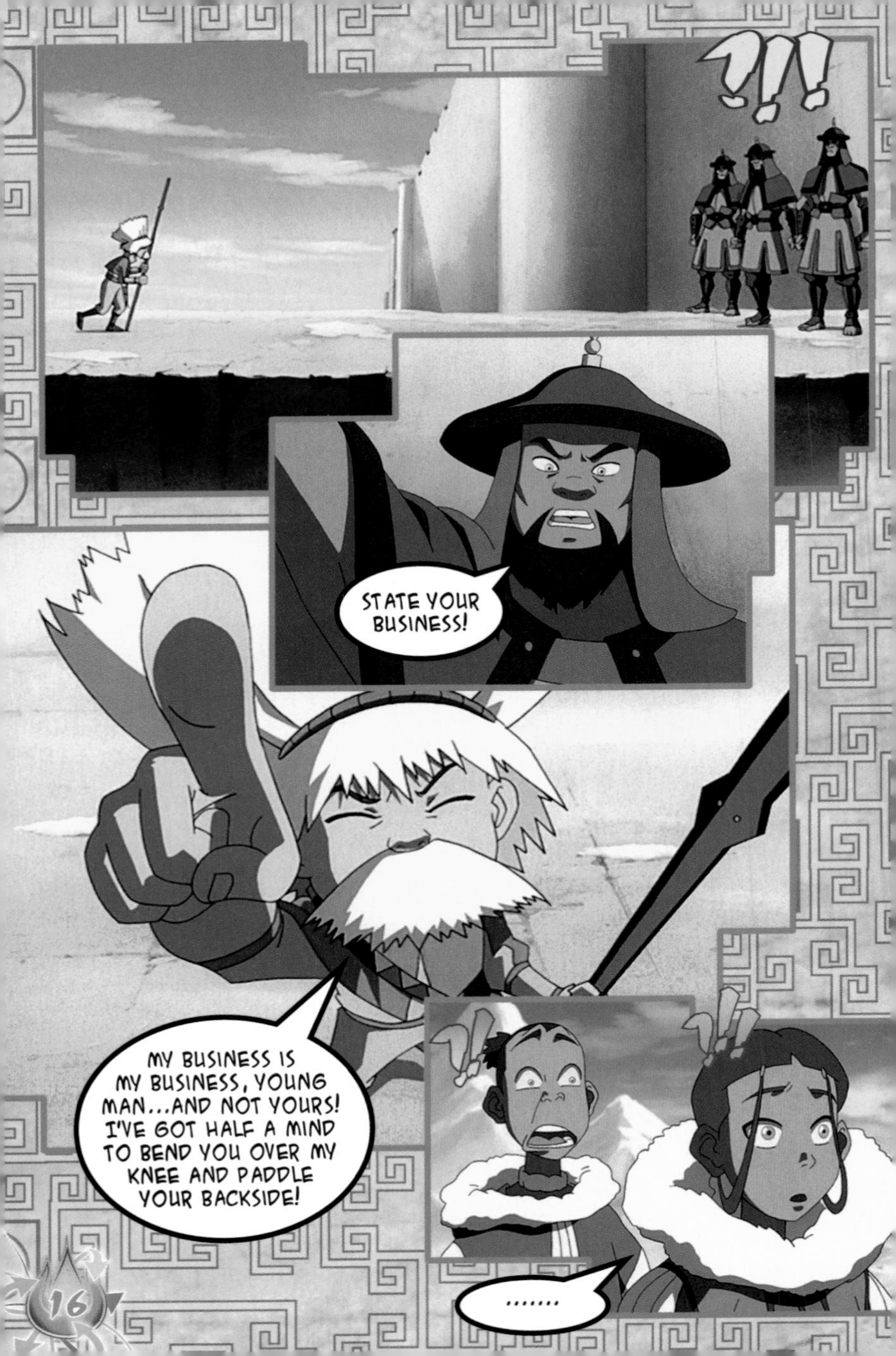
?!!
STATE YOUR BUSINESS!
MY BUSINESS IS MY BUSINESS, YOUNG MAN...AND NOT YOURS! I'VE GOT HALF A MIND TO BEND YOU OVER MY KNEE AND PADDLE YOUR BACKSIDE!
....

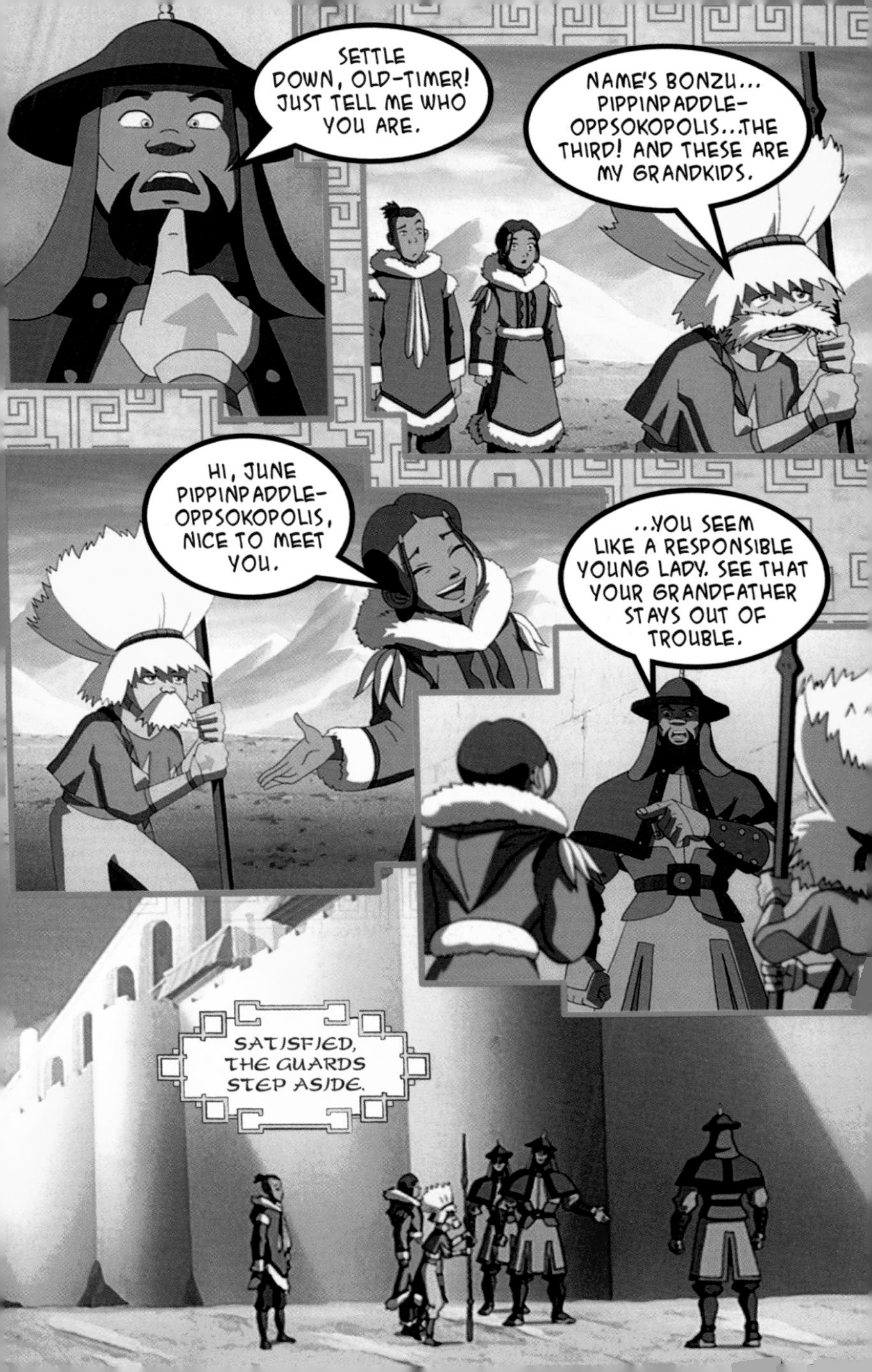
SETTLE DOWN, OLD-TIMER! JUST TELL ME WHO YOU ARE.
NAME'S BONZU... PIPPINPADDLE-OPPSOKOPOLIS...THE THIRD! AND THESE ARE MY GRANDKIDS.
HI, JUNE PIPPINPADDLE-OPPSOKOPOLIS, NICE TO MEET YOU.
...YOU SEEM LIKE A RESPONSIBLE YOUNG LADY. SEE THAT YOUR GRANDFATHER STAYS OUT OF TROUBLE.
SATISFIED, THE GUARDS STEP ASIDE.

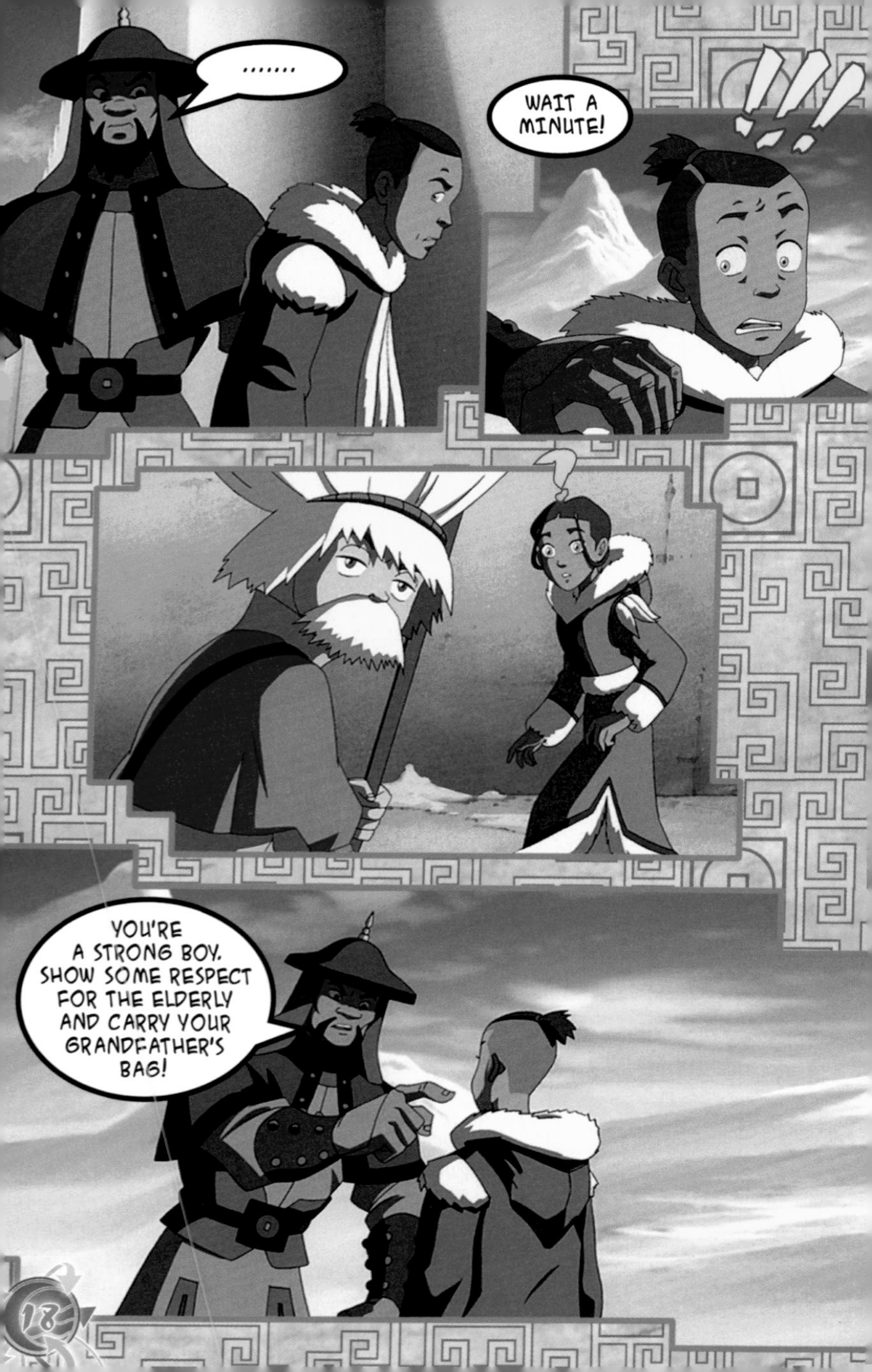
....
WAIT A MINUTE!
!!!
YOU'RE A STRONG BOY. SHOW SOME RESPECT FOR THE ELDERLY AND CARRY YOUR GRANDFATHER'S BAG!

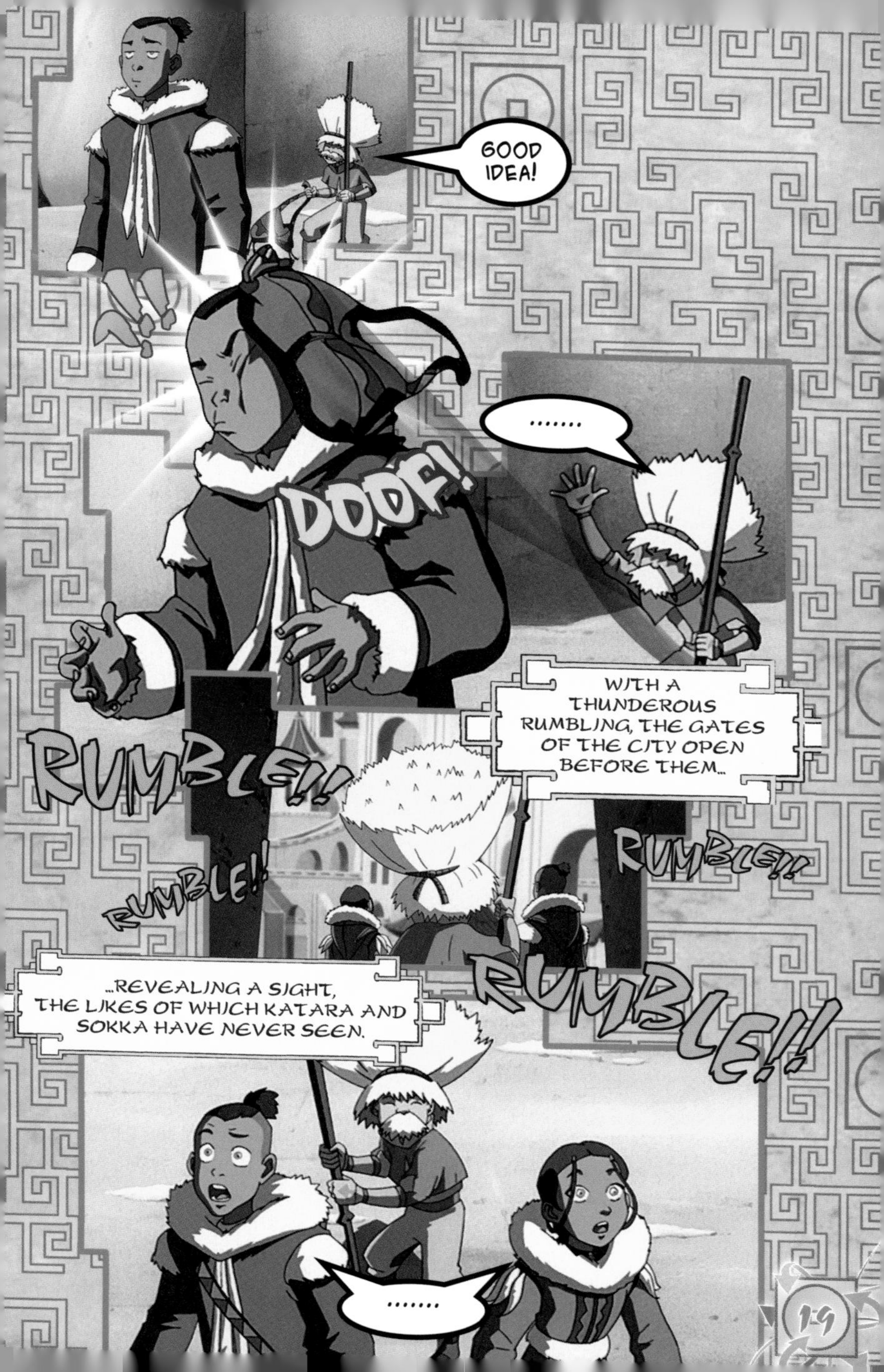
GOOD IDEA!
DOOF!
....
WITH A THUNDEROUS RUMBLING, THE GATES OF THE CITY OPEN BEFORE THEM...
RUMBLE!!
RUMBLE!!
RUMBLE!!
...REVEALING A SIGHT, THE LIKES OF WHICH KATARA AND SOKKA HAVE NEVER SEEN.
RUMBLE!!
....

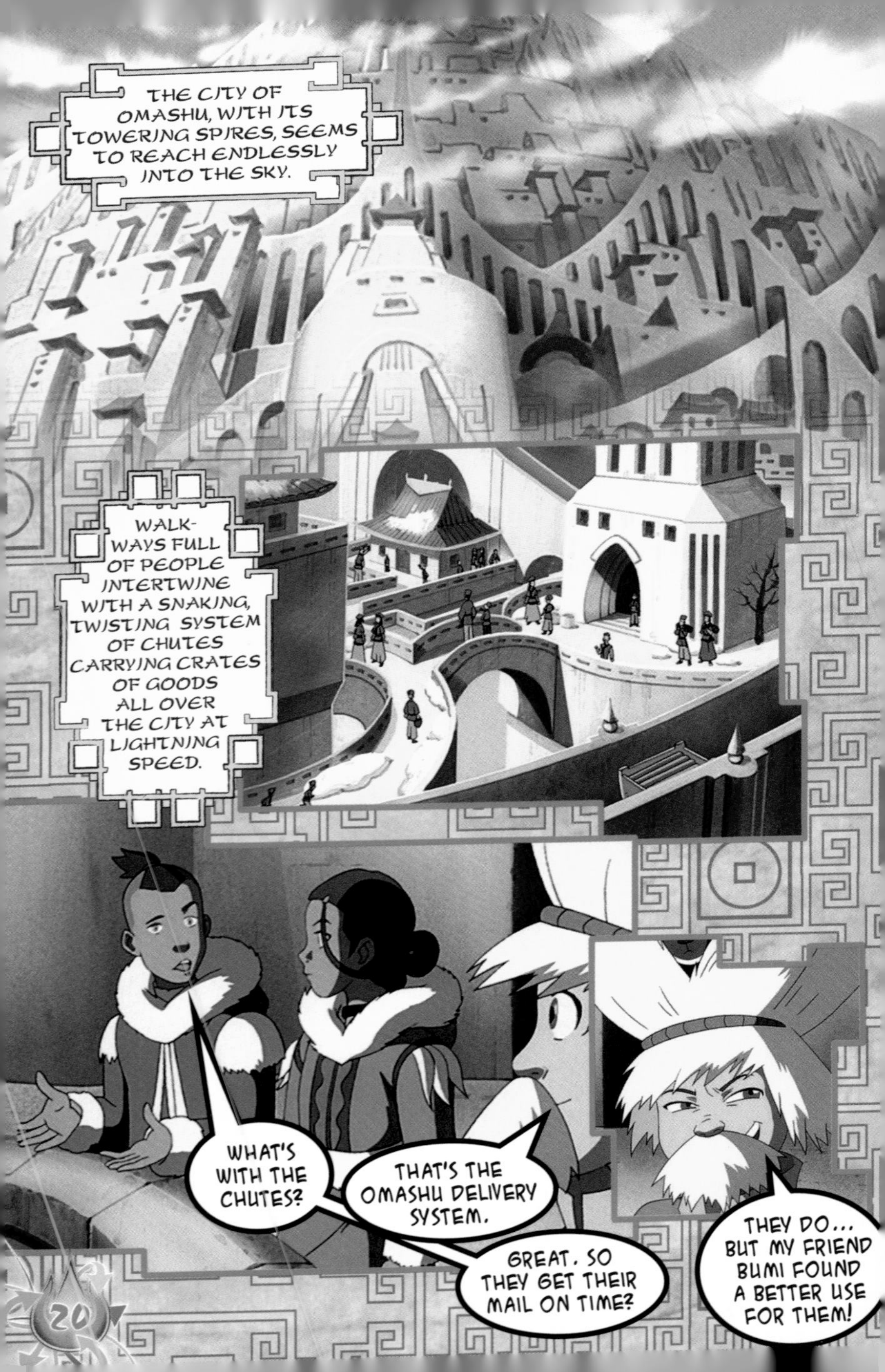
THE CITY OF OMASHU, WITH ITS TOWERING SPIRES, SEEMS TO REACH ENDLESSLY INTO THE SKY.
WALK-WAYS FULL OF PEOPLE INTERTWINE WITH A SNAKING, TWISTING SYSTEM OF CHUTES CARRYING CRATES OF GOODS ALL OVER THE CITY AT LIGHTNING SPEED.
WHAT'S WITH THE CHUTES?
THAT'S THE OMASHU DELIVERY SYSTEM.
GREAT. SO THEY GET THEIR MAIL ON TIME?
THEY DO... BUT MY FRIEND BUMI FOUND A BETTER USE FOR THEM!

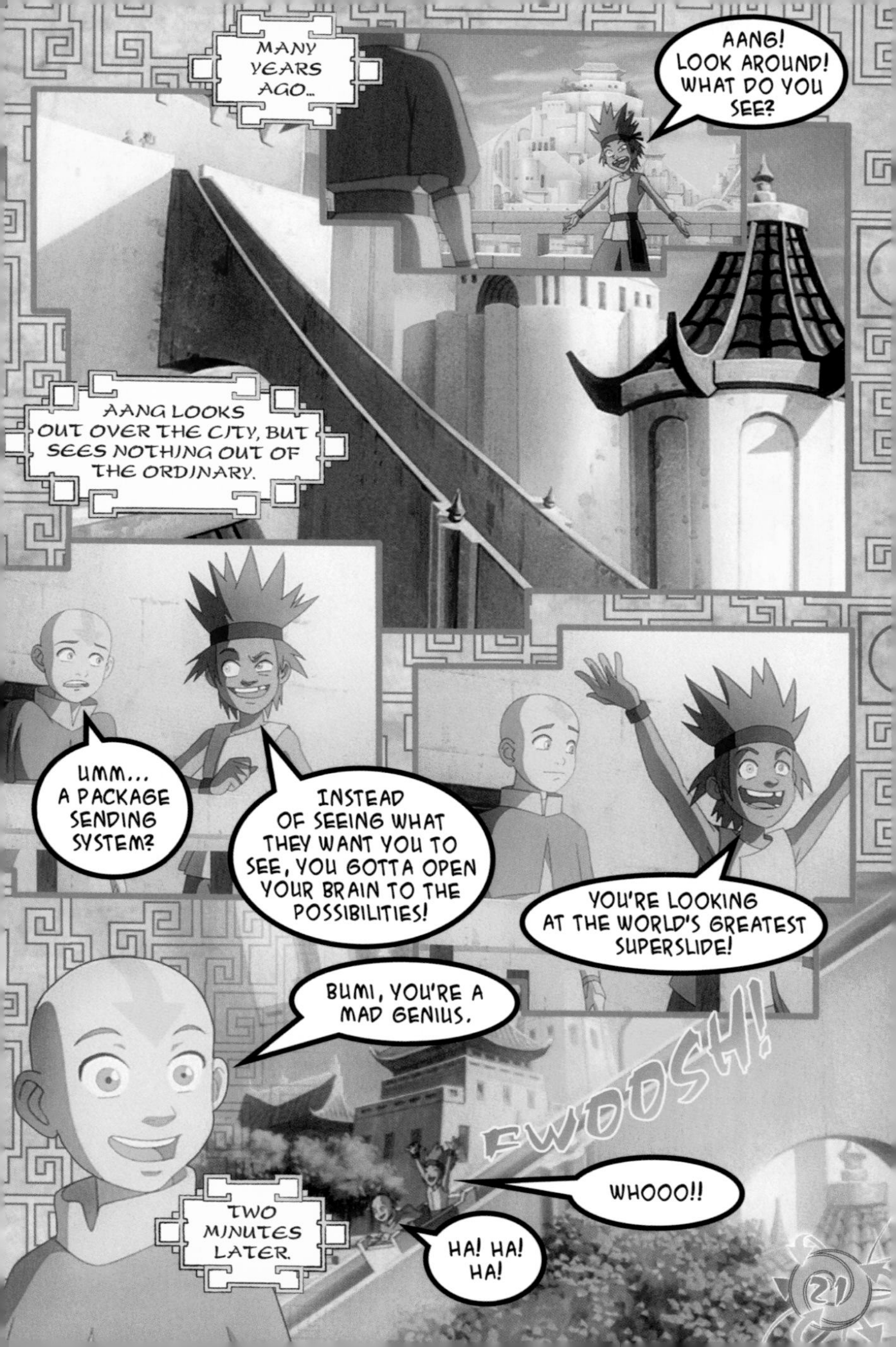
MANY YEARS AGO...
AANG! LOOK AROUND! WHAT DO YOU SEE?
AANG LOOKS OUT OVER THE CITY, BUT SEES NOTHING OUT OF THE ORDINARY.
UMM... A PACKAGE SENDING SYSTEM?
INSTEAD OF SEEING WHAT THEY WANT YOU TO SEE, YOU GOTTA OPEN YOUR BRAIN TO THE POSSIBILITIES!
YOU'RE LOOKING AT THE WORLD'S GREATEST SUPERSLIDE!
BUMI, YOU'RE A MAD GENIUS.
FWOOSH!
TWO MINUTES LATER.
WHOOO!!
HA! HA! HA!

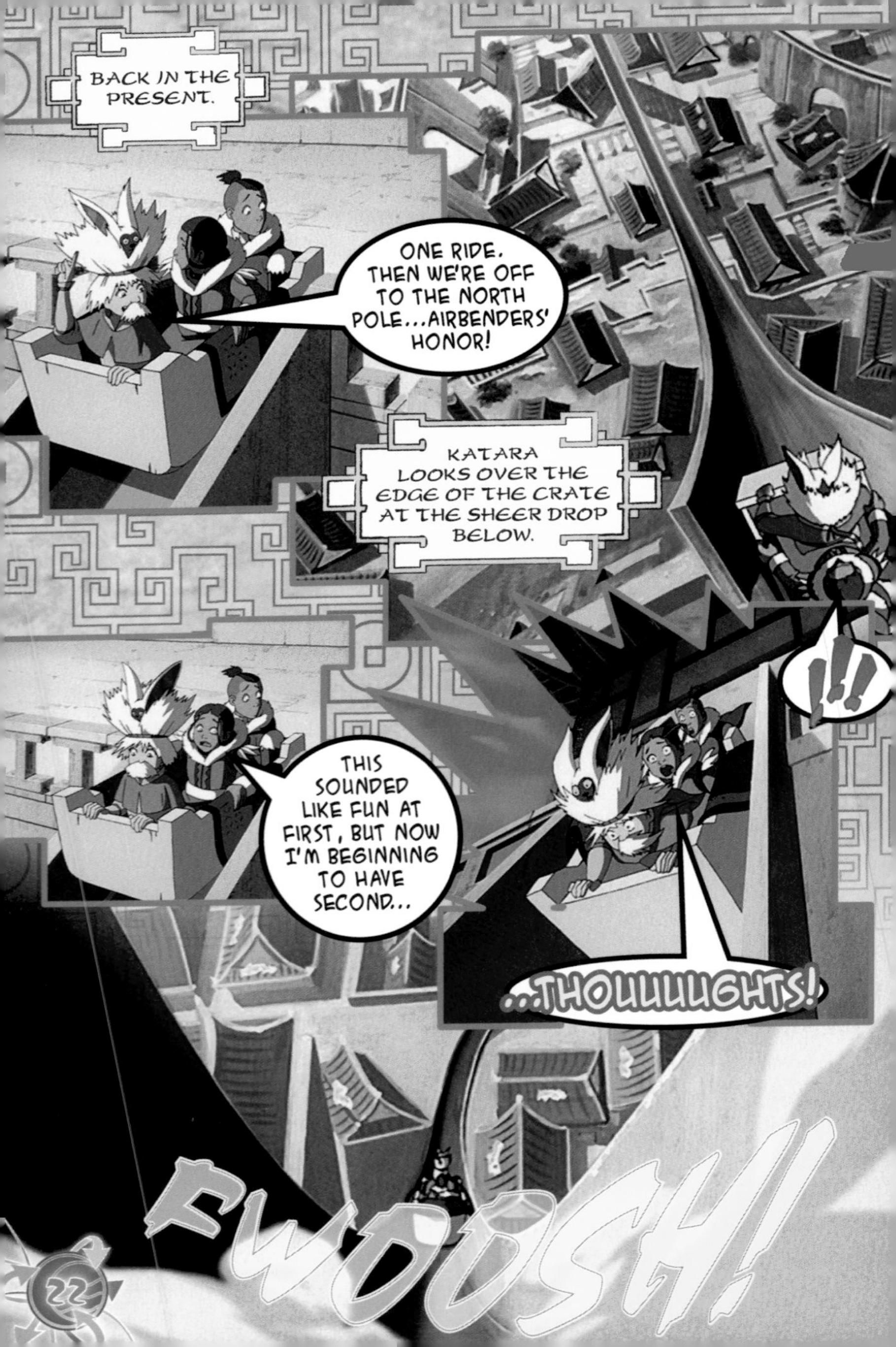
BACK IN THE PRESENT.
ONE RIDE. THEN WE'RE OFF TO THE NORTH POLE...AIRBENDERS' HONOR!
KATARA LOOKS OVER THE EDGE OF THE CRATE AT THE SHEER DROP BELOW.
THIS SOUNDED LIKE FUN AT FIRST, BUT NOW I'M BEGINNING TO HAVE SECOND...
!!
...THOUUUUGHTS!
FWOOSH!
22

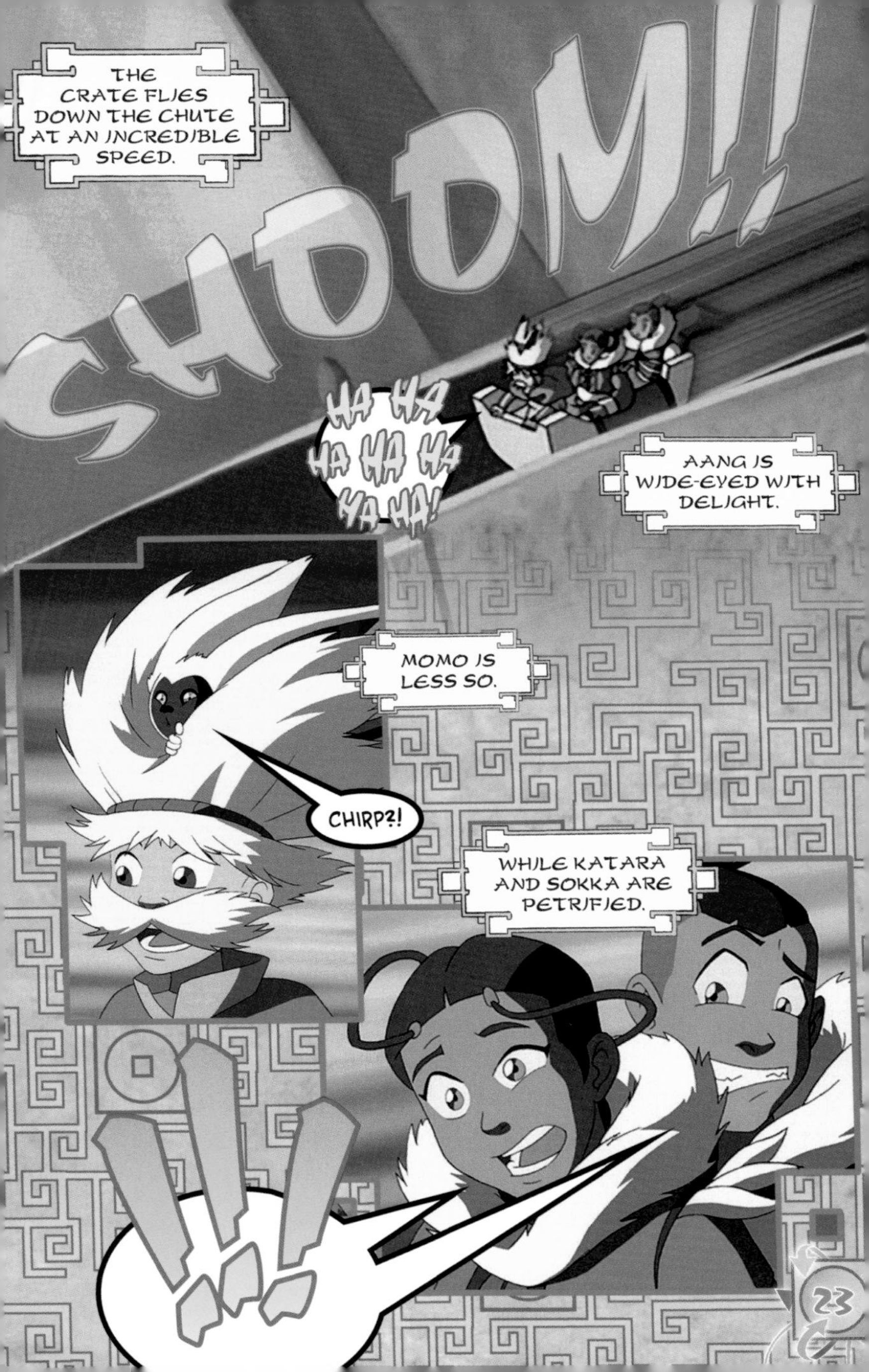

THE CRATE FLIES DOWN THE CHUTE AT AN INCREDIBLE SPEED.
SHOOM!!
HA HA HA HA HA HA HA!
AANG IS WIDE-EYED WITH DELIGHT.
MOMO IS LESS SO.
CHIRP?!
WHILE KATARA AND SOKKA ARE PETRIFIED.
!!

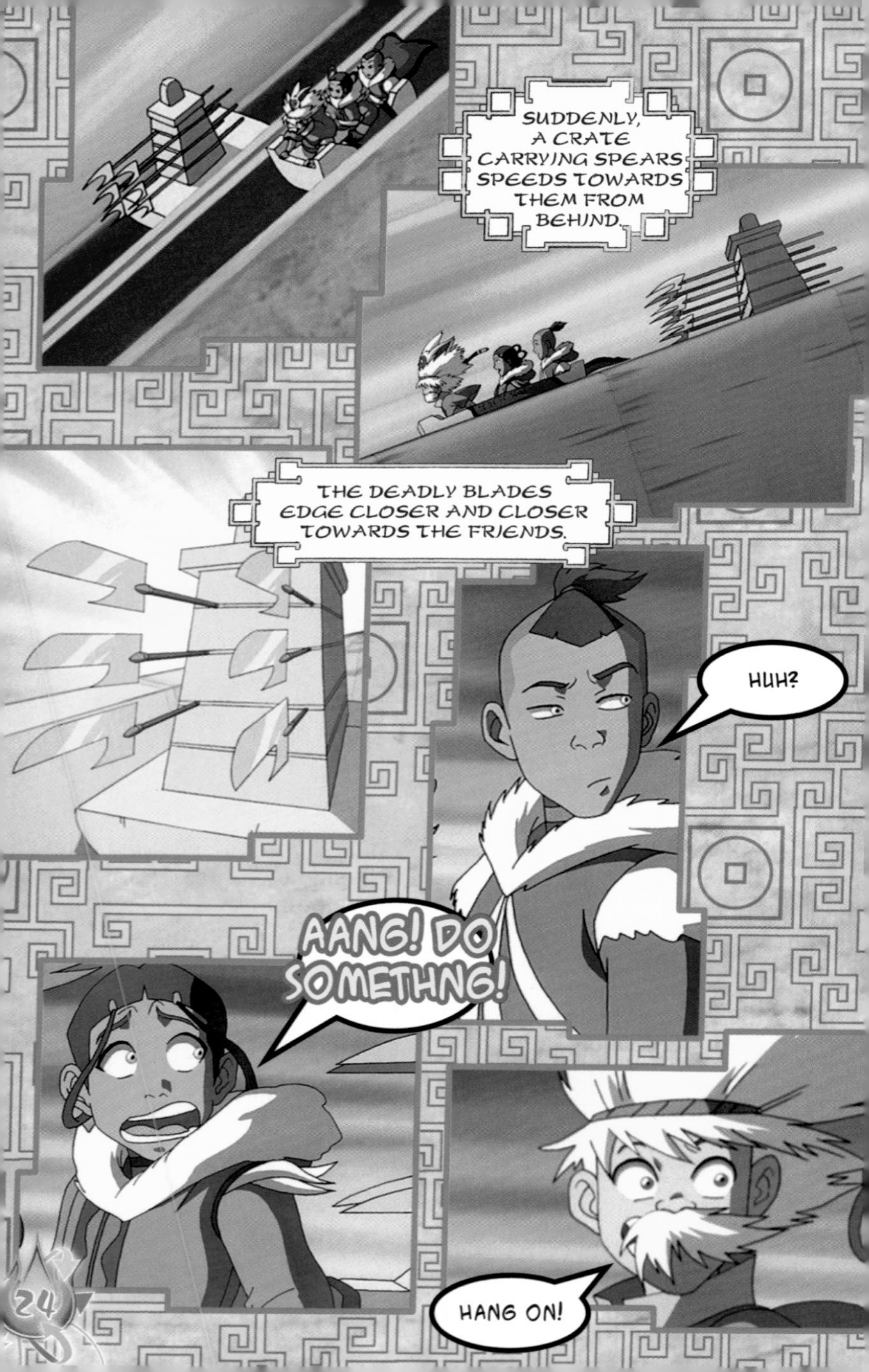
SUDDENLY, A CRATE CARRYING SPEARS SPEEDS TOWARDS THEM FROM BEHIND.
THE DEADLY BLADES EDGE CLOSER AND CLOSER TOWARDS THE FRIENDS.
HUH?
AANG! DO SOMETHNG!
HANG ON!

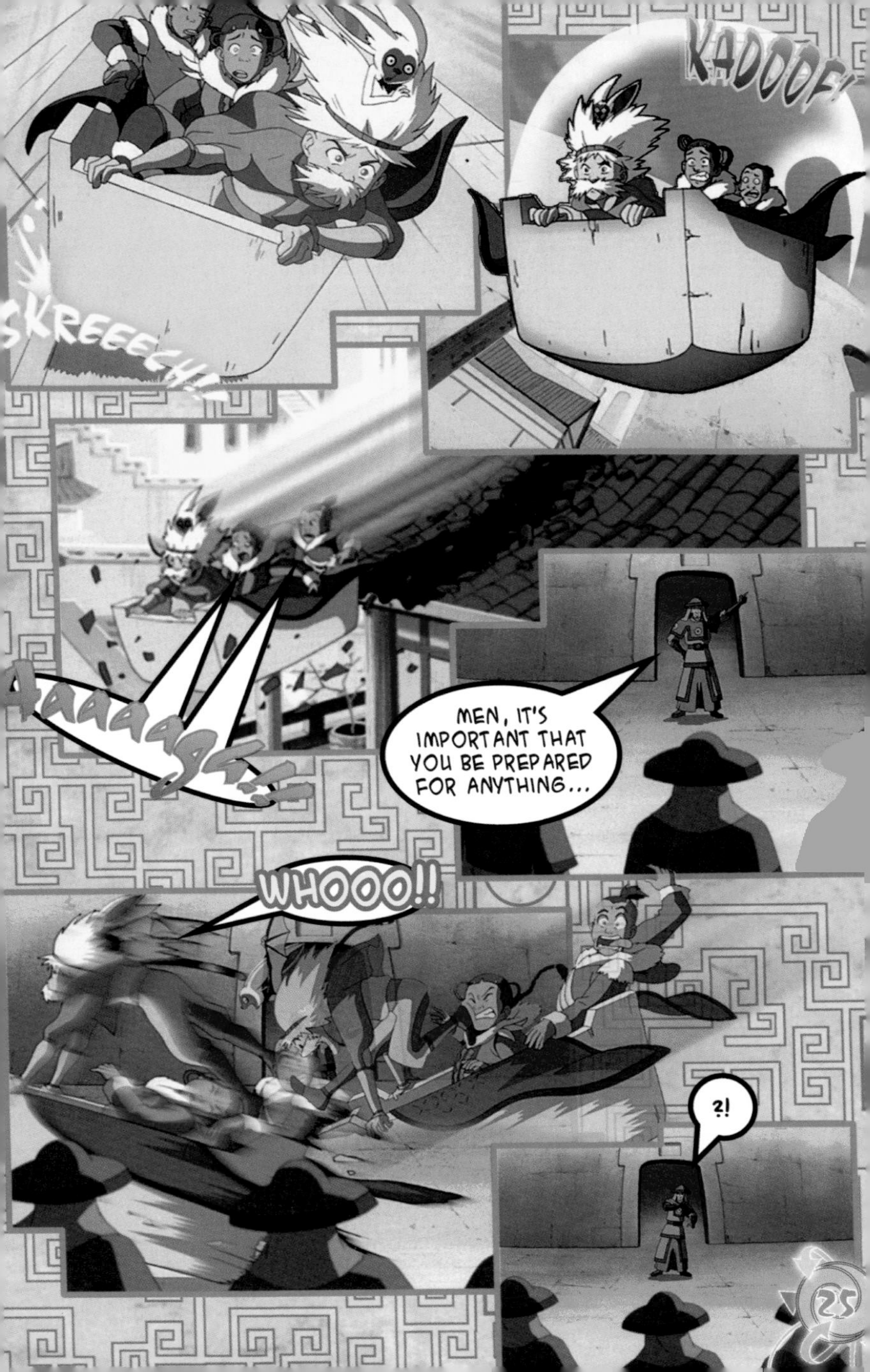
SKREEECH!!
KADOOOF!
AAAAAAGH!!
MEN, IT'S IMPORTANT THAT YOU BE PREPARED FOR ANYTHING...
WHOOO!!
?!
25

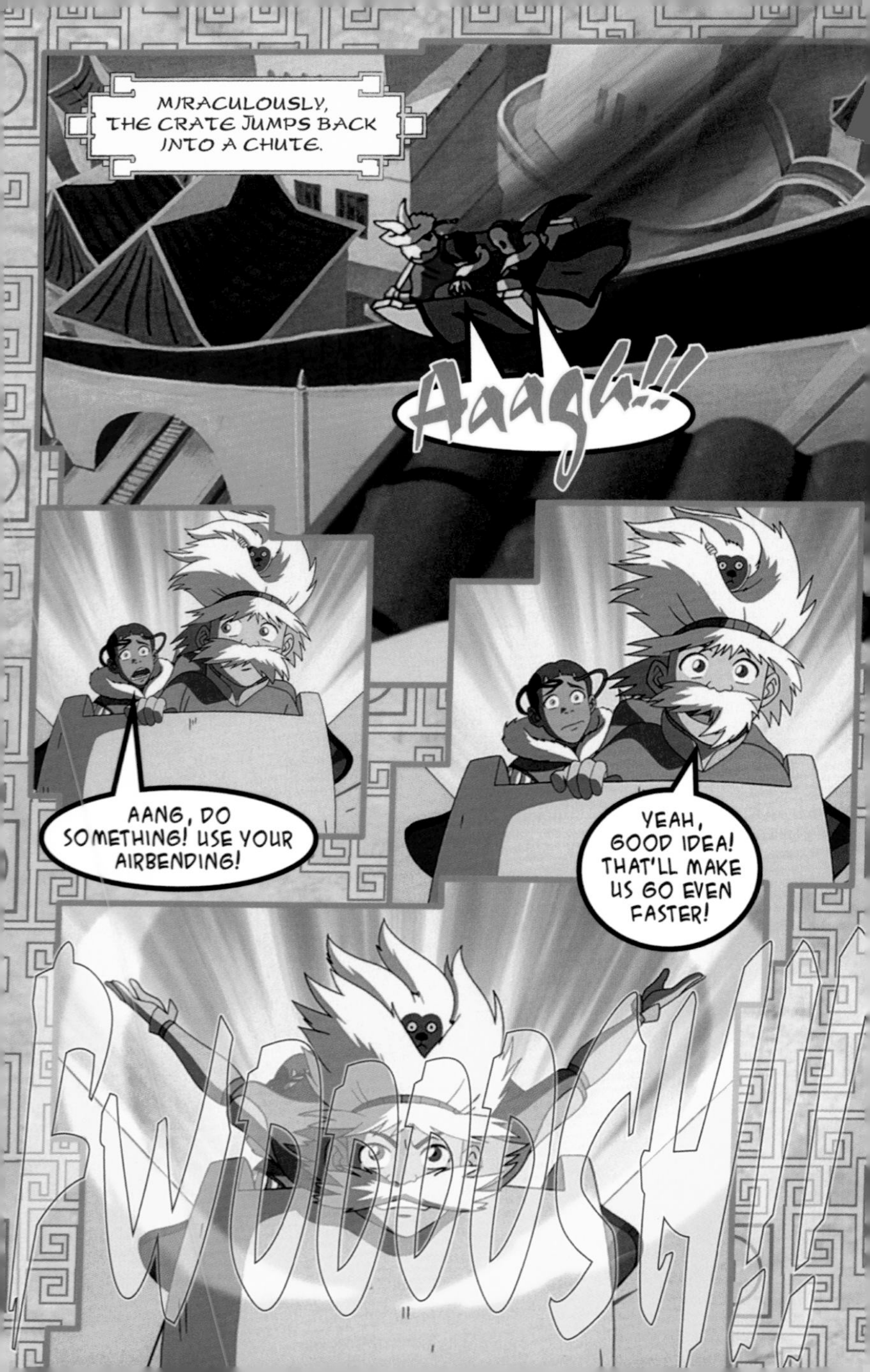
MIRACULOUSLY, THE CRATE JUMPS BACK INTO A CHUTE.
Aaagh!!
AANG, DO SOMETHING! USE YOUR AIRBENDING!
YEAH, GOOD IDEA! THAT'LL MAKE US GO EVEN FASTER!
FWOOOOSCH!!

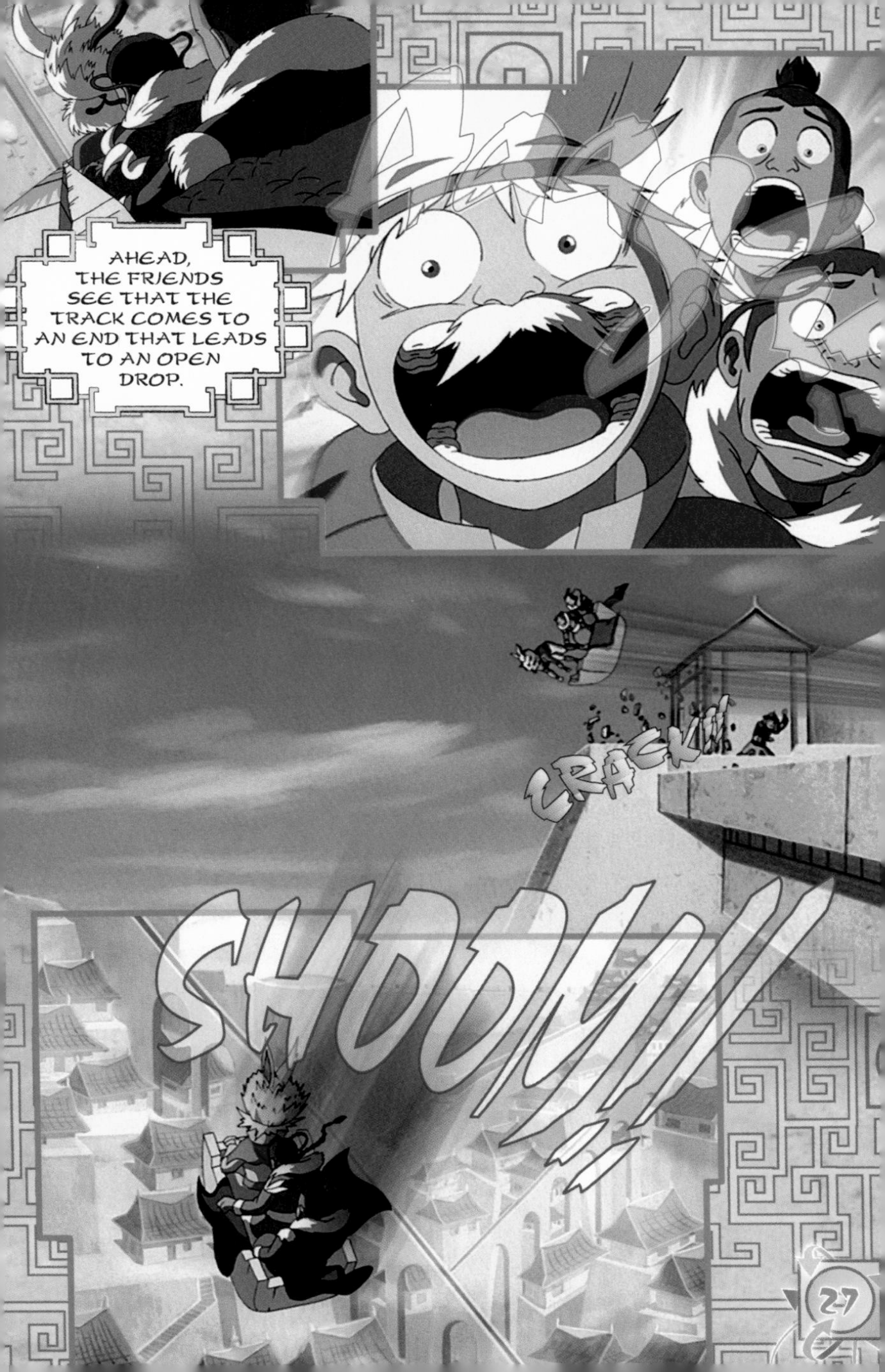
AHEAD, THE FRIENDS SEE THAT THE TRACK COMES TO AN END THAT LEADS TO AN OPEN DROP.
CRACK!!
SHOOM!!
27

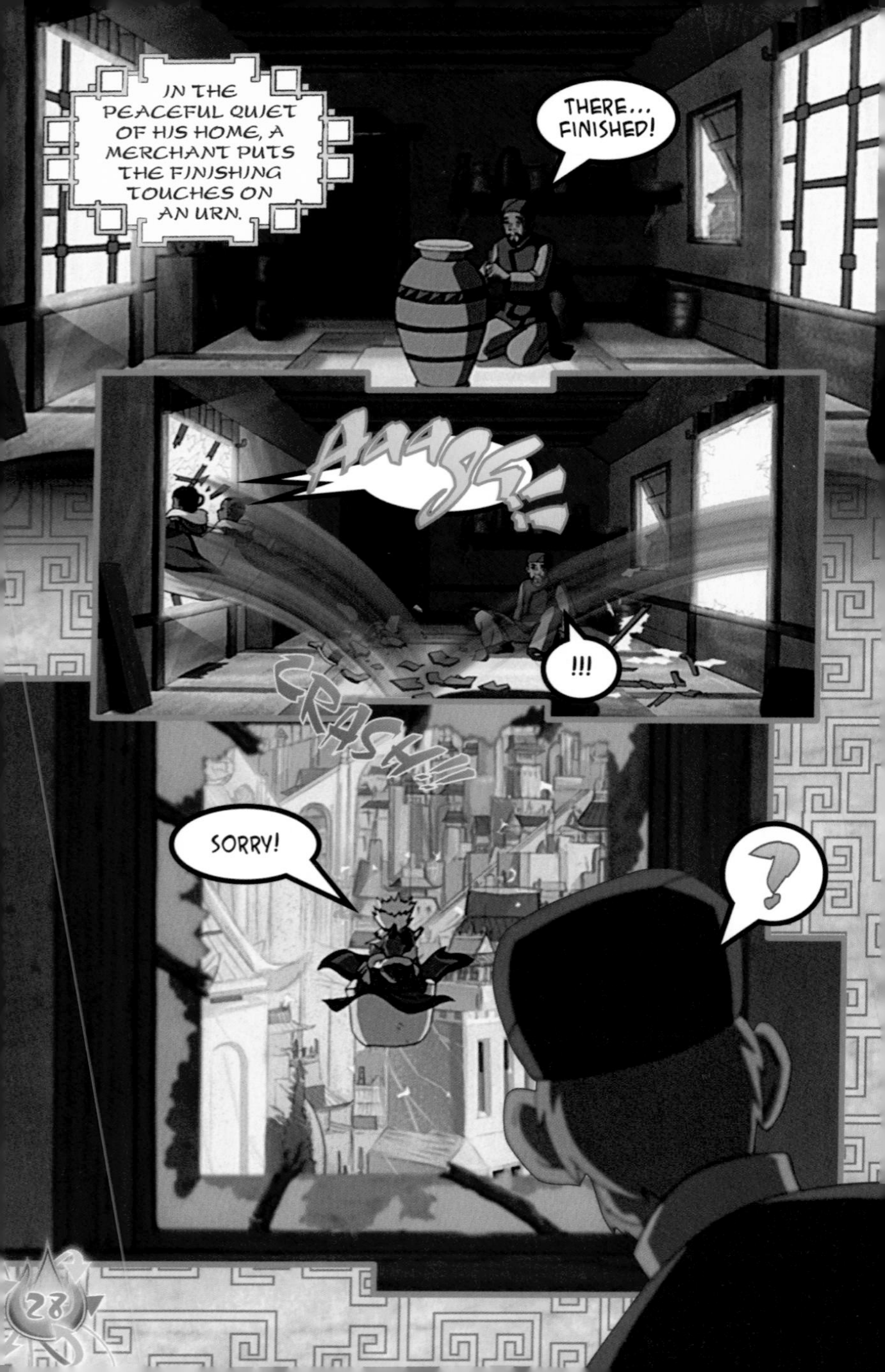
IN THE PEACEFUL QUIET OF HIS HOME, A MERCHANT PUTS THE FINISHING TOUCHES ON AN URN.
THERE... FINISHED!
AAAAGG!!
!!!
CRASH!!!
SORRY!
?

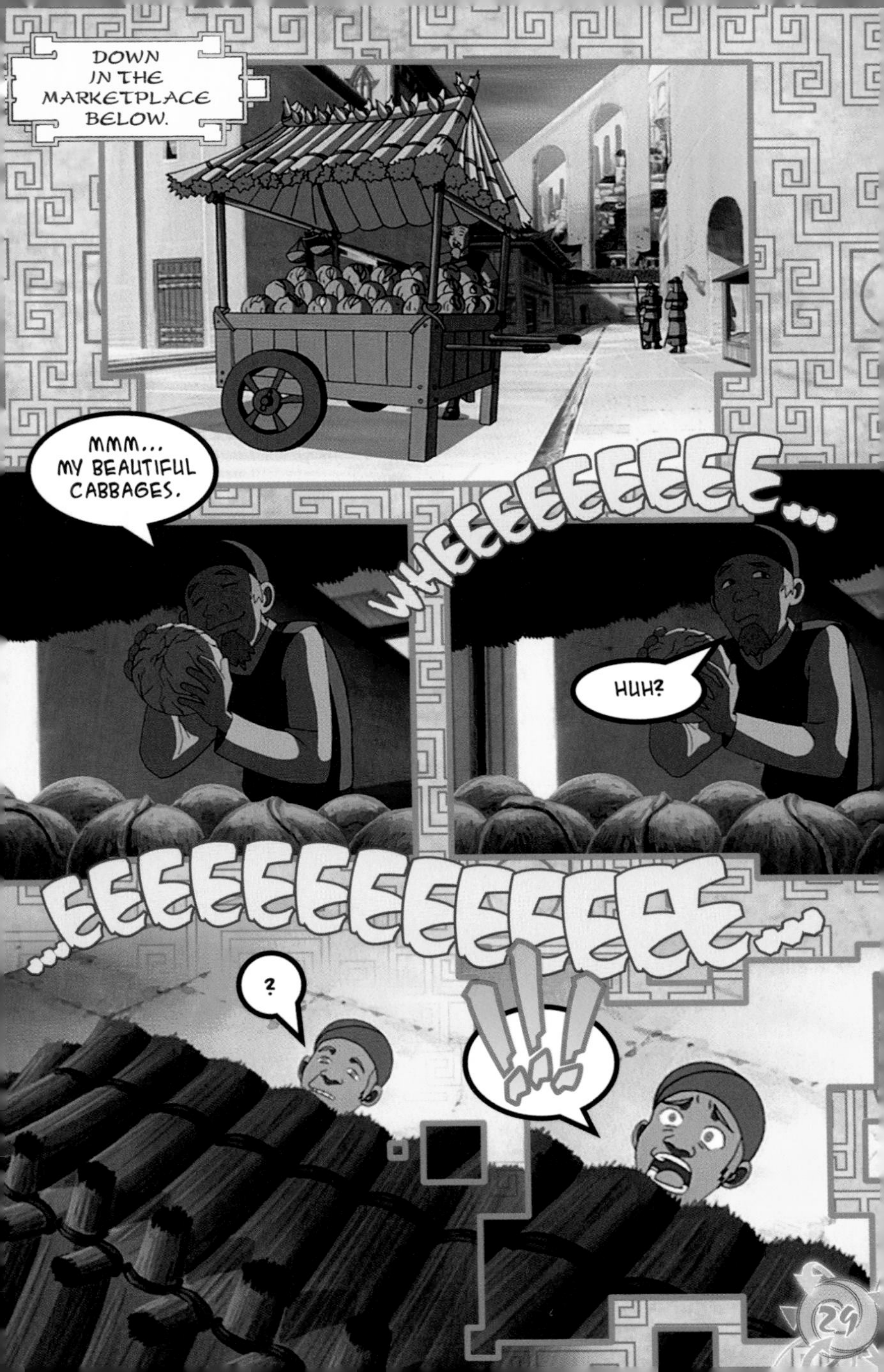
DOWN IN THE MARKETPLACE BELOW.
MMM... MY BEAUTIFUL CABBAGES.
WHEEEEEEEEEEE...
HUH?
...EEEEEEEEEEEEEEE...
?
!!!

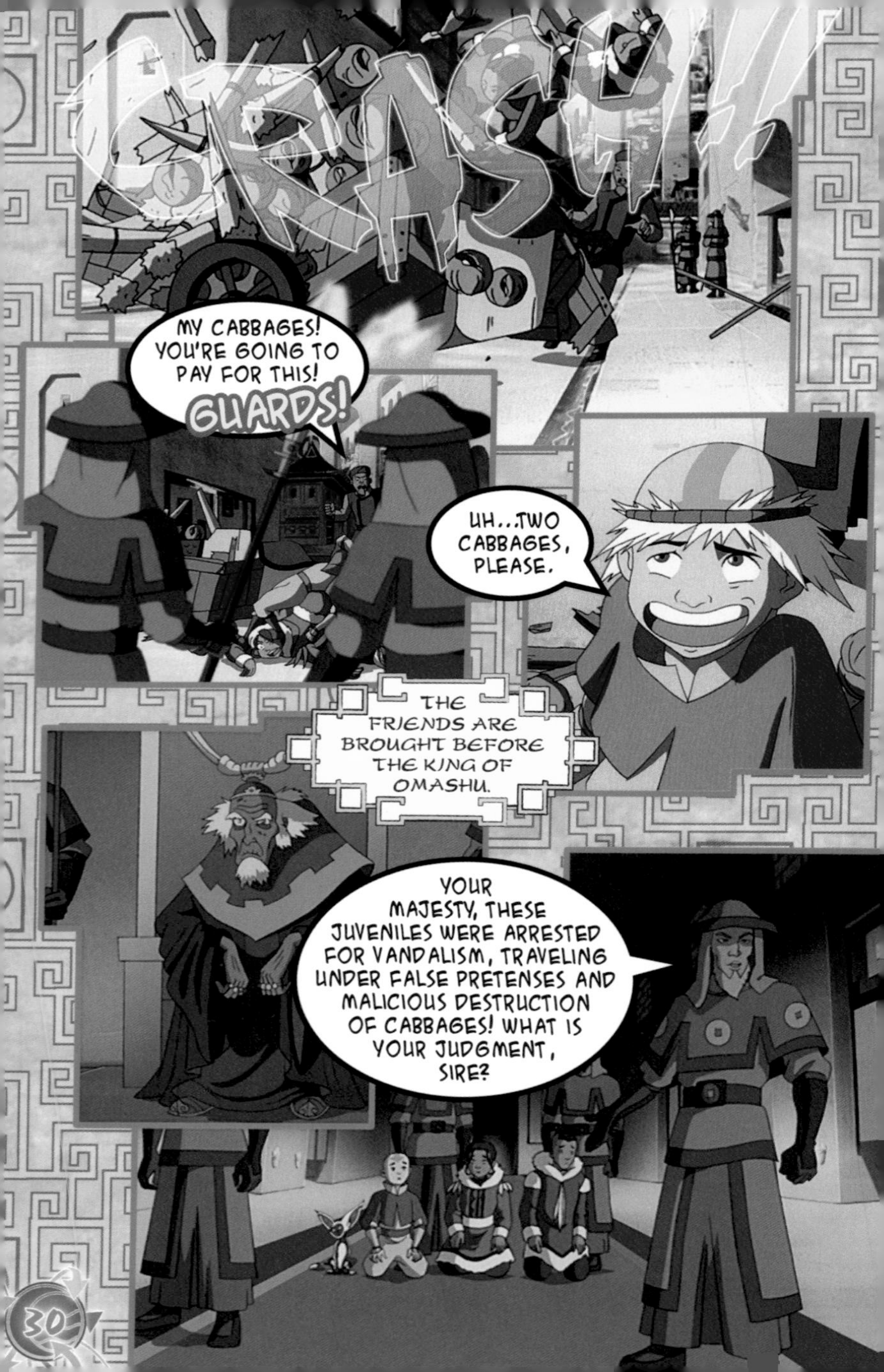
CRASH!!
MY CABBAGES! YOU'RE GOING TO PAY FOR THIS! GUARDS!
UH...TWO CABBAGES, PLEASE.
THE FRIENDS ARE BROUGHT BEFORE THE KING OF OMASHU.
YOUR MAJESTY, THESE JUVENILES WERE ARRESTED FOR VANDALISM, TRAVELING UNDER FALSE PRETENSES AND MALICIOUS DESTRUCTION OF CABBAGES! WHAT IS YOUR JUDGMENT, SIRE?

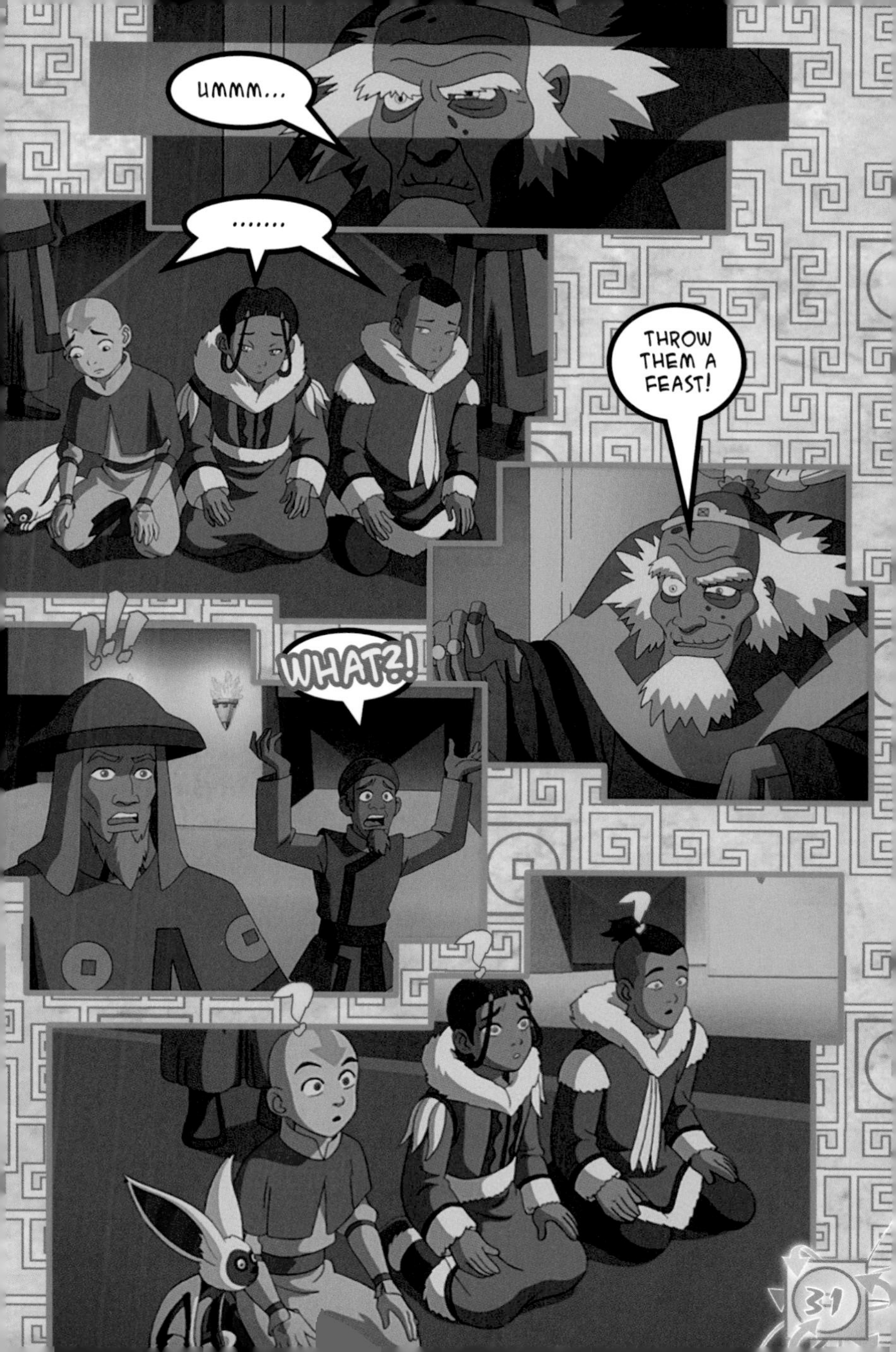
UMMM...
....
THROW THEM A FEAST!
WHAT?!

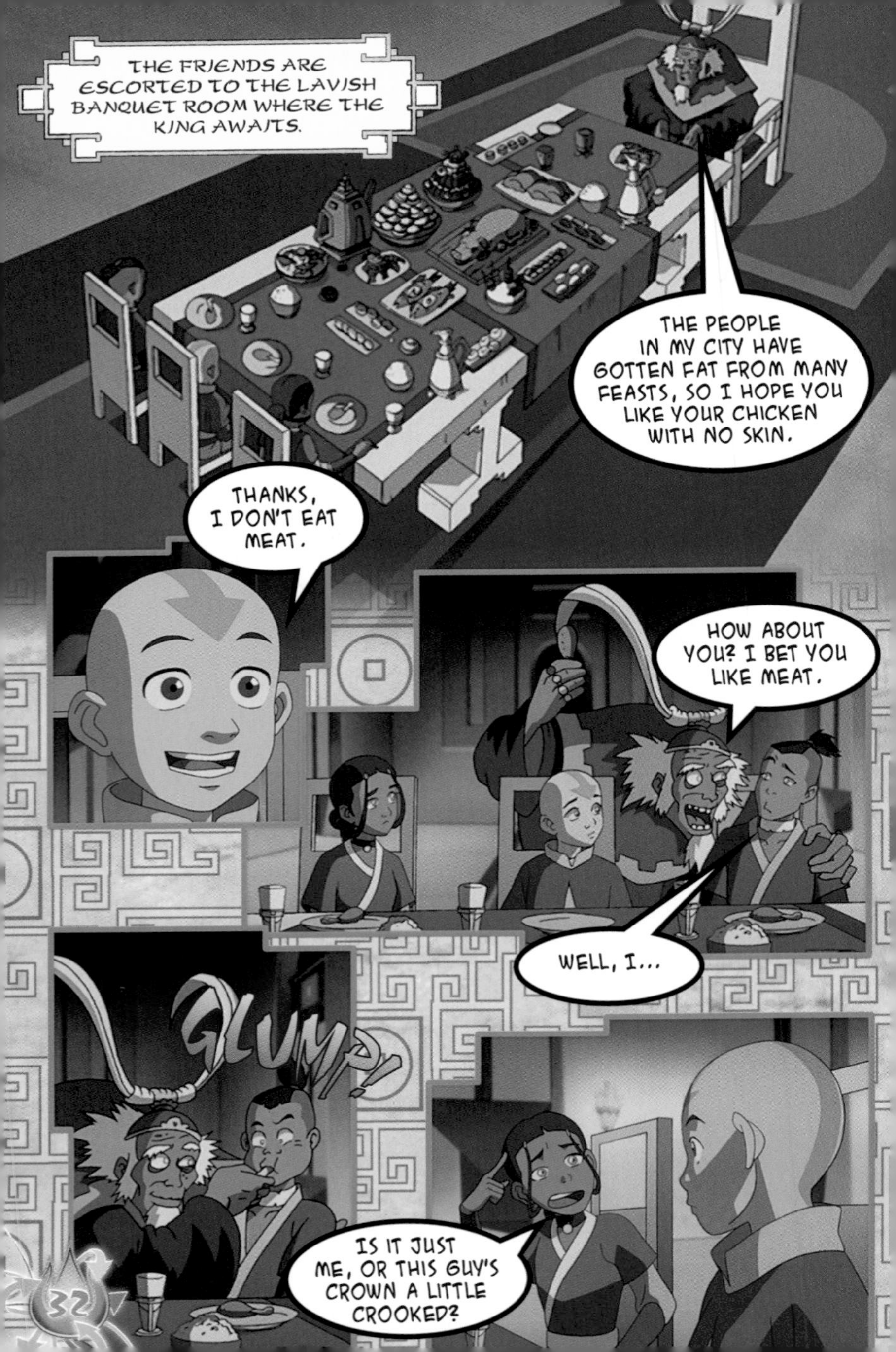
THE FRIENDS ARE ESCORTED TO THE LAVISH BANQUET ROOM WHERE THE KING AWAITS.
THE PEOPLE IN MY CITY HAVE GOTTEN FAT FROM MANY FEASTS, SO I HOPE YOU LIKE YOUR CHICKEN WITH NO SKIN.
THANKS, I DON'T EAT MEAT.
HOW ABOUT YOU? I BET YOU LIKE MEAT.
WELL, I...
GLUMP!
IS IT JUST ME, OR THIS GUY'S CROWN A LITTLE CROOKED?

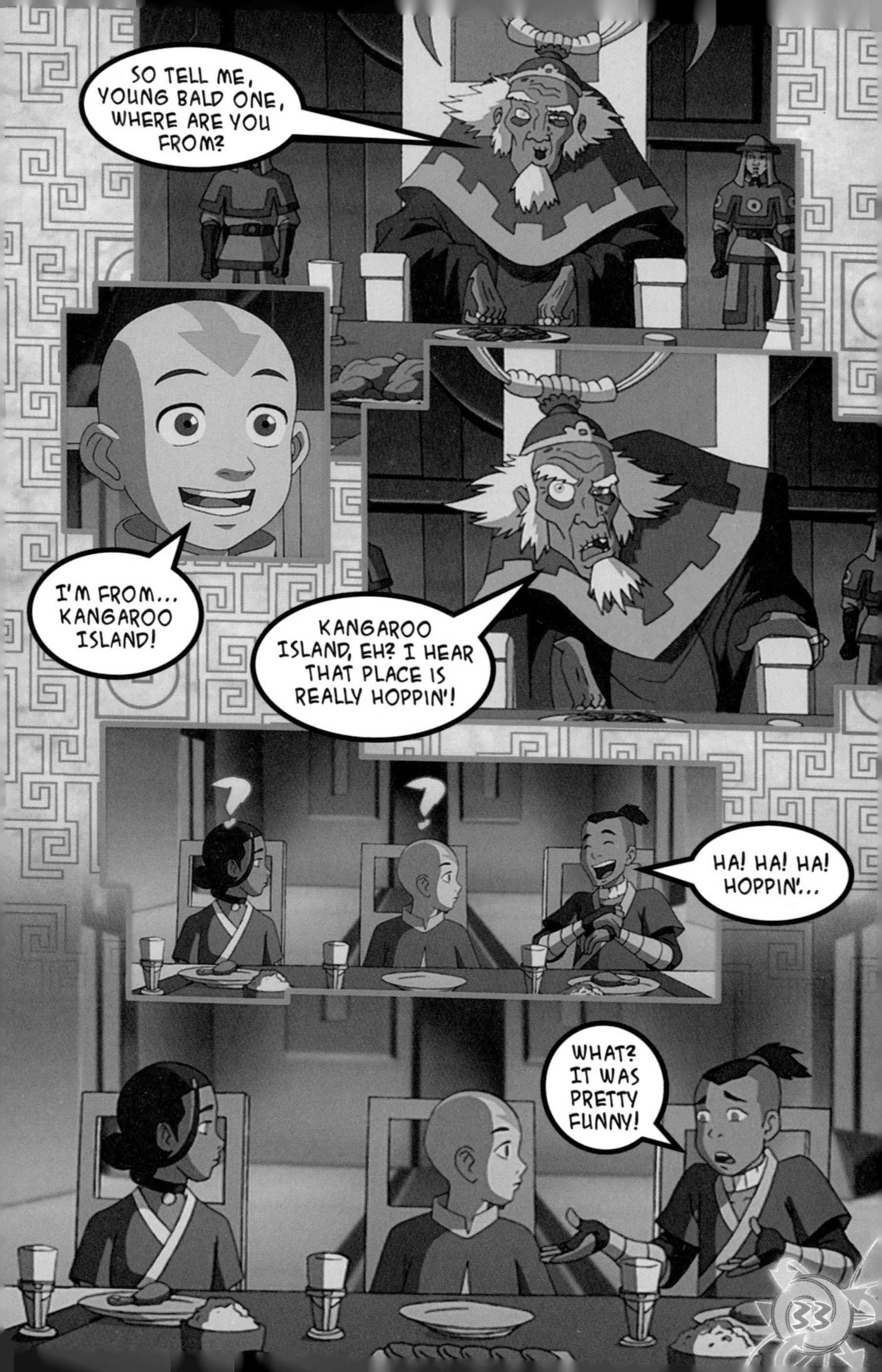
SO TELL ME, YOUNG BALD ONE, WHERE ARE YOU FROM?
I'M FROM... KANGAROO ISLAND!
KANGAROO ISLAND, EH? I HEAR THAT PLACE IS REALLY HOPPIN'!
HA! HA! HA! HOPPIN'...
WHAT? IT WAS PRETTY FUNNY!

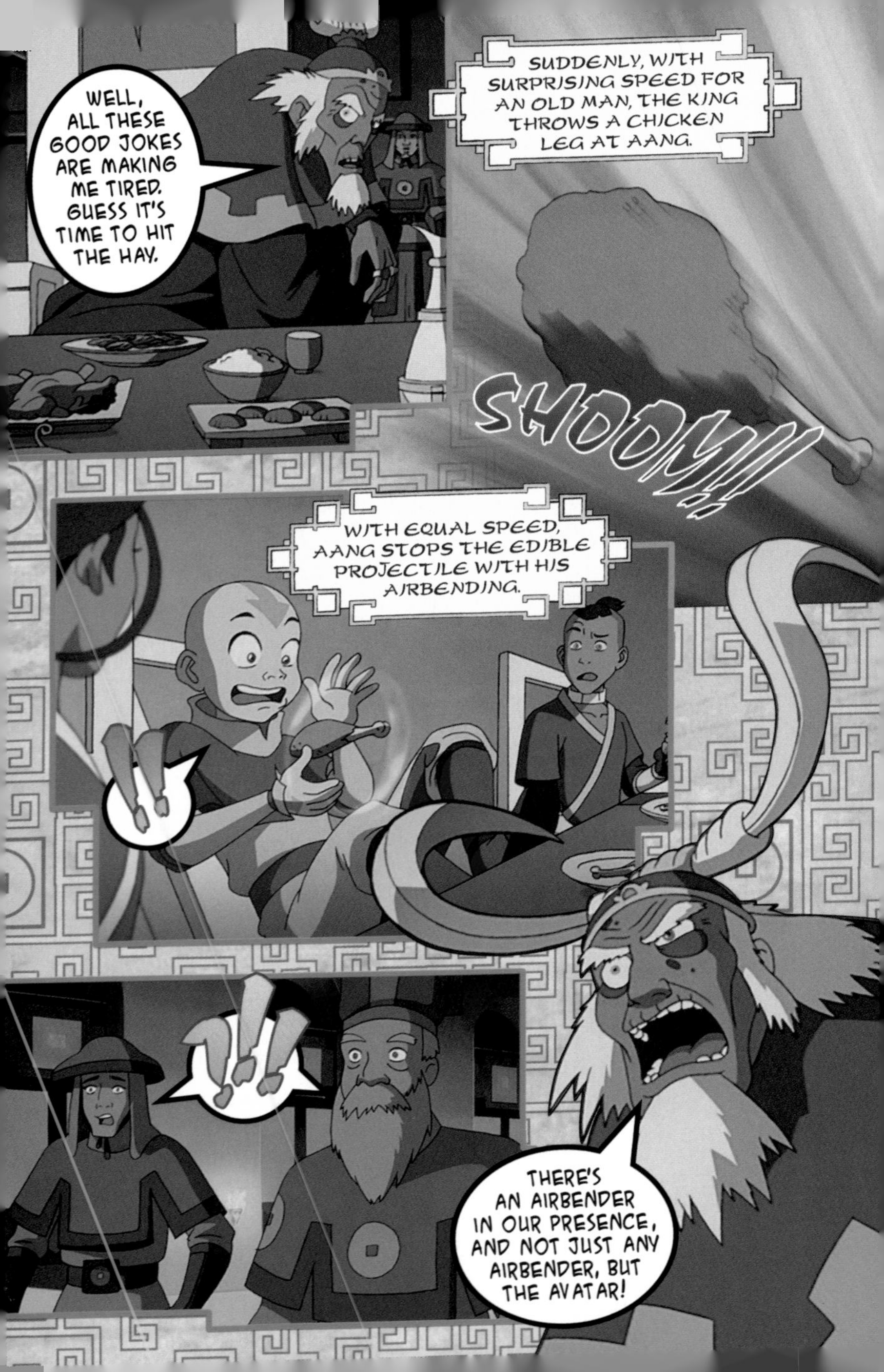
WELL, ALL THESE GOOD JOKES ARE MAKING ME TIRED. GUESS IT'S TIME TO HIT THE HAY.
SUDDENLY, WITH SURPRISING SPEED FOR AN OLD MAN, THE KING THROWS A CHICKEN LEG AT AANG.
SHOOM!!
WITH EQUAL SPEED, AANG STOPS THE EDIBLE PROJECTILE WITH HIS AIRBENDING.
THERE'S AN AIRBENDER IN OUR PRESENCE, AND NOT JUST ANY AIRBENDER, BUT THE AVATAR!

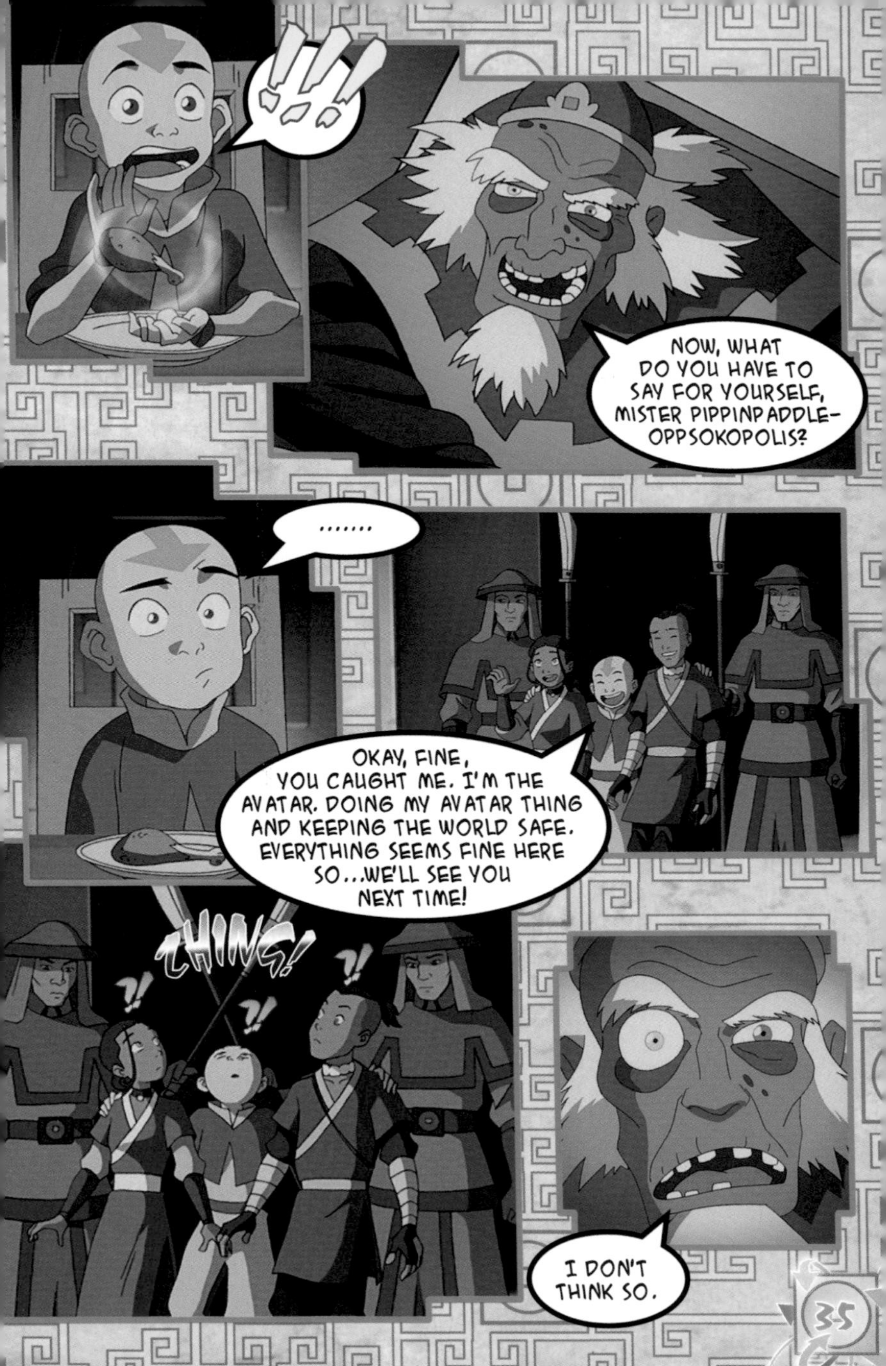
!!!
NOW, WHAT DO YOU HAVE TO SAY FOR YOURSELF, MISTER PIPPINPADDLE-OPPSOKOPOLIS?
....
OKAY, FINE, YOU CAUGHT ME. I'M THE AVATAR. DOING MY AVATAR THING AND KEEPING THE WORLD SAFE. EVERYTHING SEEMS FINE HERE SO...WE'LL SEE YOU NEXT TIME!
CHING!
?!
?!
?!
I DON'T THINK SO.

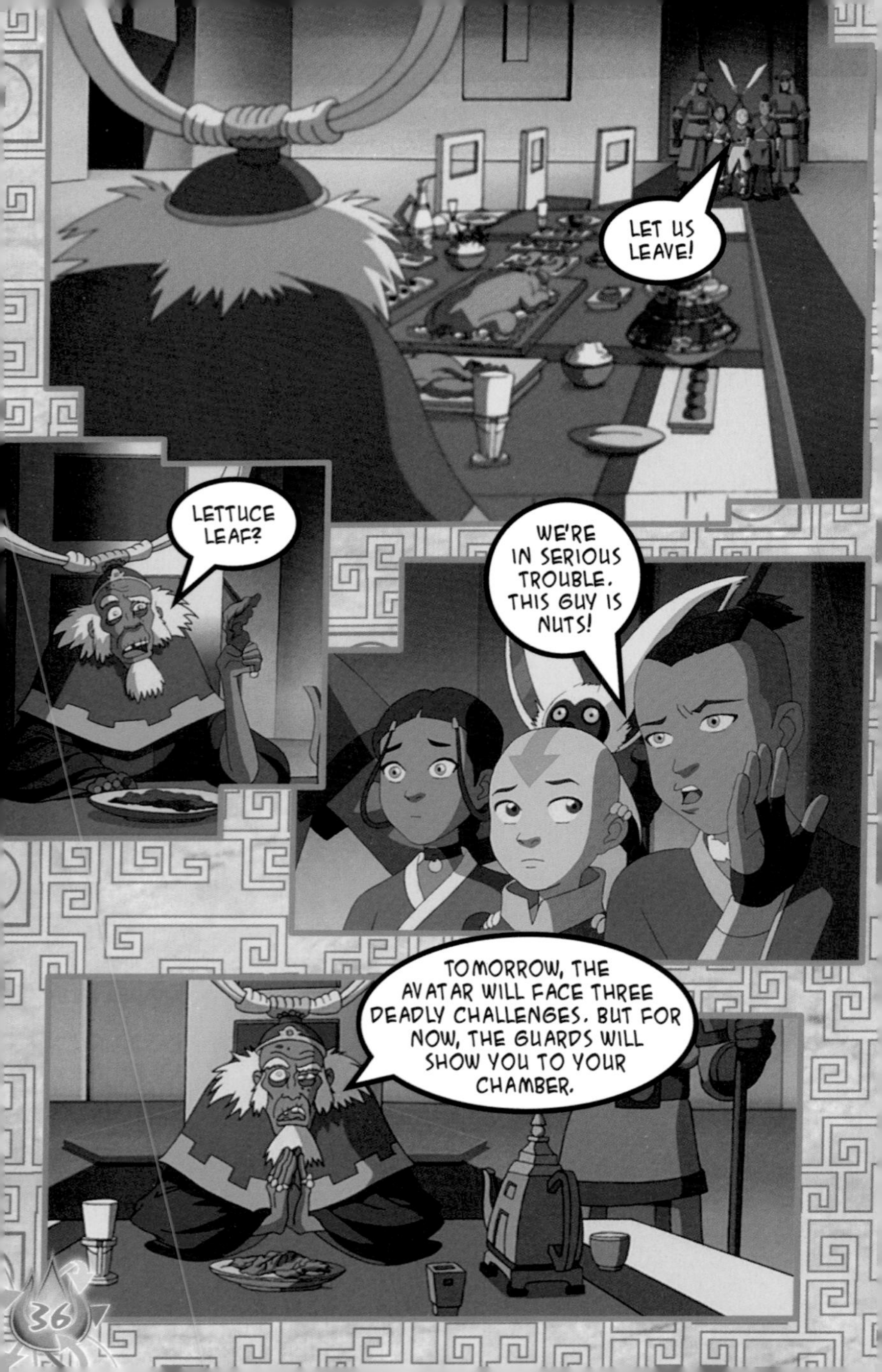
LET US LEAVE!
LETTUCE LEAF?
WE'RE IN SERIOUS TROUBLE. THIS GUY IS NUTS!
TOMORROW, THE AVATAR WILL FACE THREE DEADLY CHALLENGES. BUT FOR NOW, THE GUARDS WILL SHOW YOU TO YOUR CHAMBER.

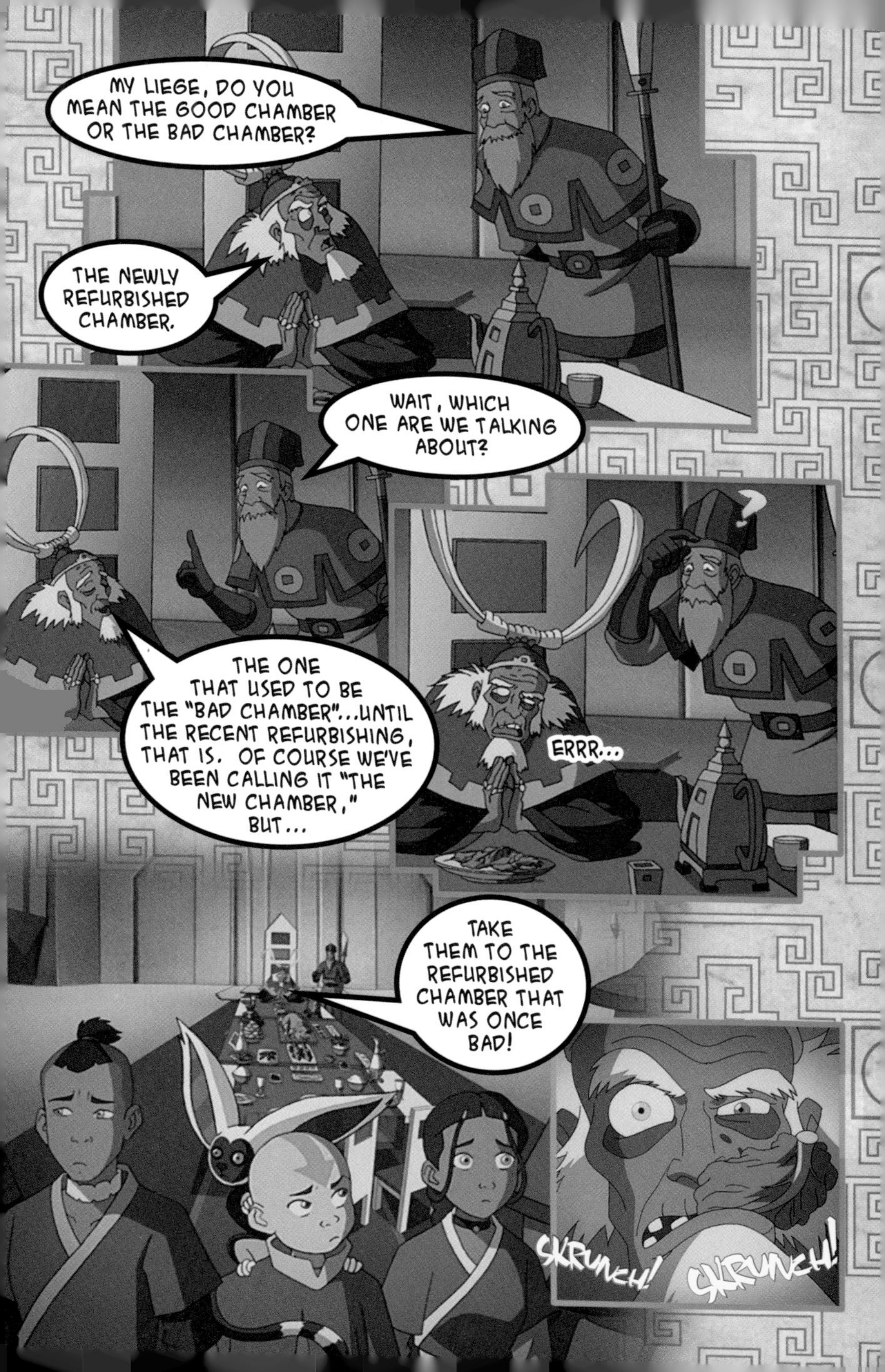
MY LIEGE, DO YOU MEAN THE GOOD CHAMBER OR THE BAD CHAMBER?
THE NEWLY REFURBISHED CHAMBER.
WAIT, WHICH ONE ARE WE TALKING ABOUT?
THE ONE THAT USED TO BE THE "BAD CHAMBER"...UNTIL THE RECENT REFURBISHING, THAT IS. OF COURSE WE'VE BEEN CALLING IT "THE NEW CHAMBER," BUT...
?
ERRR...
TAKE THEM TO THE REFURBISHED CHAMBER THAT WAS ONCE BAD!
SKRUNCH! SKRUNCH!

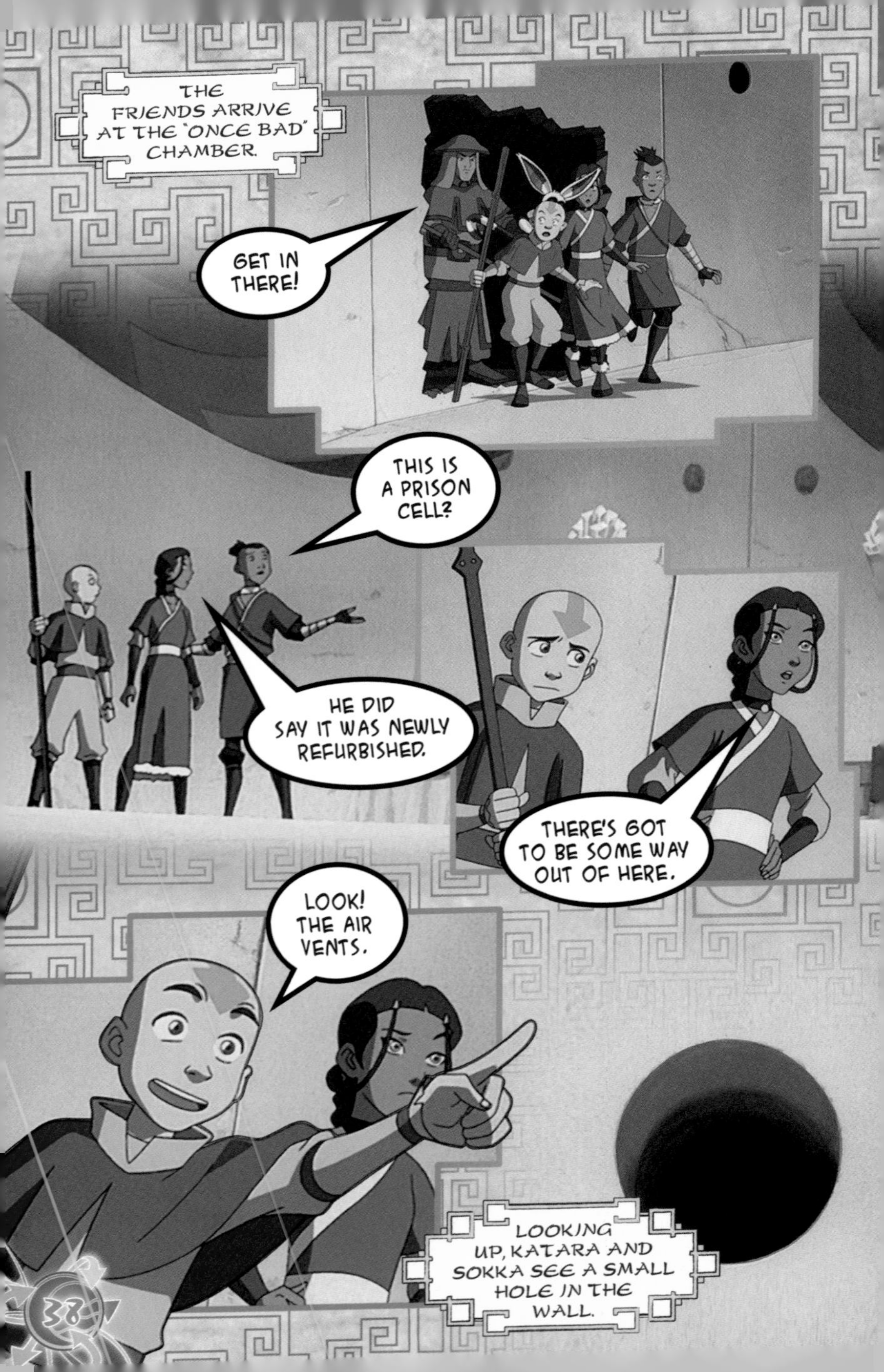
THE FRIENDS ARRIVE AT THE "ONCE BAD" CHAMBER.
GET IN THERE!
THIS IS A PRISON CELL?
HE DID SAY IT WAS NEWLY REFURBISHED.
THERE'S GOT TO BE SOME WAY OUT OF HERE.
LOOK! THE AIR VENTS.
LOOKING UP, KATARA AND SOKKA SEE A SMALL HOLE IN THE WALL.

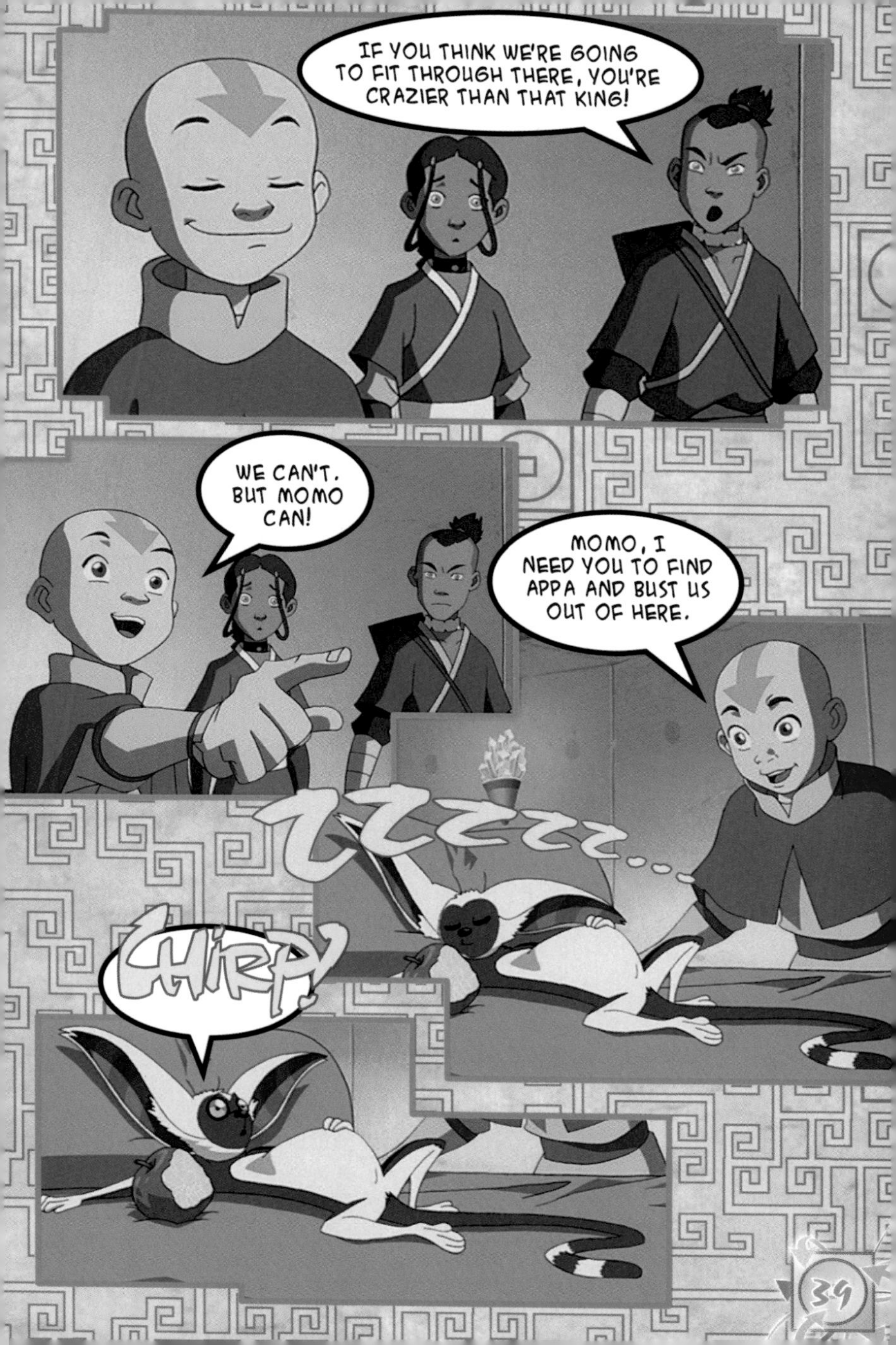
IF YOU THINK WE'RE GOING TO FIT THROUGH THERE, YOU'RE CRAZIER THAN THAT KING!
WE CAN'T. BUT MOMO CAN!
MOMO, I NEED YOU TO FIND APPA AND BUST US OUT OF HERE.
ZZZZZZ...
CHIRP!

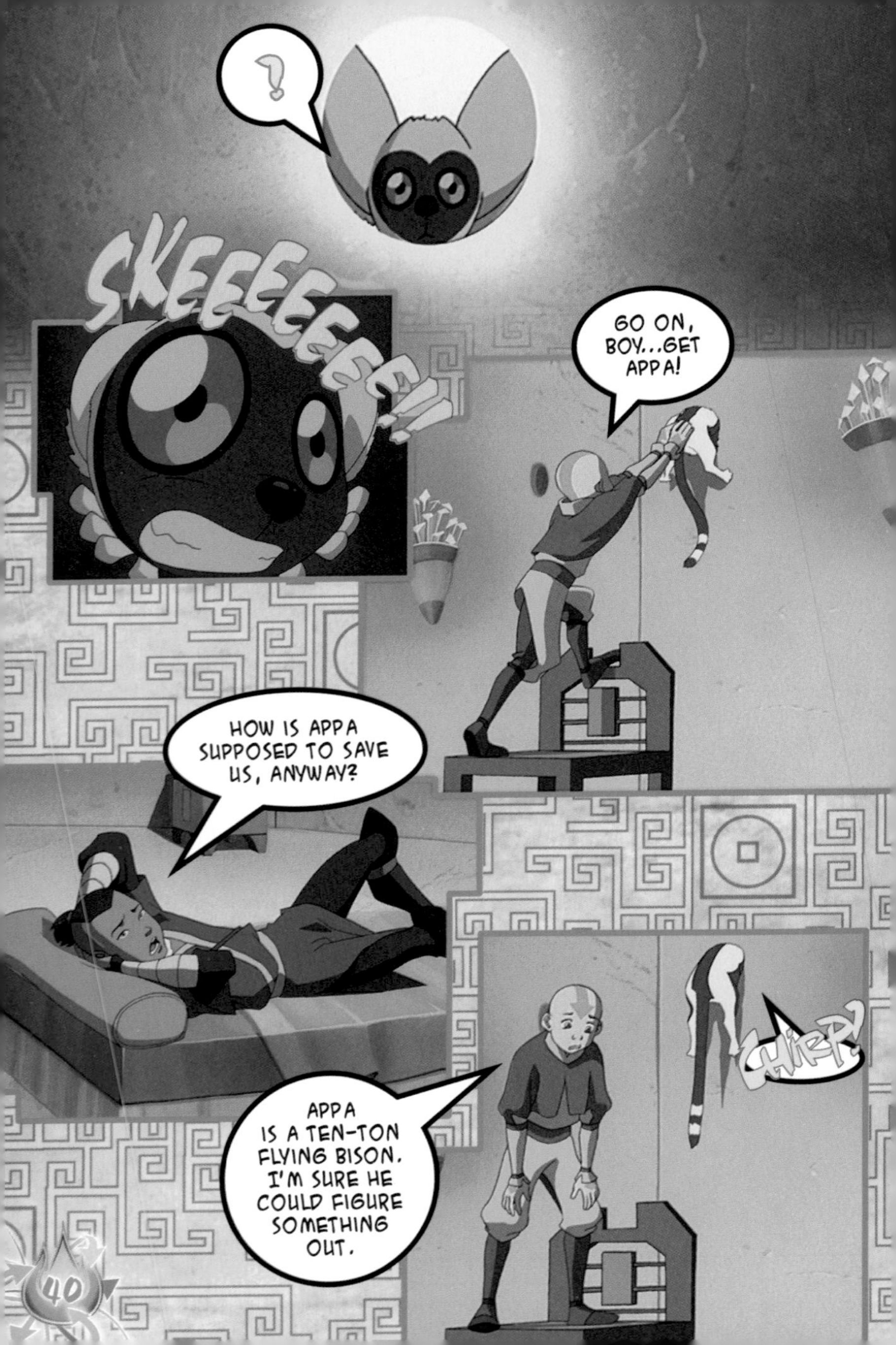
?
SKEEEEEEE!!
GO ON, BOY...GET APPA!
HOW IS APPA SUPPOSED TO SAVE US, ANYWAY?
APPA IS A TEN-TON FLYING BISON. I'M SURE HE COULD FIGURE SOMETHING OUT.
CHIRP?

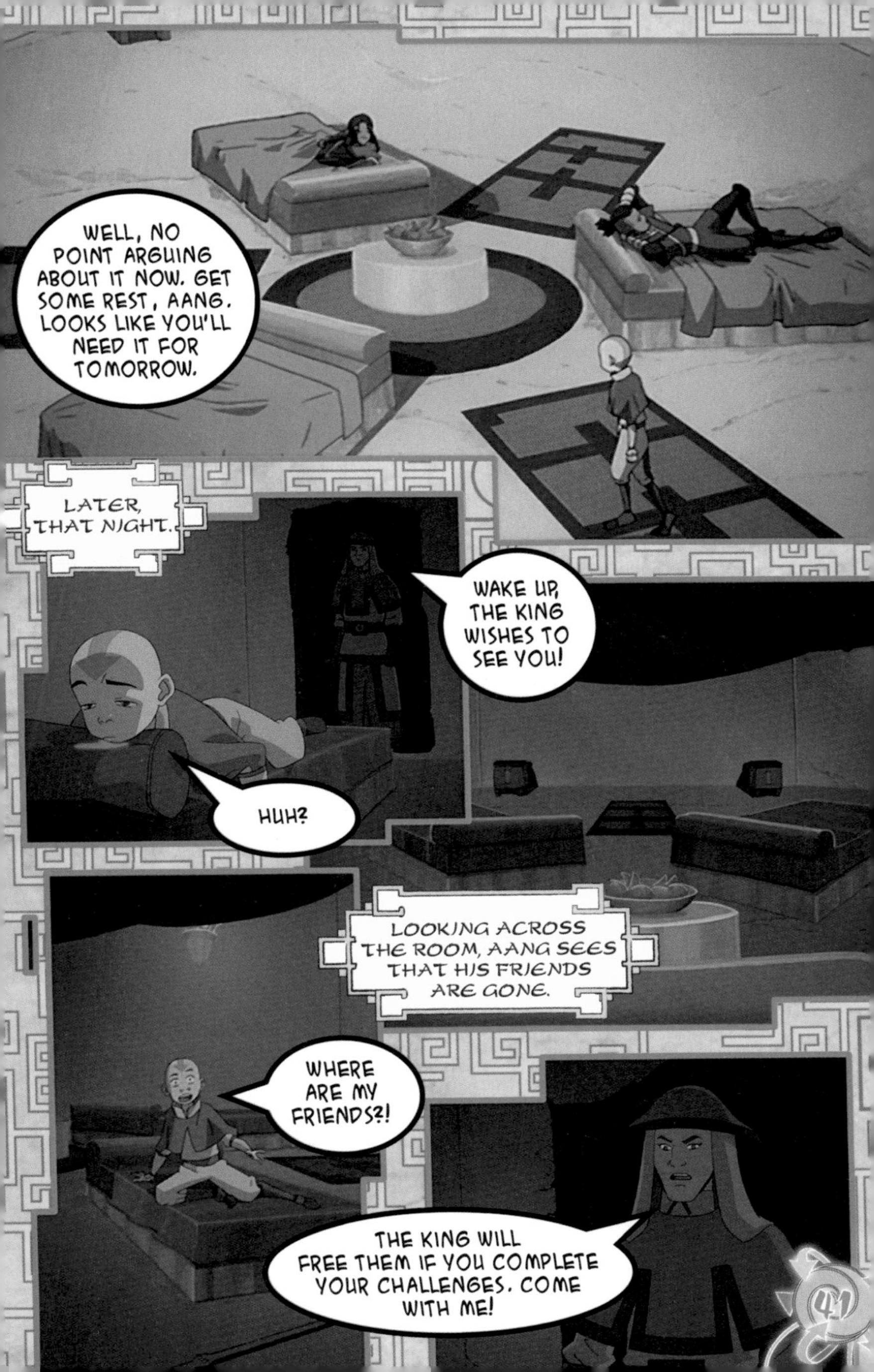
WELL, NO POINT ARGUING ABOUT IT NOW. GET SOME REST, AANG. LOOKS LIKE YOU'LL NEED IT FOR TOMORROW.
LATER, THAT NIGHT.
WAKE UP, THE KING WISHES TO SEE YOU!
HUH?
LOOKING ACROSS THE ROOM, AANG SEES THAT HIS FRIENDS ARE GONE.
WHERE ARE MY FRIENDS?!
THE KING WILL FREE THEM IF YOU COMPLETE YOUR CHALLENGES. COME WITH ME!

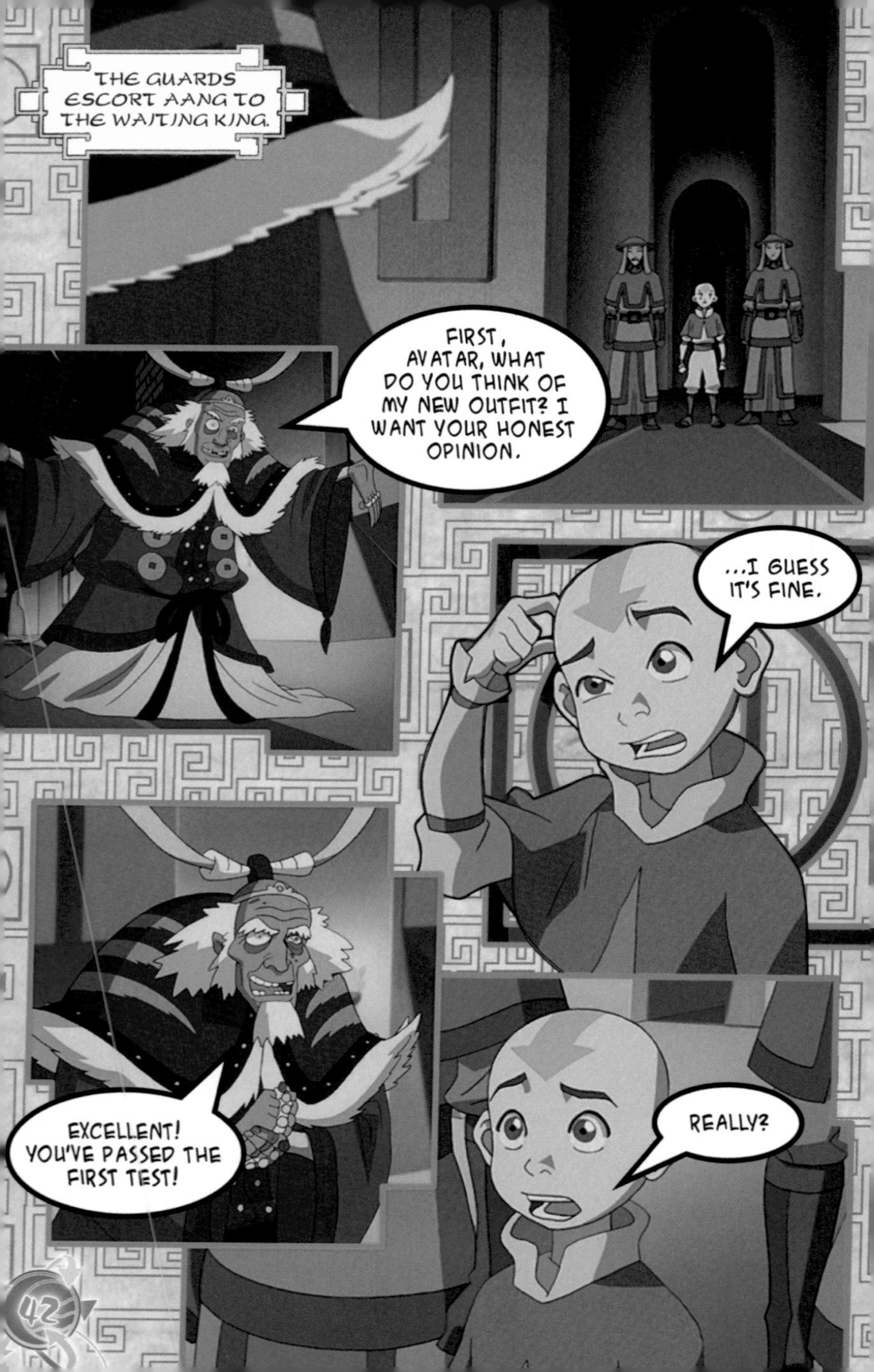
THE GUARDS ESCORT AANG TO THE WAITING KING.
FIRST, AVATAR, WHAT DO YOU THINK OF MY NEW OUTFIT? I WANT YOUR HONEST OPINION.
...I GUESS IT'S FINE.
EXCELLENT! YOU'VE PASSED THE FIRST TEST!
REALLY?
42

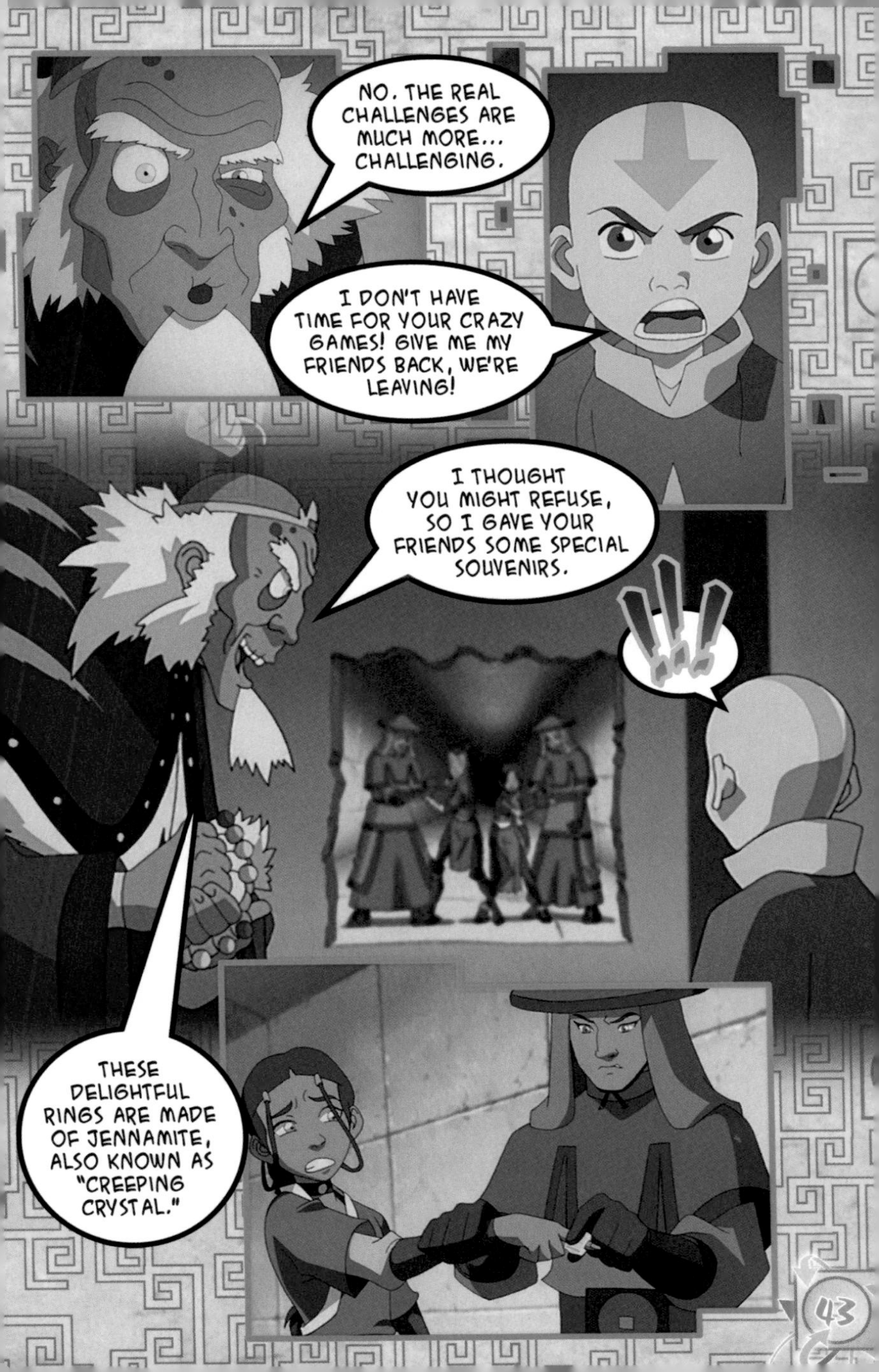
NO. THE REAL CHALLENGES ARE MUCH MORE... CHALLENGING.
I DON'T HAVE TIME FOR YOUR CRAZY GAMES! GIVE ME MY FRIENDS BACK, WE'RE LEAVING!
I THOUGHT YOU MIGHT REFUSE, SO I GAVE YOUR FRIENDS SOME SPECIAL SOUVENIRS.
!!!
THESE DELIGHTFUL RINGS ARE MADE OF JENNAMITE, ALSO KNOWN AS "CREEPING CRYSTAL."

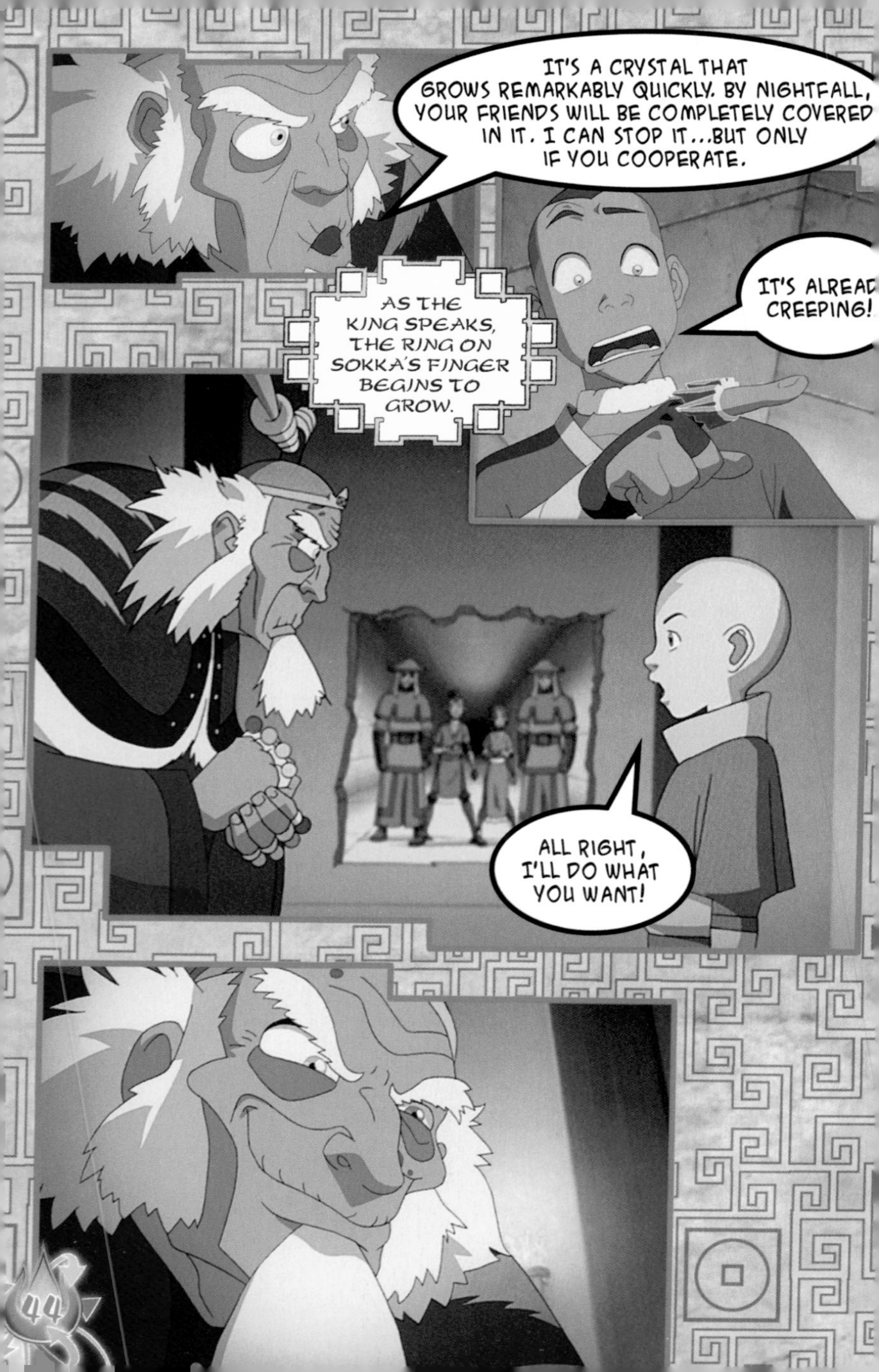
IT'S A CRYSTAL THAT GROWS REMARKABLY QUICKLY. BY NIGHTFALL, YOUR FRIENDS WILL BE COMPLETELY COVERED IN IT. I CAN STOP IT...BUT ONLY IF YOU COOPERATE.
AS THE KING SPEAKS, THE RING ON SOKKA'S FINGER BEGINS TO GROW.
IT'S ALREAD CREEPING!
ALL RIGHT, I'LL DO WHAT YOU WANT!

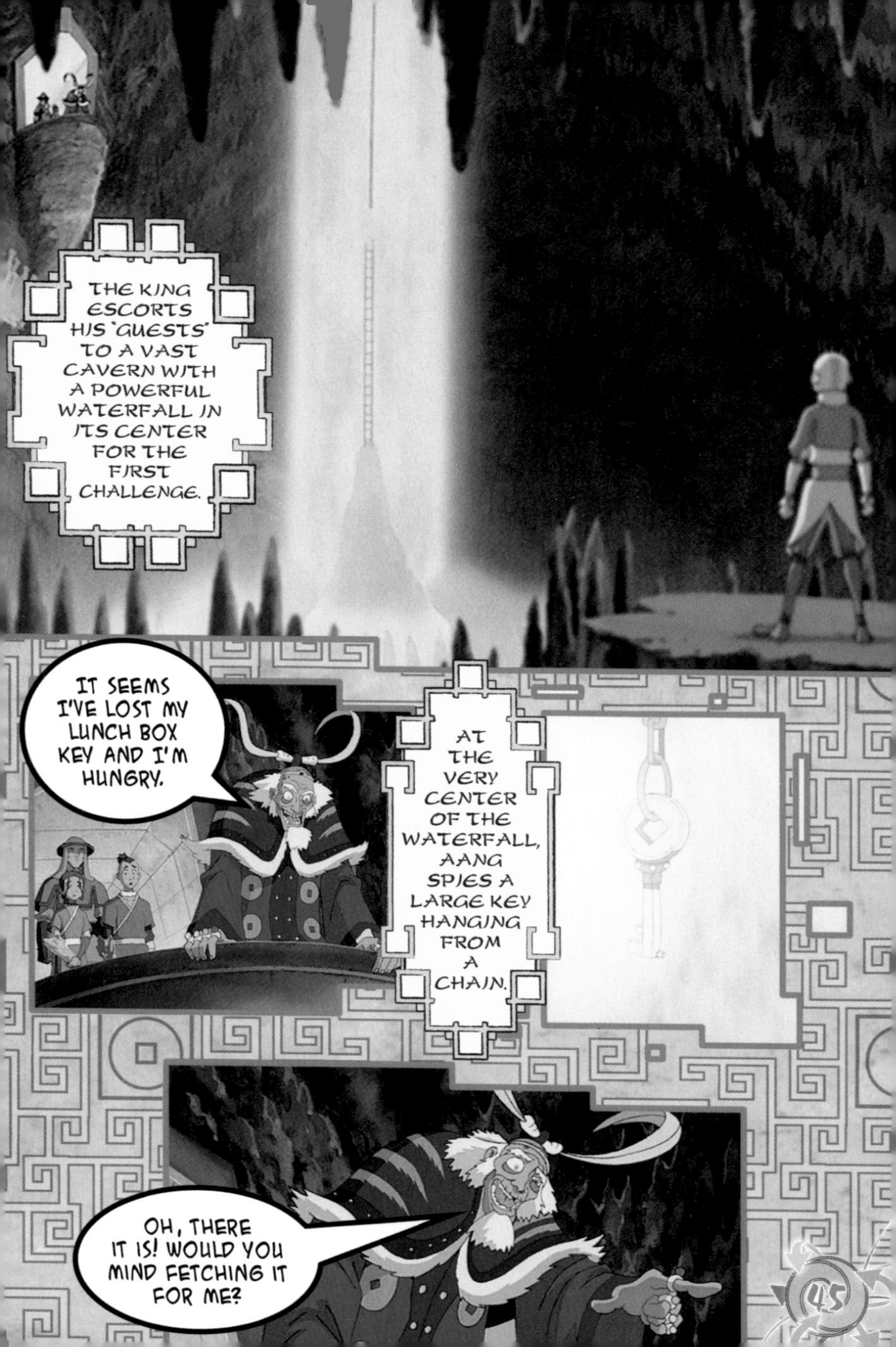
THE KING ESCORTS HIS "GUESTS" TO A VAST CAVERN WITH A POWERFUL WATERFALL IN ITS CENTER FOR THE FIRST CHALLENGE.
IT SEEMS I'VE LOST MY LUNCH BOX KEY AND I'M HUNGRY.
AT THE VERY CENTER OF THE WATERFALL, AANG SPIES A LARGE KEY HANGING FROM A CHAIN.
OH, THERE IT IS! WOULD YOU MIND FETCHING IT FOR ME?
45

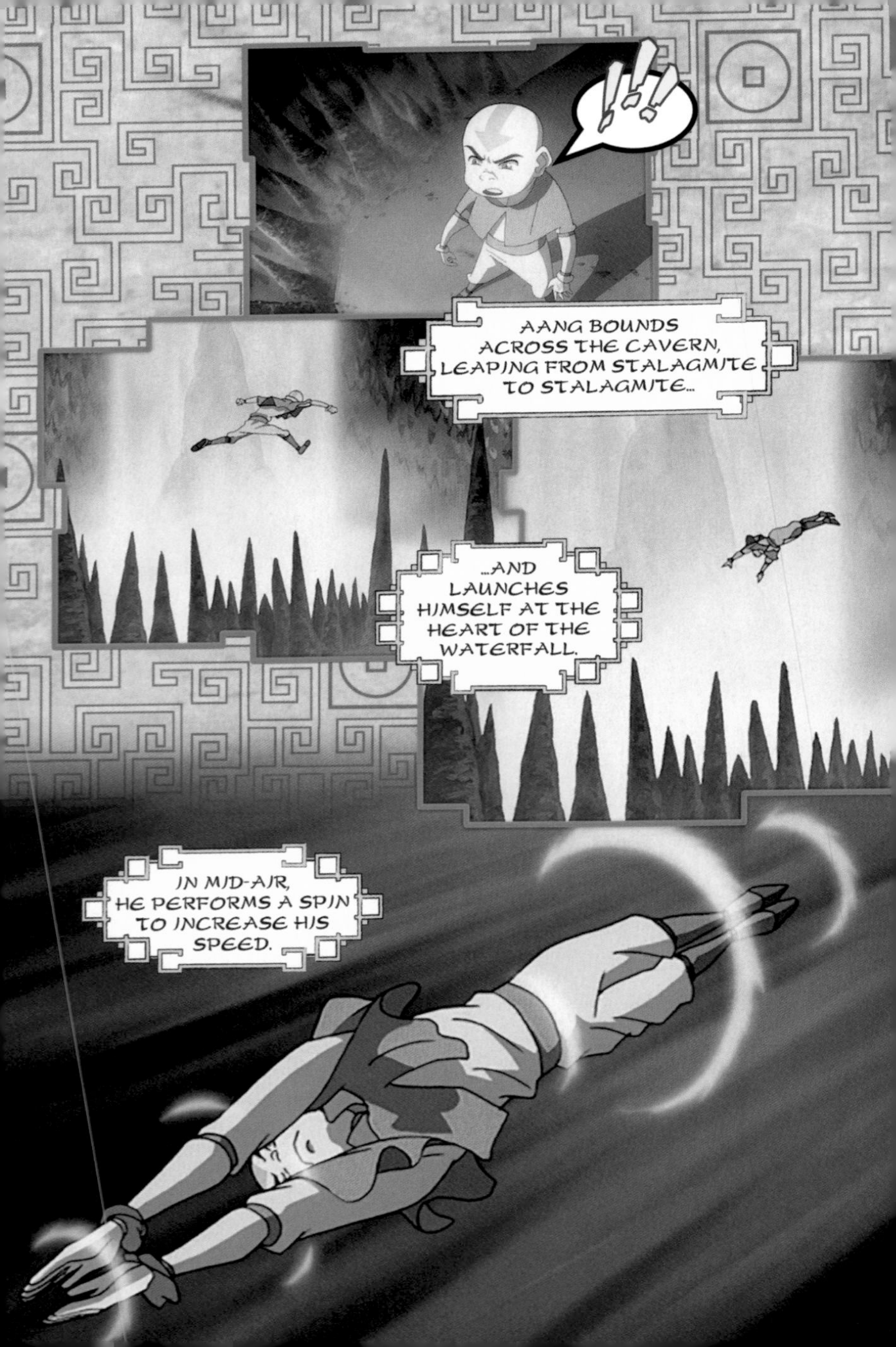
!!
AANG BOUNDS ACROSS THE CAVERN, LEAPING FROM STALAGMITE TO STALAGMITE...
...AND LAUNCHES HIMSELF AT THE HEART OF THE WATERFALL.
IN MID-AIR, HE PERFORMS A SPIN TO INCREASE HIS SPEED.

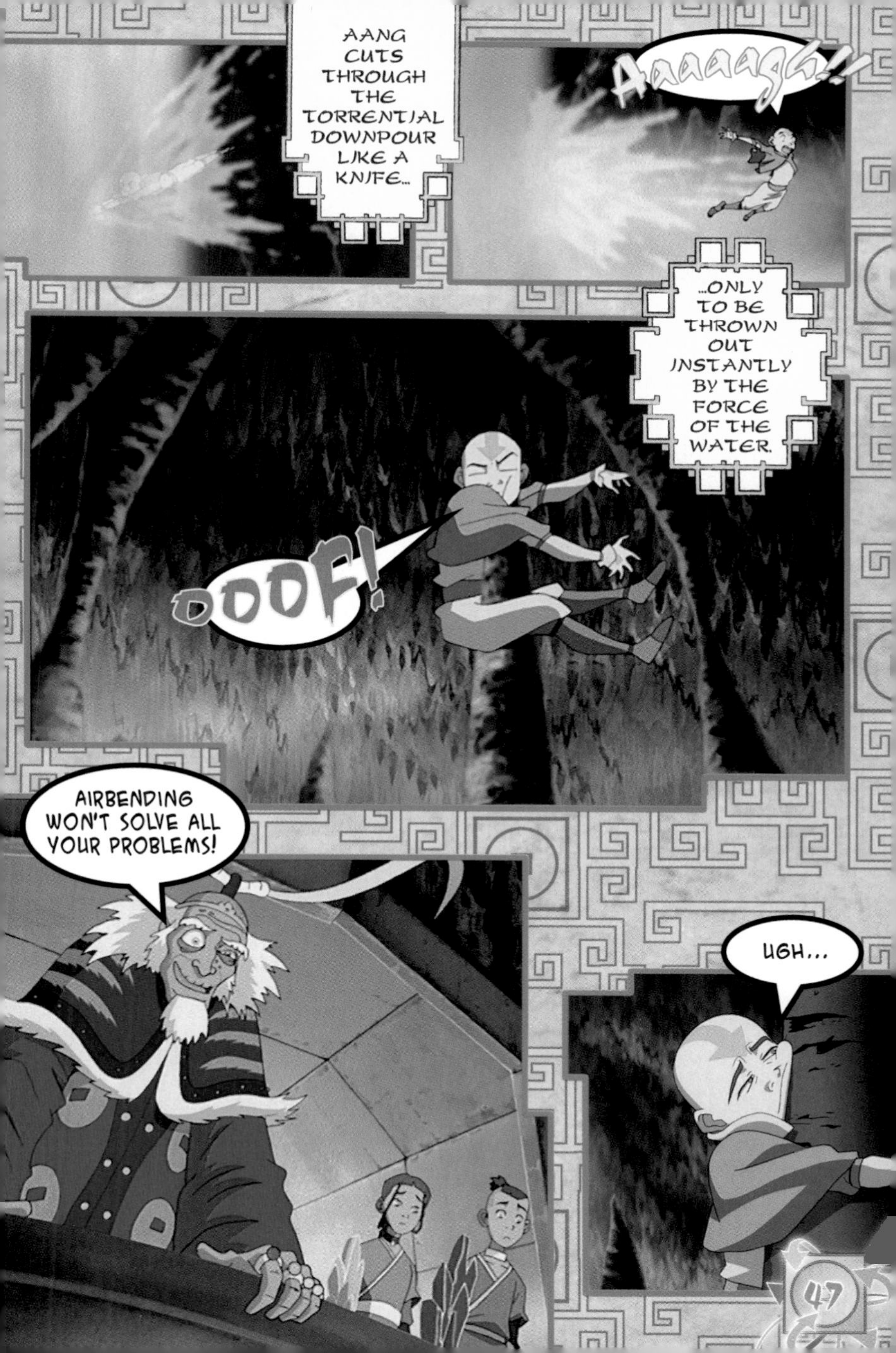
AANG CUTS THROUGH THE TORRENTIAL DOWNPOUR LIKE A KNIFE...
Aaaaagh!!
...ONLY TO BE THROWN OUT INSTANTLY BY THE FORCE OF THE WATER.
OOOF!
AIRBENDING WON'T SOLVE ALL YOUR PROBLEMS!
UGH...

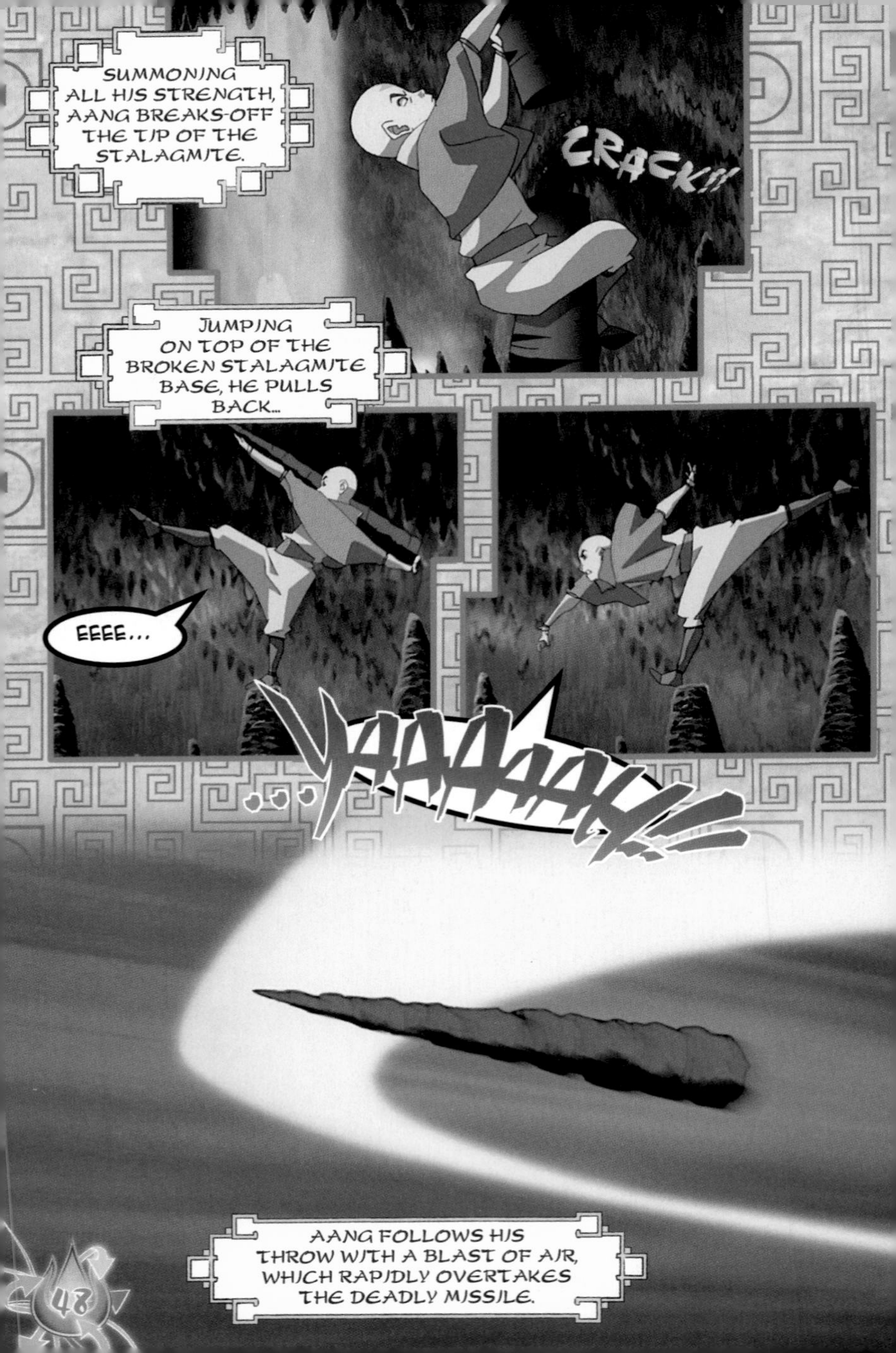
SUMMONING ALL HIS STRENGTH, AANG BREAKS-OFF THE TIP OF THE STALAGMITE.
CRACK!!
JUMPING ON TOP OF THE BROKEN STALAGMITE BASE, HE PULLS BACK...
EEEE...
...YAAAAAH!!!
AANG FOLLOWS HIS THROW WITH A BLAST OF AIR, WHICH RAPIDLY OVERTAKES THE DEADLY MISSILE.

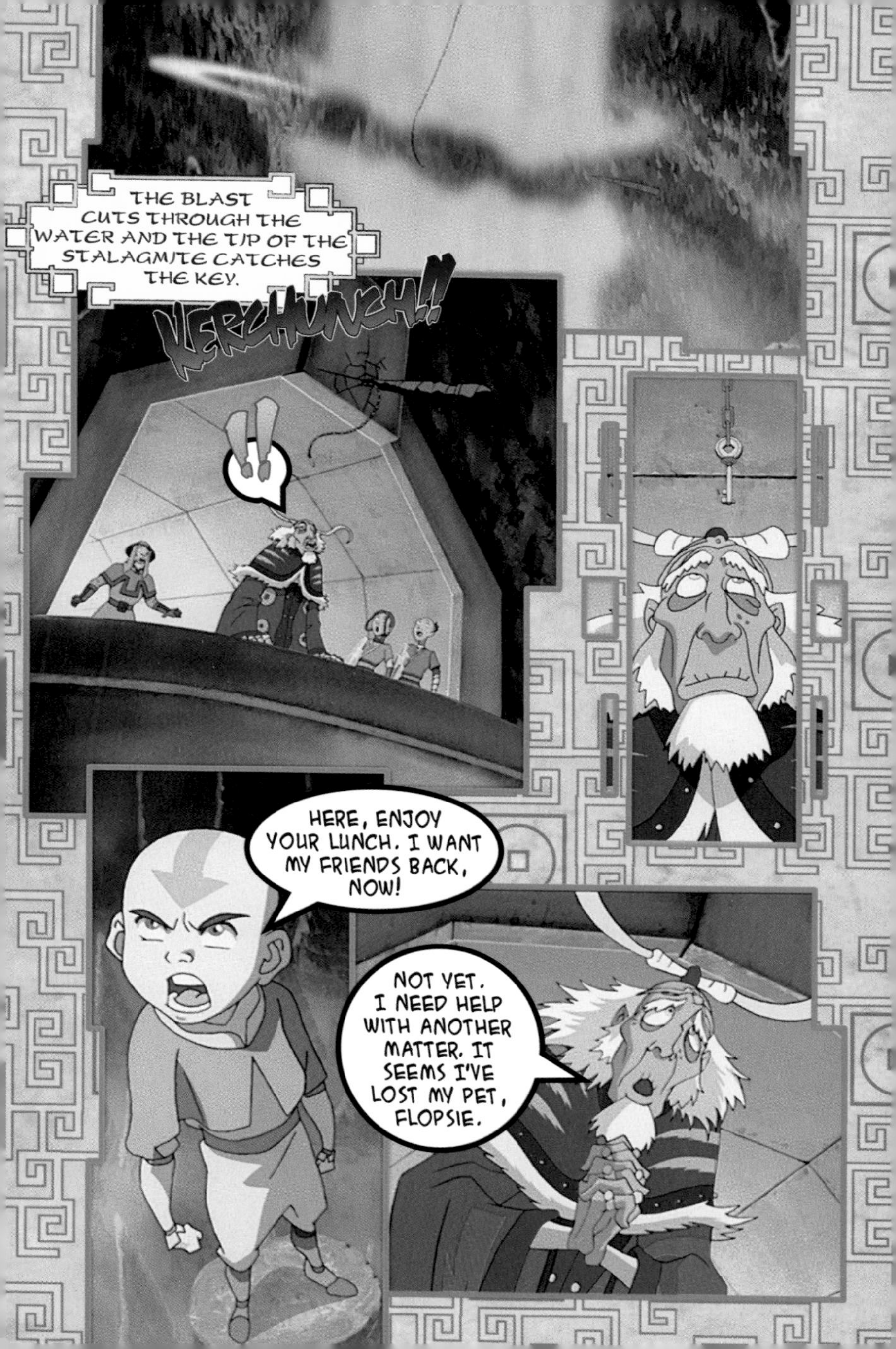
THE BLAST CUTS THROUGH THE WATER AND THE TIP OF THE STALAGMITE CATCHES THE KEY.
KERCHUNCH!!
HERE, ENJOY YOUR LUNCH. I WANT MY FRIENDS BACK, NOW!
NOT YET. I NEED HELP WITH ANOTHER MATTER. IT SEEMS I'VE LOST MY PET, FLOPSIE.

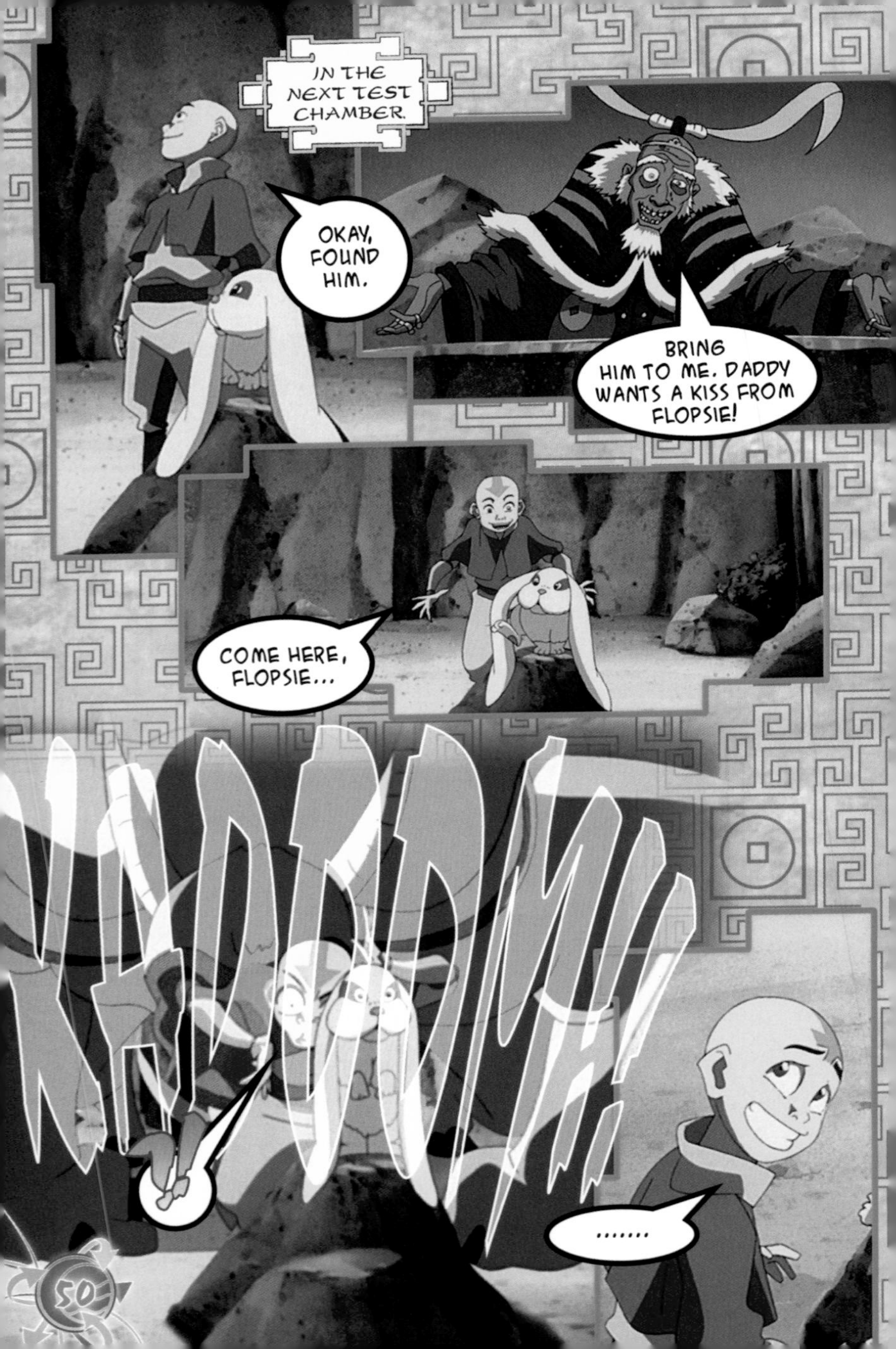
IN THE NEXT TEST CHAMBER.
OKAY, FOUND HIM.
BRING HIM TO ME. DADDY WANTS A KISS FROM FLOPSIE!
COME HERE, FLOPSIE...
....

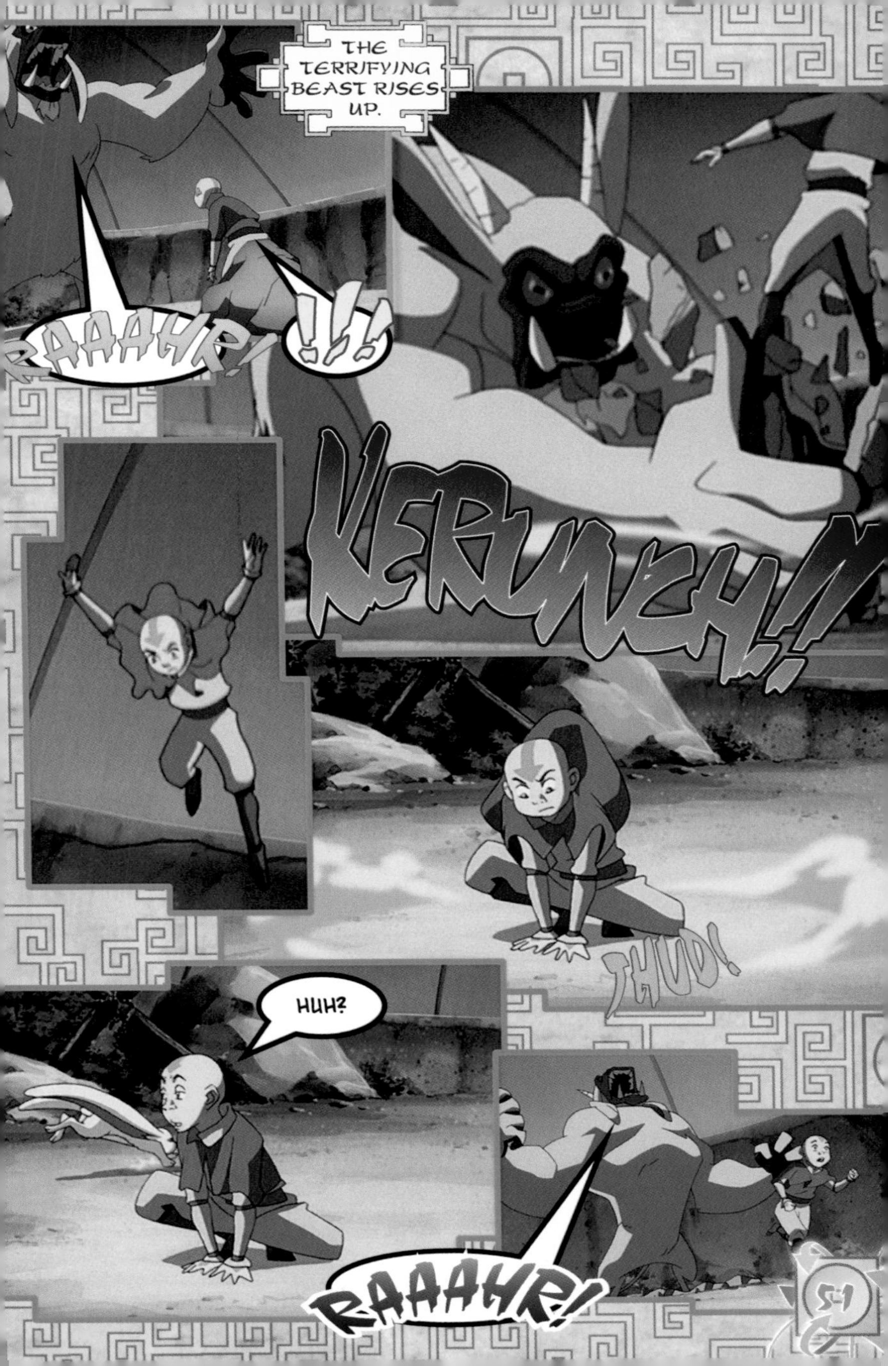
THE TERRIFYING BEAST RISES UP.
RAAAHR!
!!!
KERUNCH!!
THUD!
HUH?
RAAAHR!

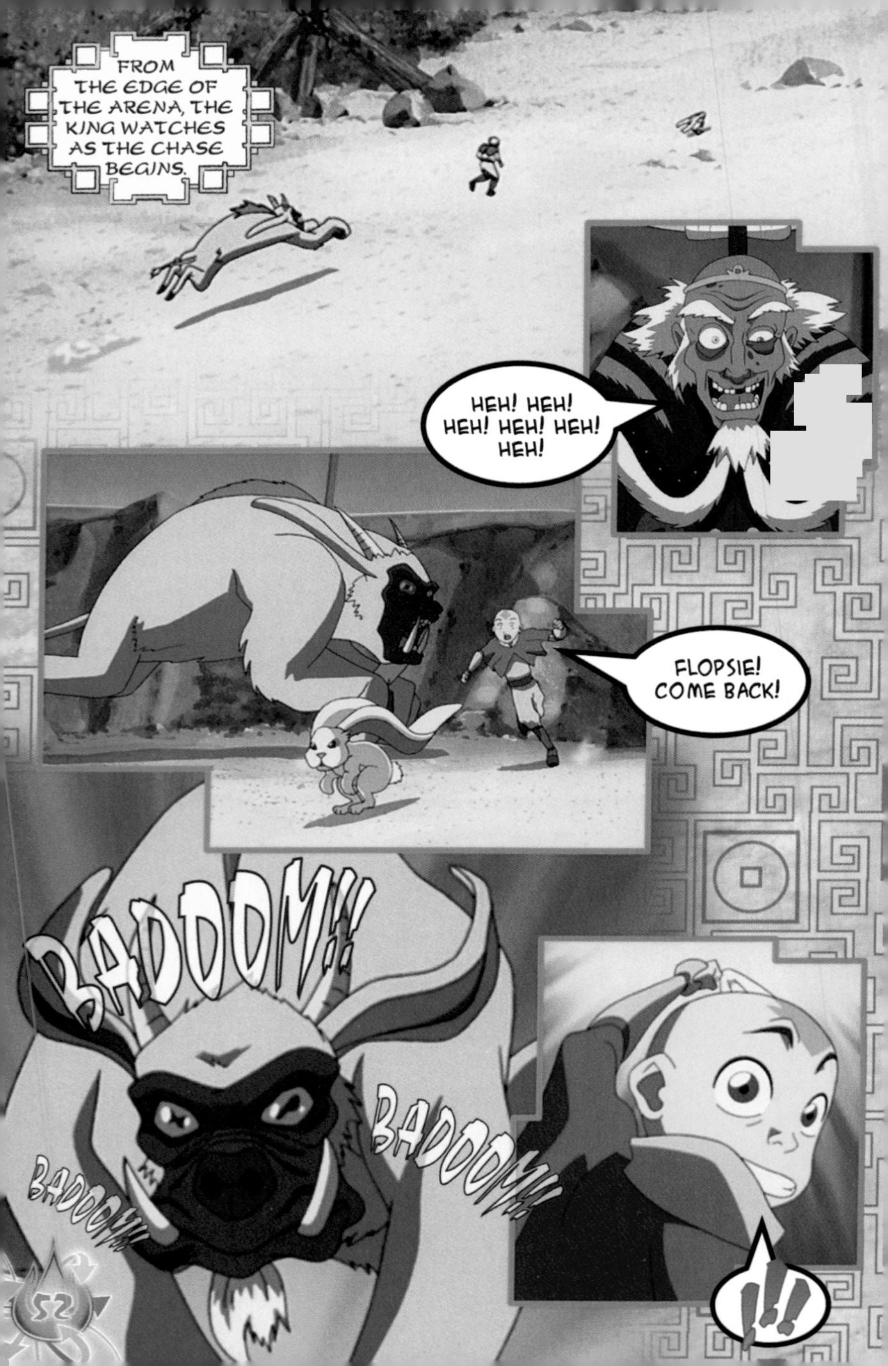
FROM THE EDGE OF THE ARENA, THE KING WATCHES AS THE CHASE BEGINS.
HEH! HEH! HEH! HEH! HEH! HEH!
FLOPSIE! COME BACK!
BADOOM!!
BADOOM!!
BADOOM!!
!!

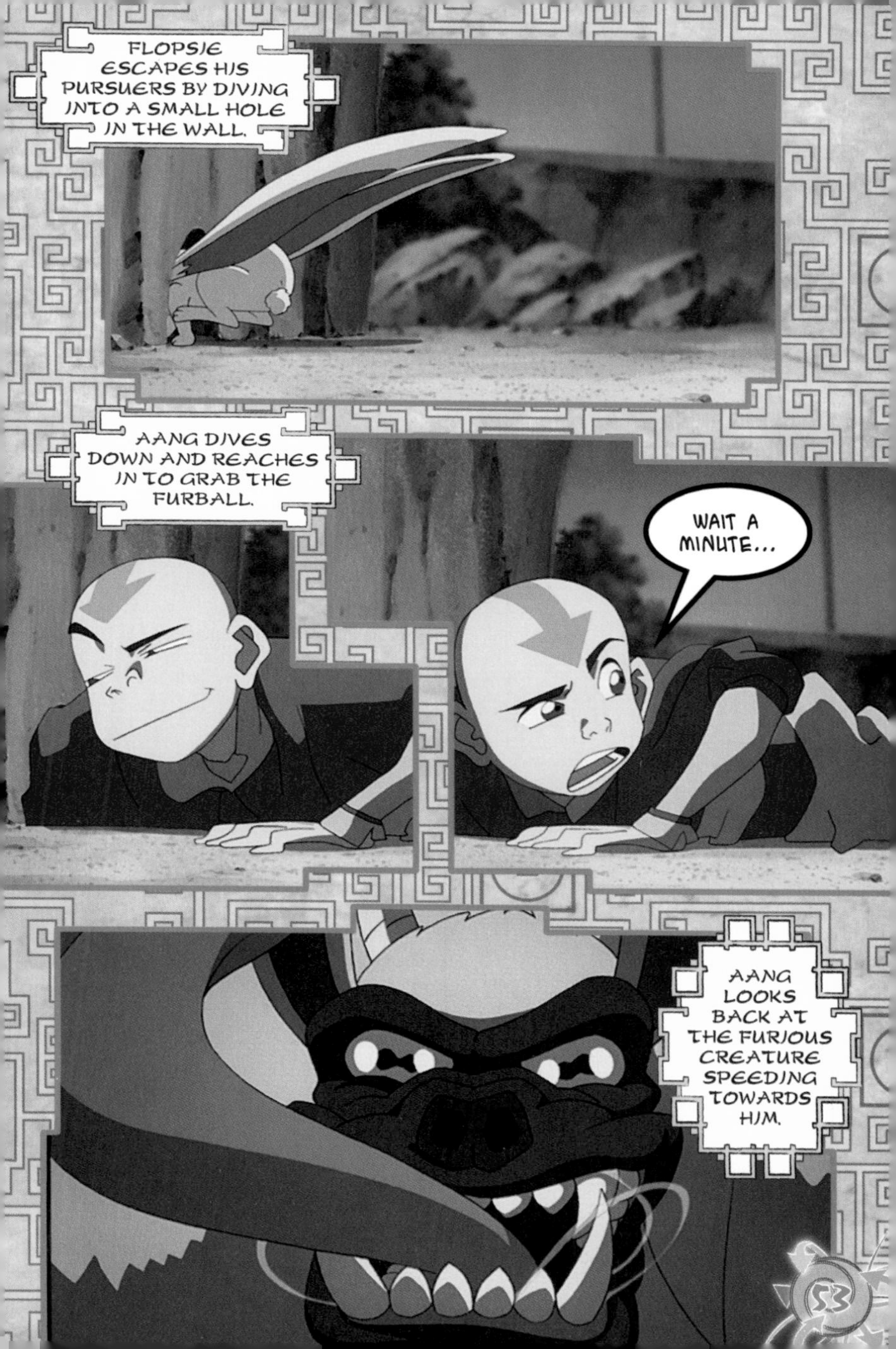
FLOPSIE ESCAPES HIS PURSUERS BY DIVING INTO A SMALL HOLE IN THE WALL.
AANG DIVES DOWN AND REACHES IN TO GRAB THE FURBALL.
WAIT A MINUTE...
AANG LOOKS BACK AT THE FURIOUS CREATURE SPEEDING TOWARDS HIM.

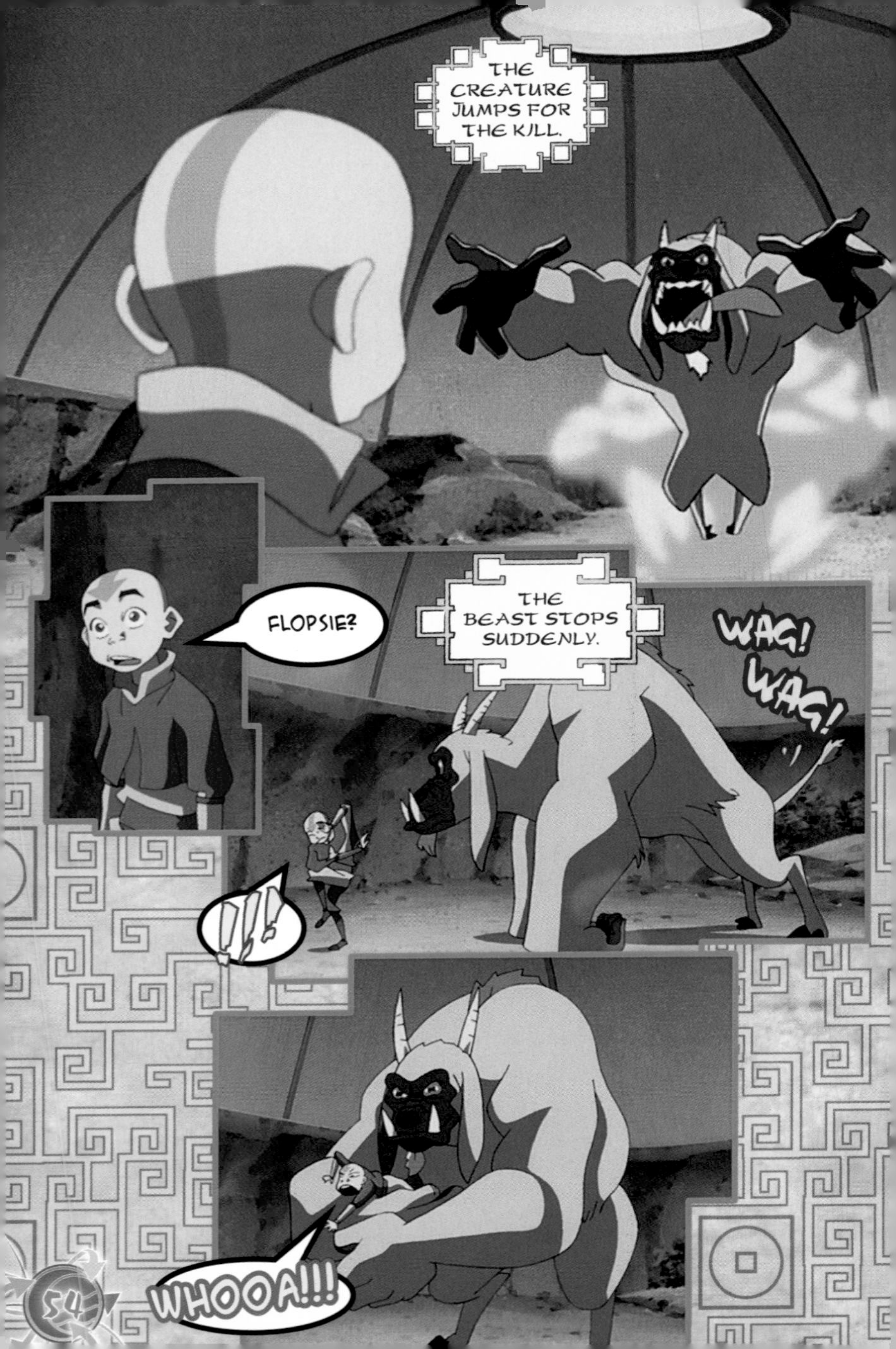
THE CREATURE JUMPS FOR THE KILL.
FLOPSIE?
THE BEAST STOPS SUDDENLY.
WAG! WAG!
!!!
WHOOA!!!

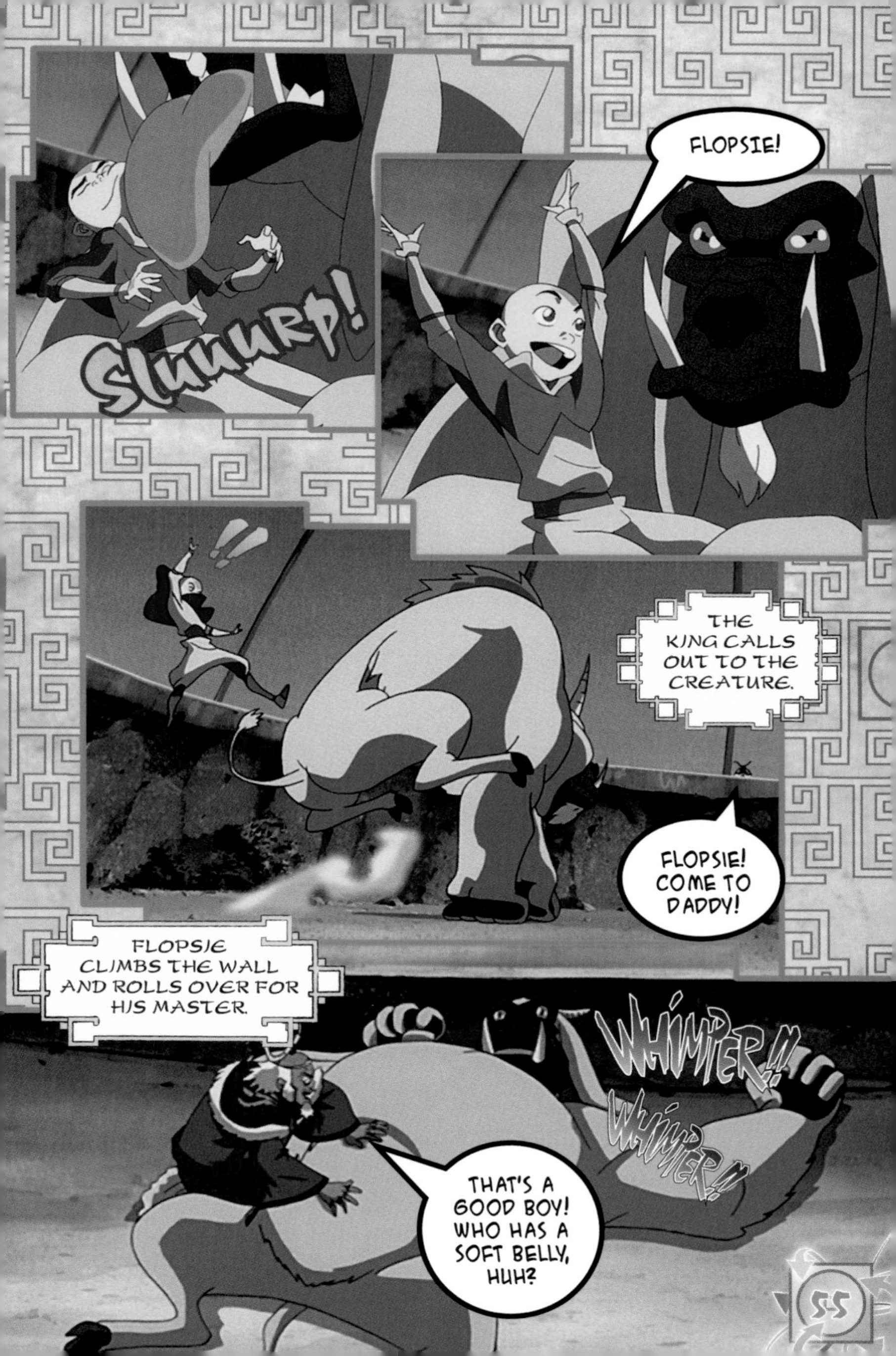
SLUUURP!
FLOPSIE!
THE KING CALLS OUT TO THE CREATURE.
FLOPSIE! COME TO DADDY!
FLOPSIE CLIMBS THE WALL AND ROLLS OVER FOR HIS MASTER.
WHIMPER!!
WHIMPER!!
THAT'S A GOOD BOY! WHO HAS A SOFT BELLY, HUH?

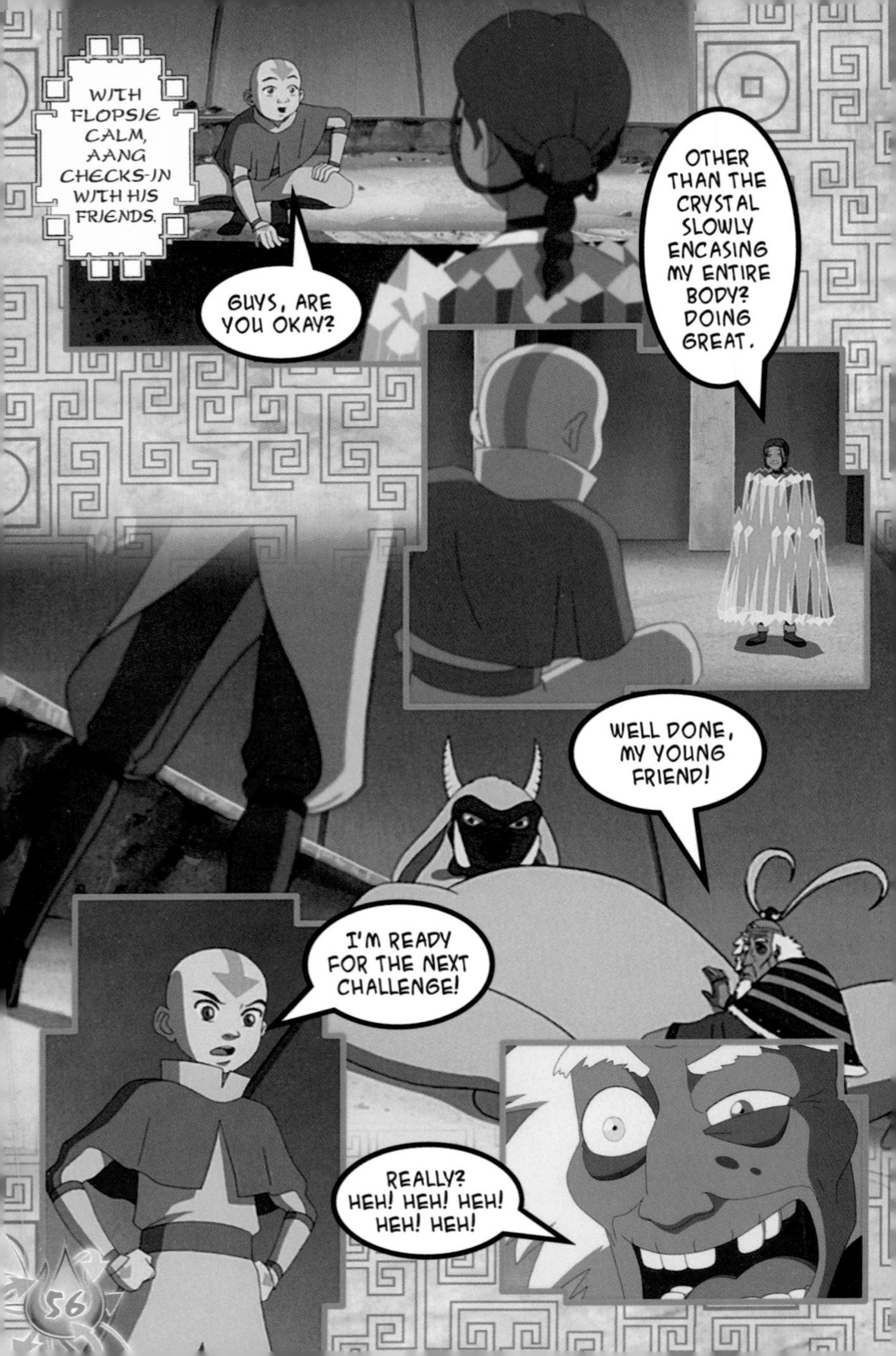
WITH FLOPSIE CALM, AANG CHECKS-IN WITH HIS FRIENDS.
GUYS, ARE YOU OKAY?
OTHER THAN THE CRYSTAL SLOWLY ENCASING MY ENTIRE BODY? DOING GREAT.
WELL DONE, MY YOUNG FRIEND!
I'M READY FOR THE NEXT CHALLENGE!
REALLY? HEH! HEH! HEH! HEH! HEH!
56

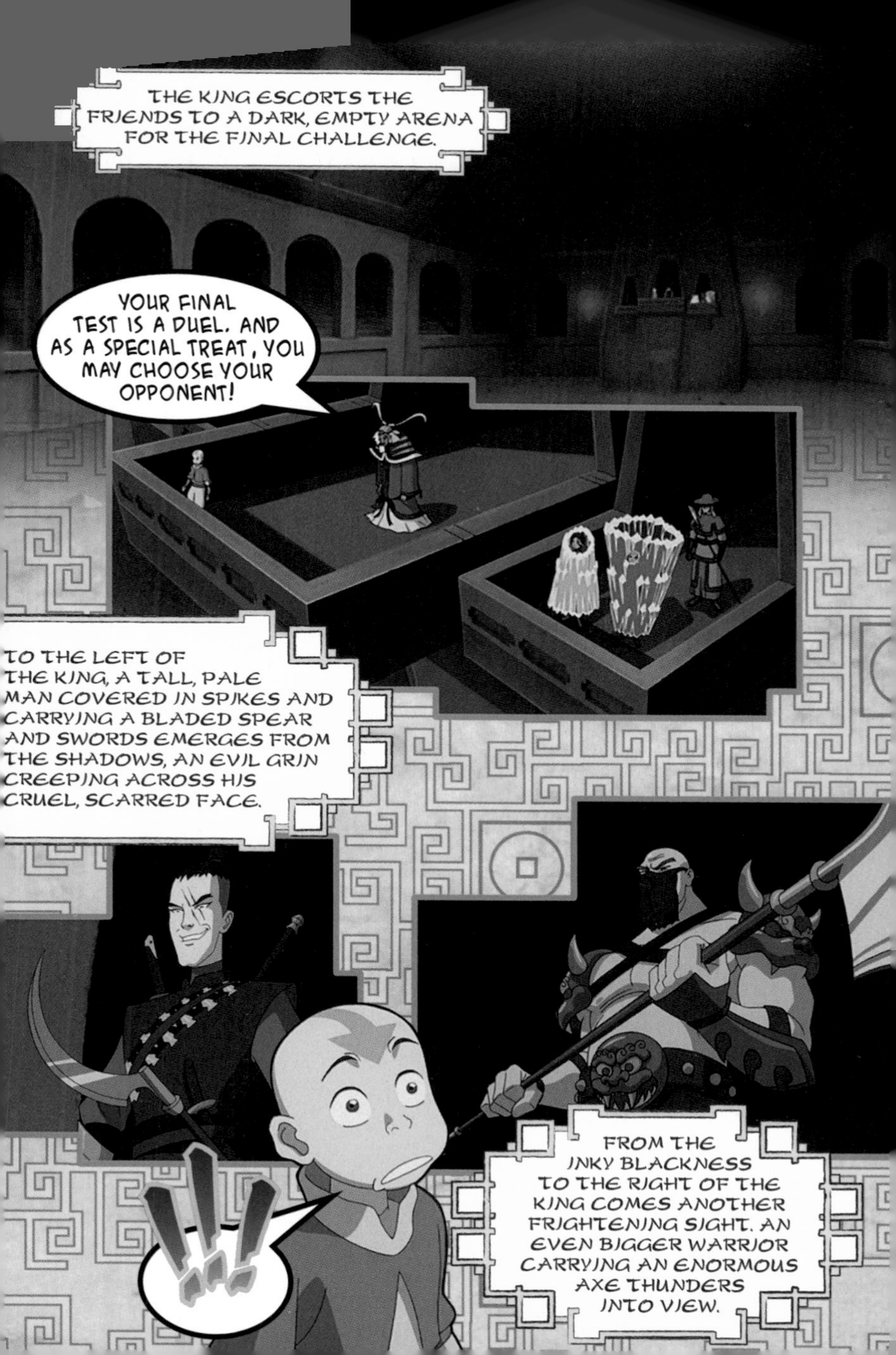
THE KING ESCORTS THE FRIENDS TO A DARK, EMPTY ARENA FOR THE FINAL CHALLENGE.
YOUR FINAL TEST IS A DUEL. AND AS A SPECIAL TREAT, YOU MAY CHOOSE YOUR OPPONENT!
TO THE LEFT OF THE KING, A TALL, PALE MAN COVERED IN SPIKES AND CARRYING A BLADED SPEAR AND SWORDS EMERGES FROM THE SHADOWS, AN EVIL GRIN CREEPING ACROSS HIS CRUEL, SCARRED FACE.
!!!
FROM THE INKY BLACKNESS TO THE RIGHT OF THE KING COMES ANOTHER FRIGHTENING SIGHT. AN EVEN BIGGER WARRIOR CARRYING AN ENORMOUS AXE THUNDERS INTO VIEW.

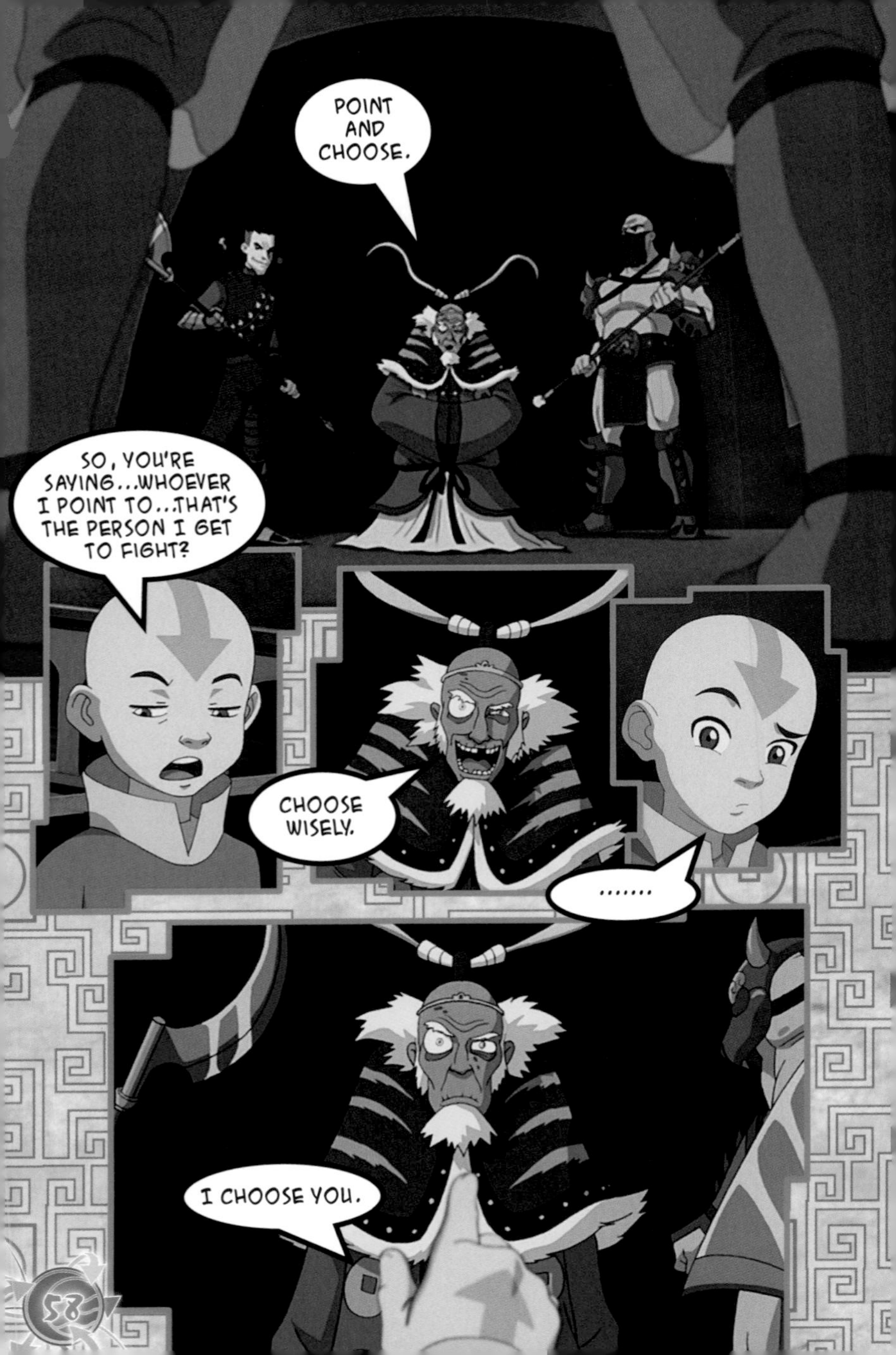
POINT AND CHOOSE.
SO, YOU'RE SAYING...WHOEVER I POINT TO...THAT'S THE PERSON I GET TO FIGHT?
CHOOSE WISELY.
....
I CHOOSE YOU.

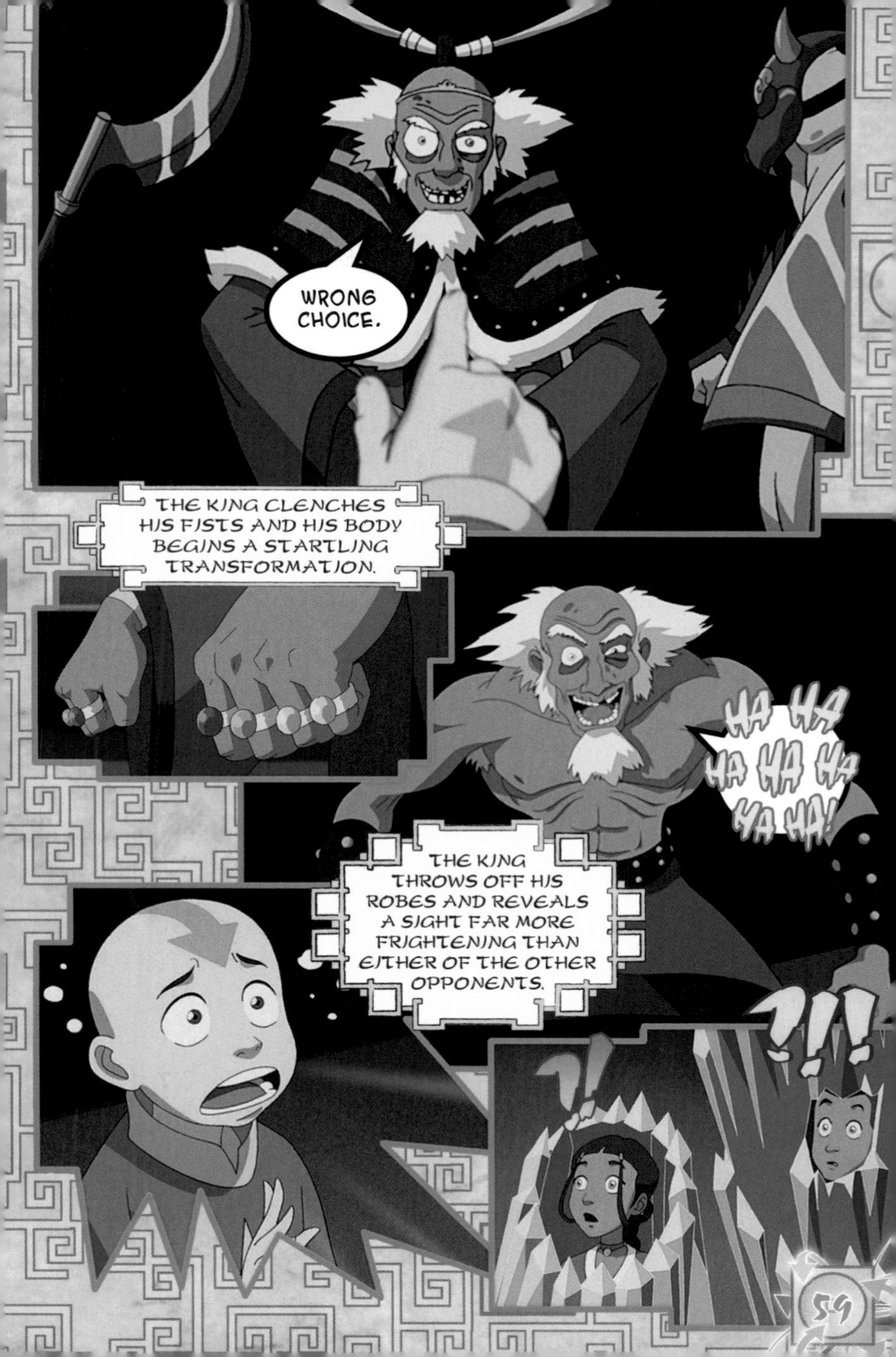
WRONG CHOICE.
THE KING CLENCHES HIS FISTS AND HIS BODY BEGINS A STARTLING TRANSFORMATION.
HA HA HA HA HA HA HA!
THE KING THROWS OFF HIS ROBES AND REVEALS A SIGHT FAR MORE FRIGHTENING THAN EITHER OF THE OTHER OPPONENTS.
?!
?!!

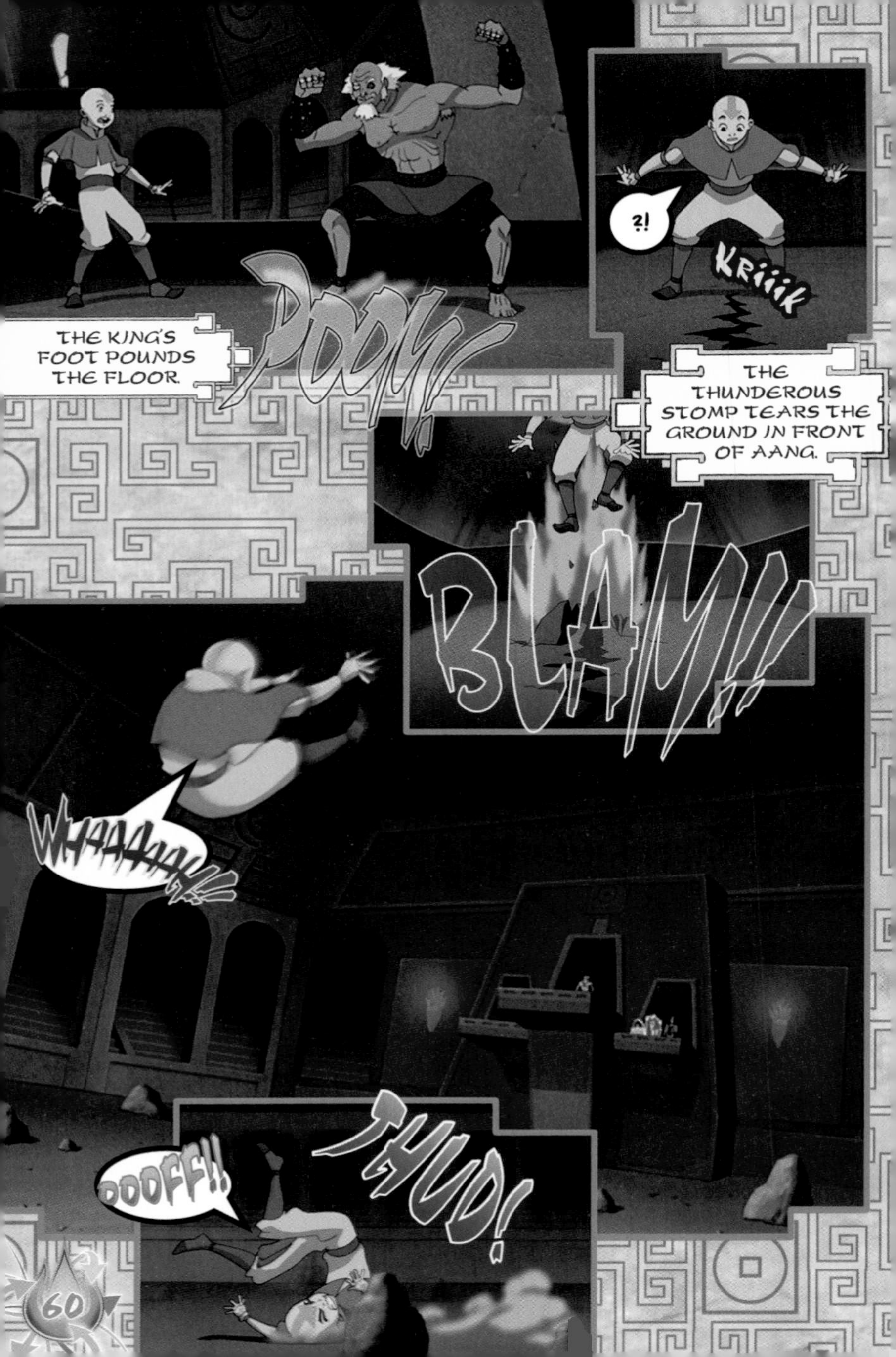
THE KING'S FOOT POUNDS THE FLOOR.
DOOM!!
?!
KRIIIK
THE THUNDEROUS STOMP TEARS THE GROUND IN FRONT OF AANG.
BLAM!!
WHAAAAAH!!
OOOFF!!
THUD!

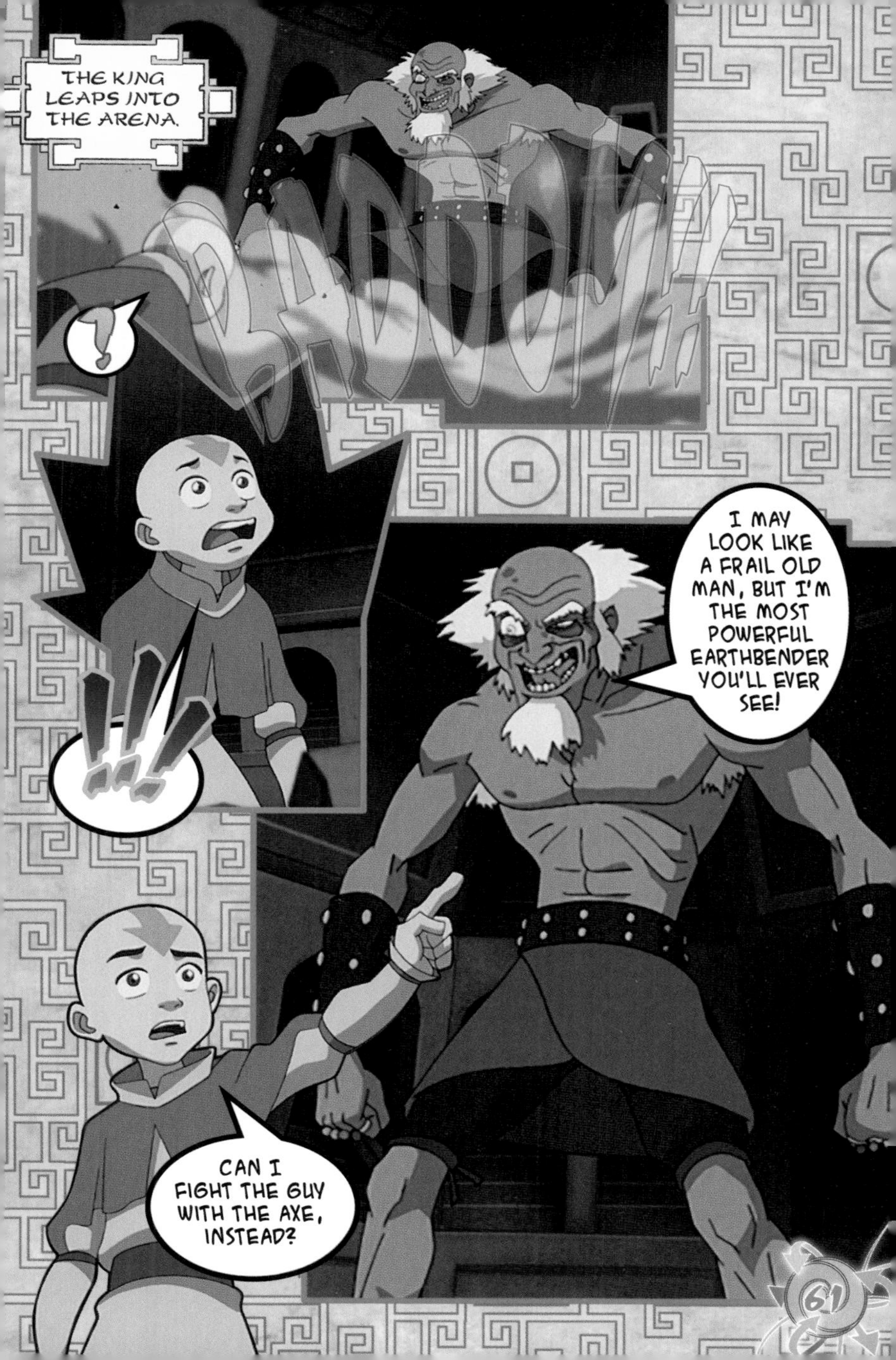
THE KING LEAPS INTO THE ARENA.
BADOOM!
?
!!!
I MAY LOOK LIKE A FRAIL OLD MAN, BUT I'M THE MOST POWERFUL EARTHBENDER YOU'LL EVER SEE!
CAN I FIGHT THE GUY WITH THE AXE, INSTEAD?

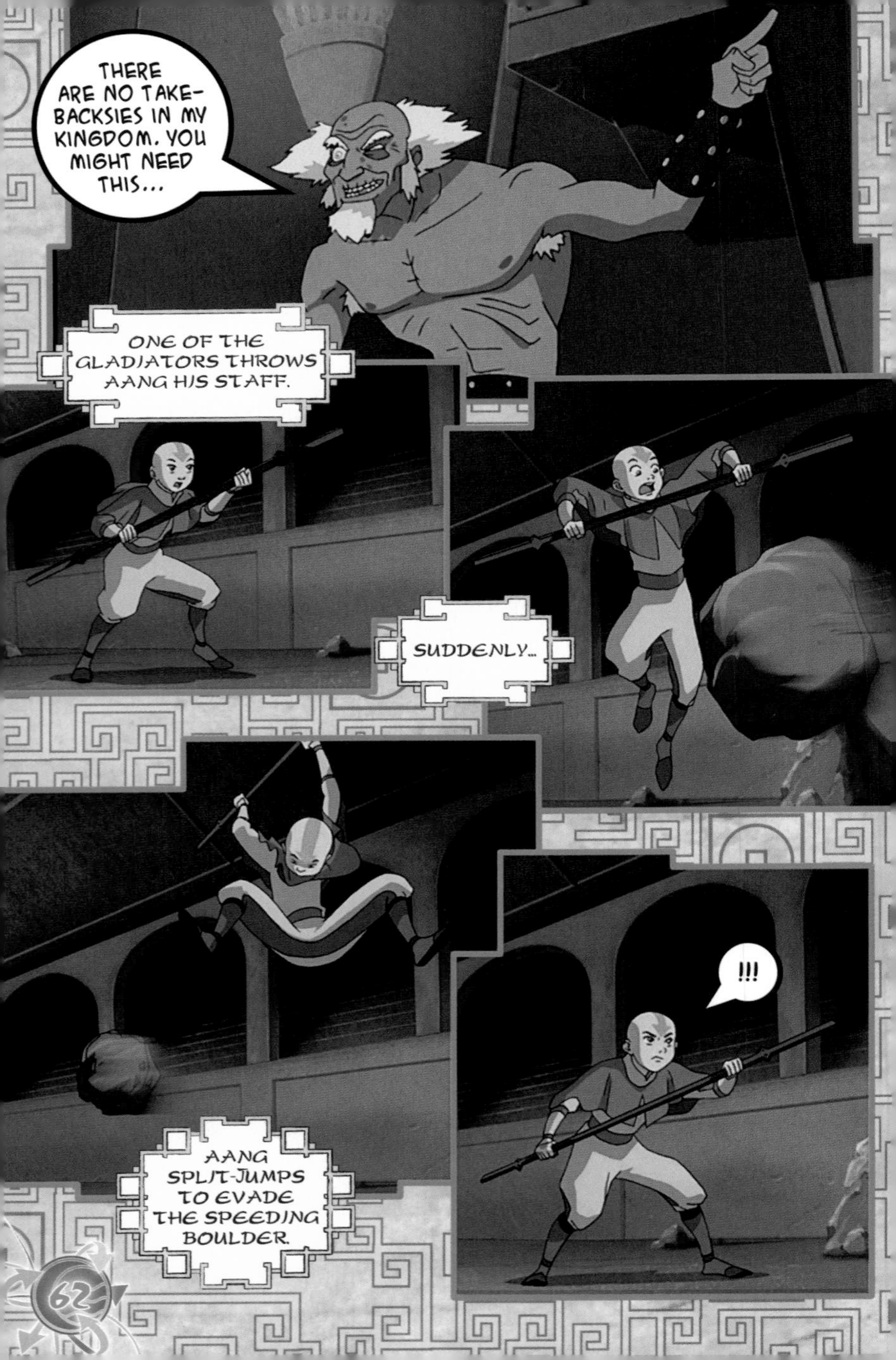
THERE ARE NO TAKE-BACKSIES IN MY KINGDOM. YOU MIGHT NEED THIS...
ONE OF THE GLADIATORS THROWS AANG HIS STAFF.
SUDDENLY...
AANG SPLIT-JUMPS TO EVADE THE SPEEDING BOULDER.
!!!

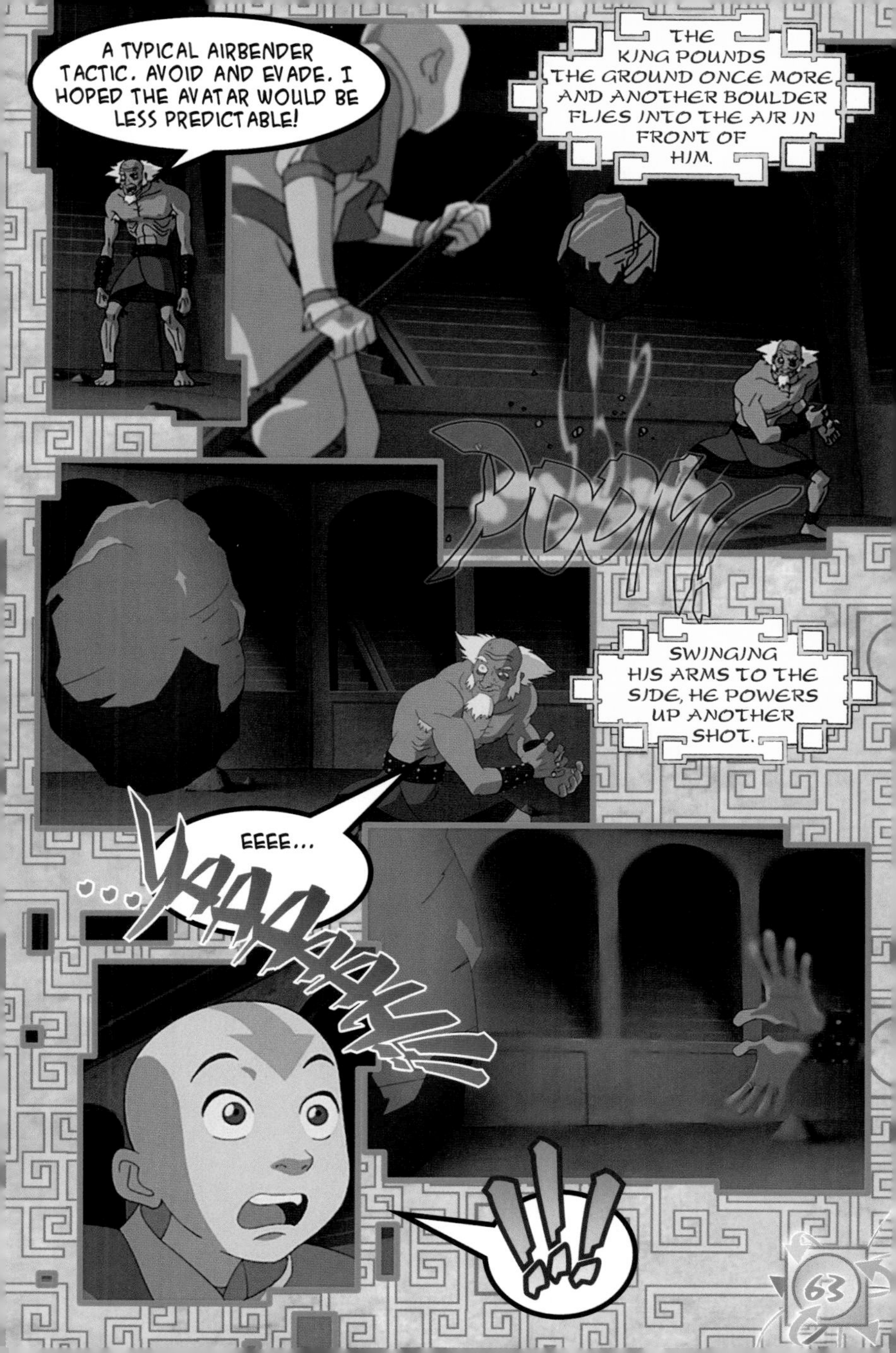
A TYPICAL AIRBENDER TACTIC. AVOID AND EVADE. I HOPED THE AVATAR WOULD BE LESS PREDICTABLE!
THE KING POUNDS THE GROUND ONCE MORE AND ANOTHER BOULDER FLIES INTO THE AIR IN FRONT OF HIM.
DOOM!
SWINGING HIS ARMS TO THE SIDE, HE POWERS UP ANOTHER SHOT.
EEEE...
...YAAAHHH!!
!!!

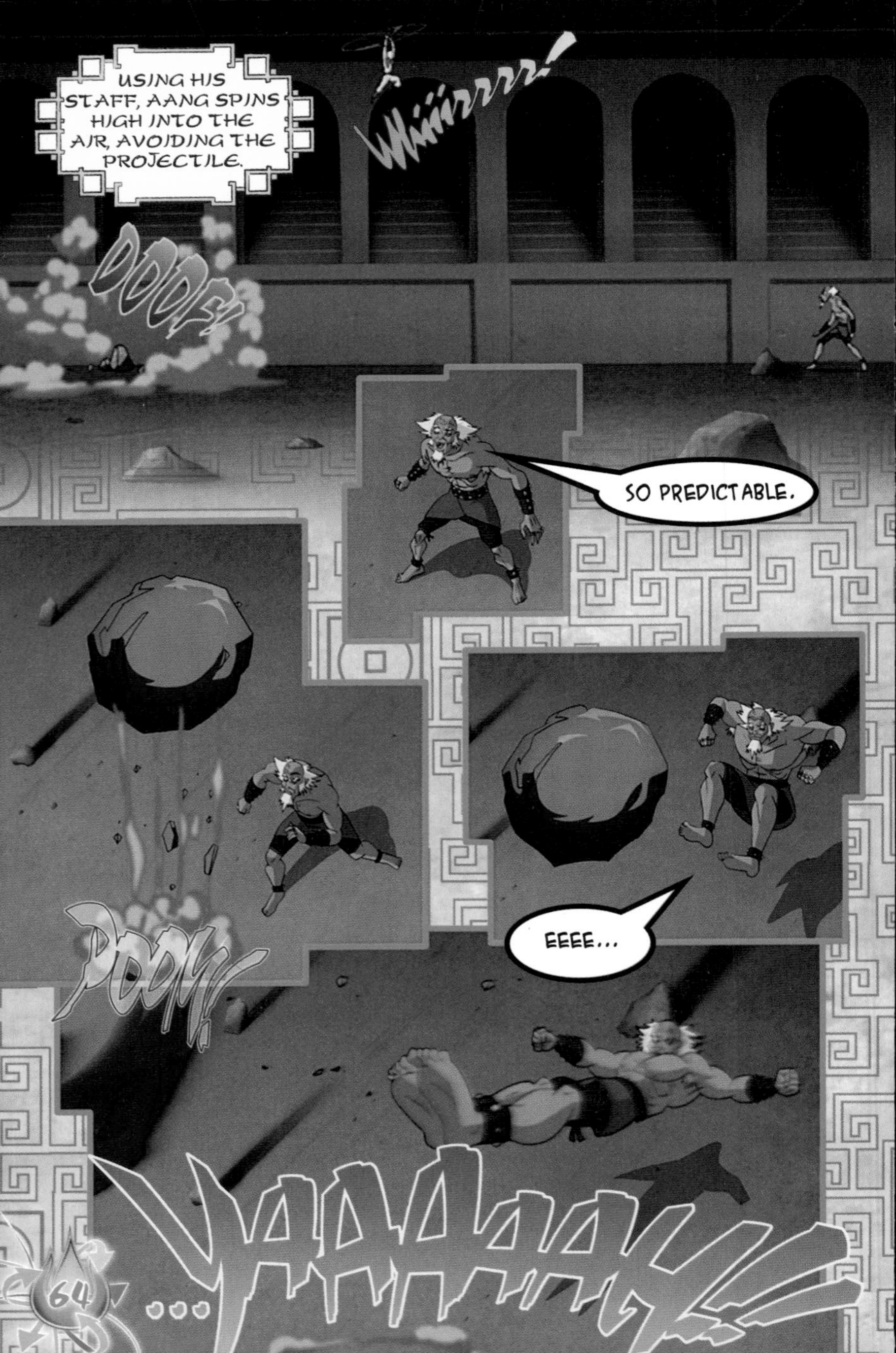
USING HIS STAFF, AANG SPINS HIGH INTO THE AIR, AVOIDING THE PROJECTILE.
WHiiiRRRR!
DOOOF!
SO PREDICTABLE.
EEEE...
POOM!
...YAAAAAAH!

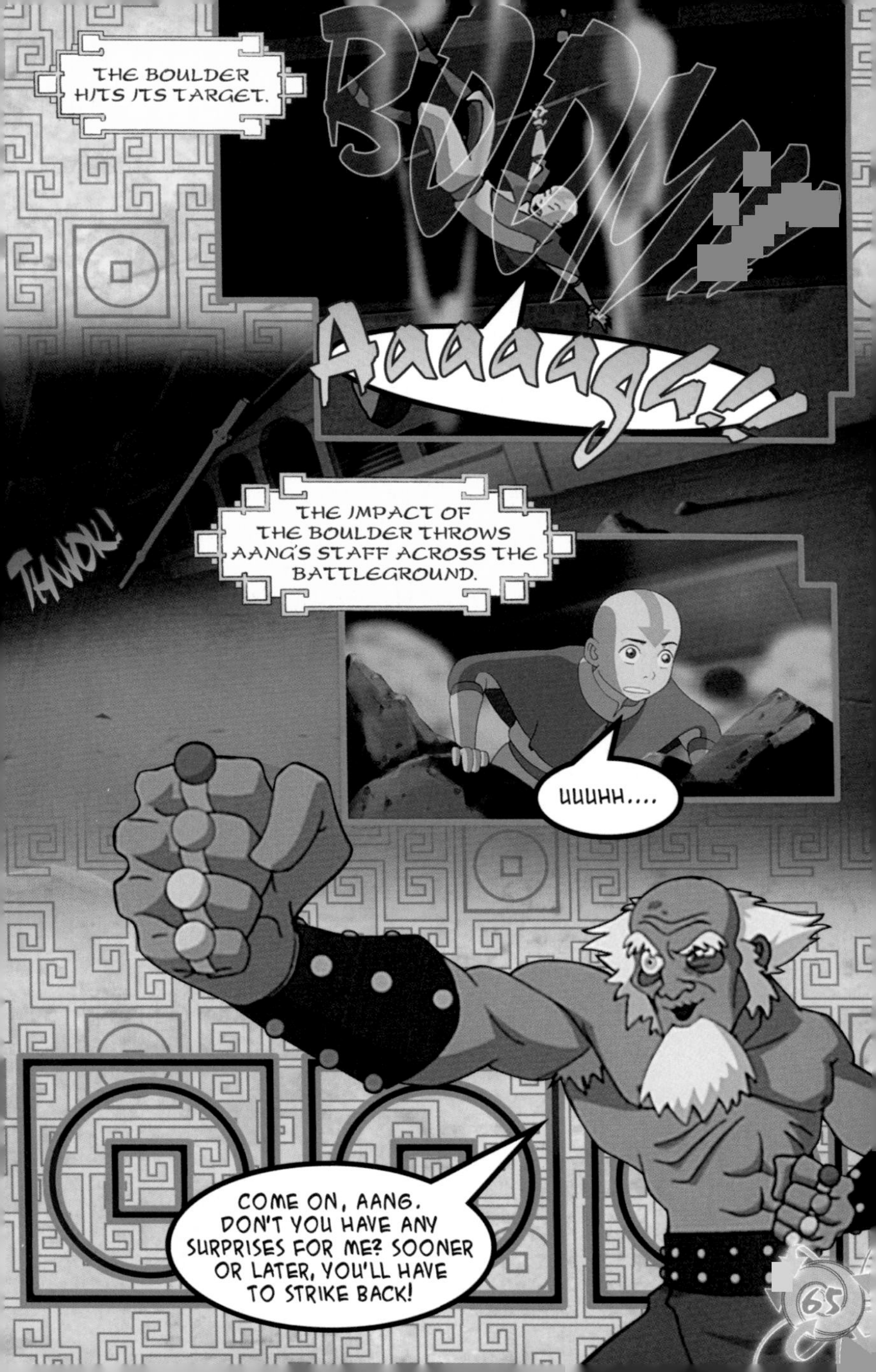
THE BOULDER HITS ITS TARGET.
BOOM
Aaaaagh!!!
THWOK!
THE IMPACT OF THE BOULDER THROWS AANG'S STAFF ACROSS THE BATTLEGROUND.
UUUHH....
COME ON, AANG. DON'T YOU HAVE ANY SURPRISES FOR ME? SOONER OR LATER, YOU'LL HAVE TO STRIKE BACK!

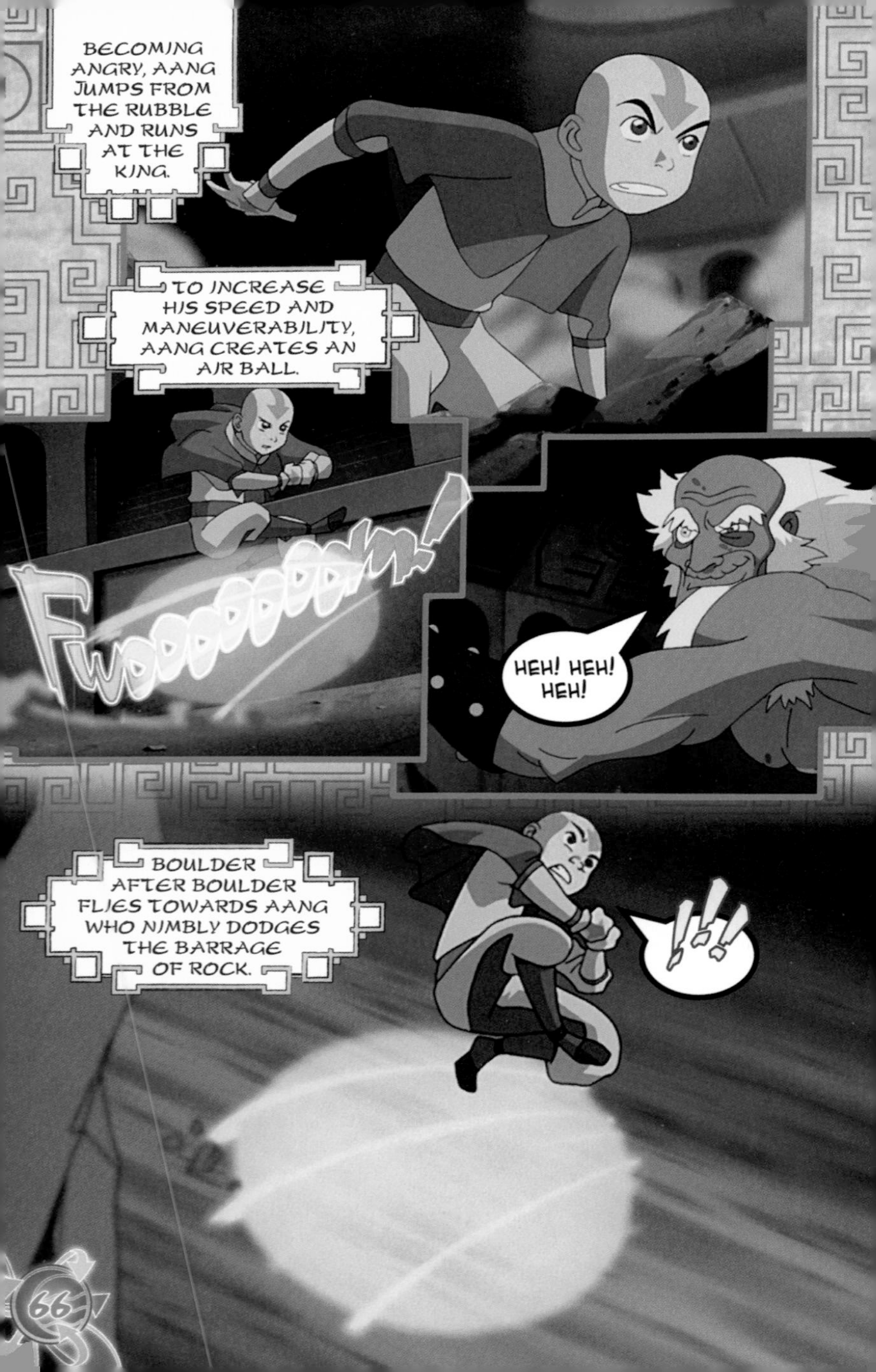
BECOMING ANGRY, AANG JUMPS FROM THE RUBBLE AND RUNS AT THE KING.
TO INCREASE HIS SPEED AND MANEUVERABILITY, AANG CREATES AN AIR BALL.
FWOOOOOOOM!
HEH! HEH! HEH!
BOULDER AFTER BOULDER FLIES TOWARDS AANG WHO NIMBLY DODGES THE BARRAGE OF ROCK.
!!

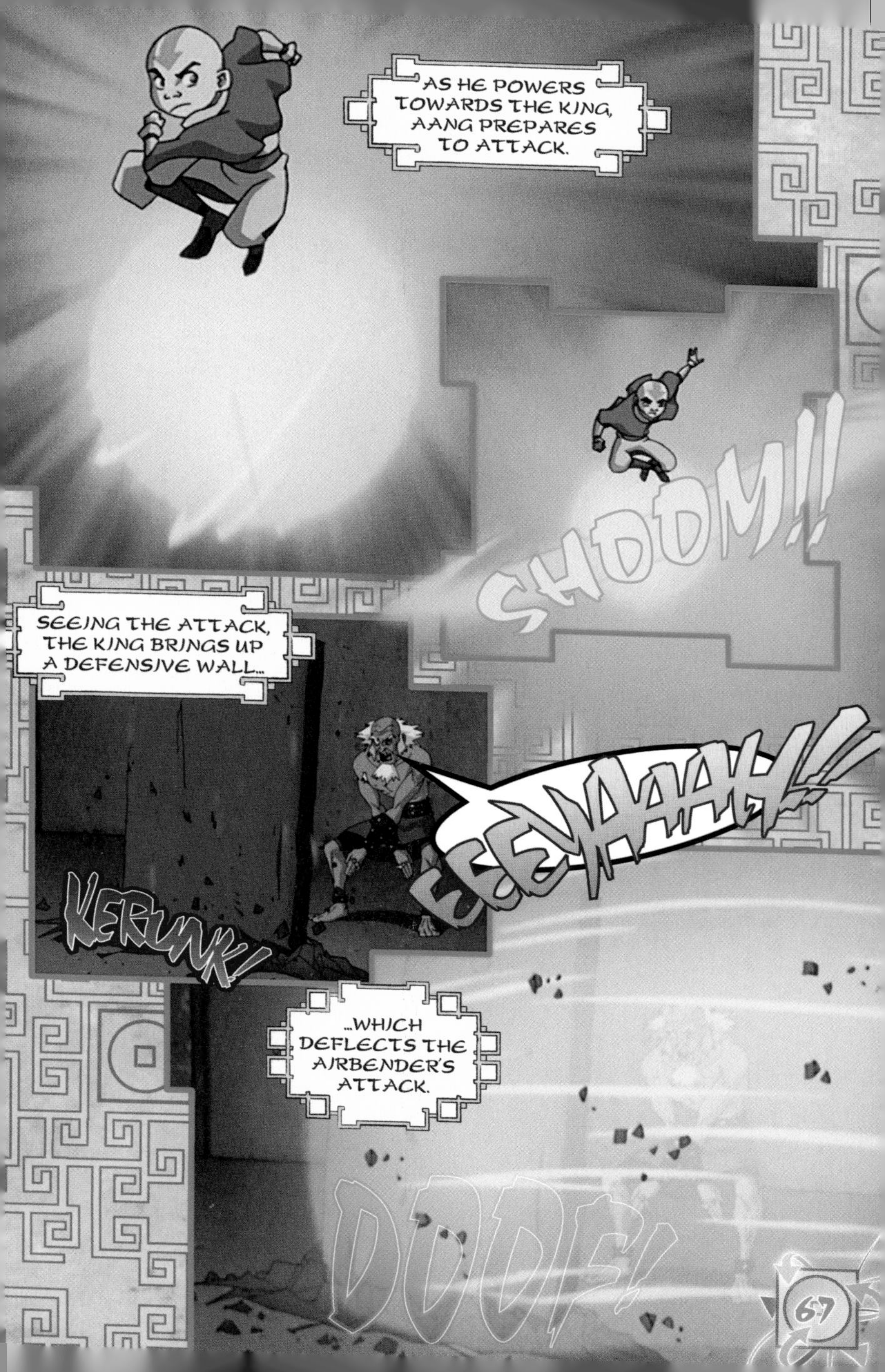
AS HE POWERS TOWARDS THE KING, AANG PREPARES TO ATTACK.
SHOOM!!
SEEING THE ATTACK, THE KING BRINGS UP A DEFENSIVE WALL...
EEEYAAAAH!!
KERUNK!
...WHICH DEFLECTS THE AIRBENDER'S ATTACK.
DOOF!

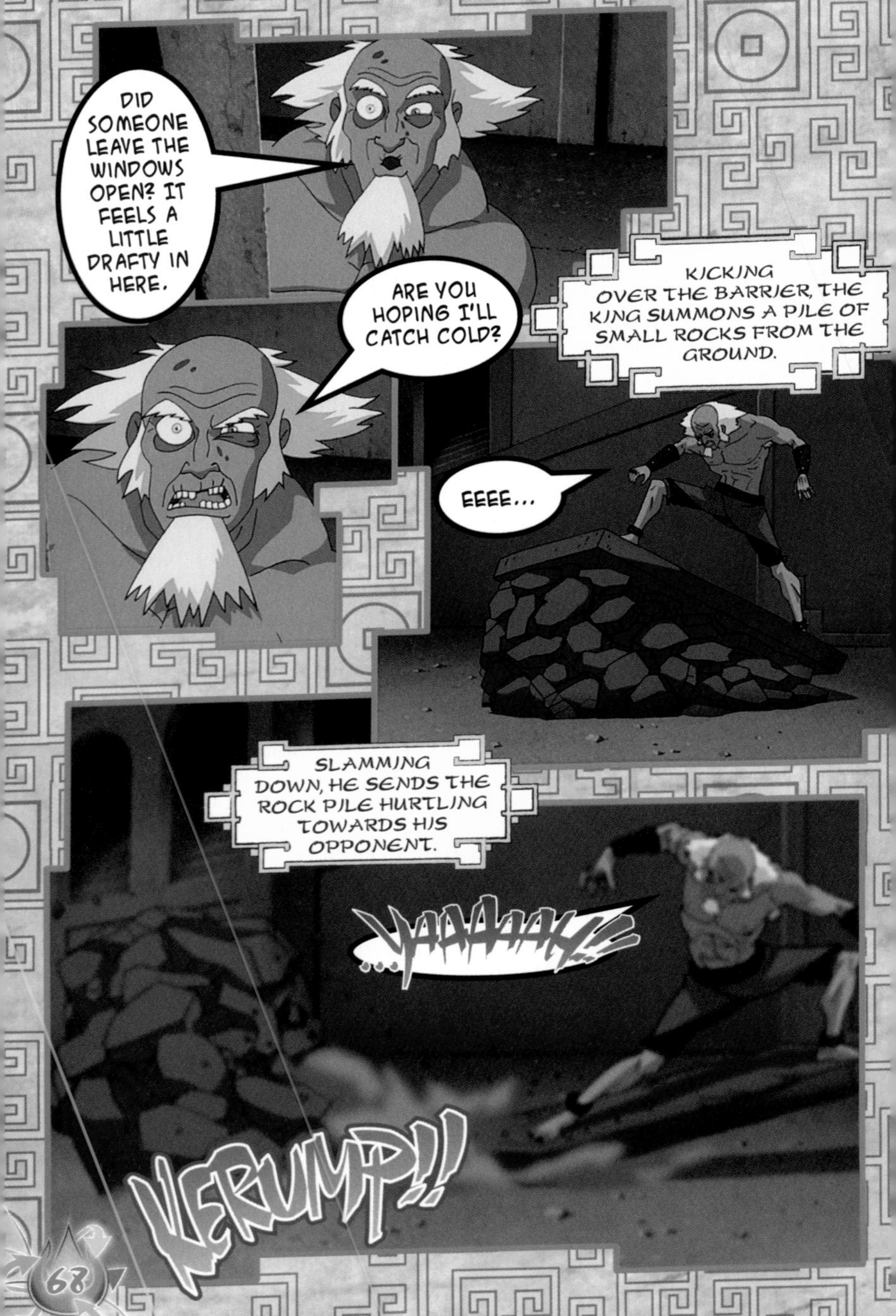
DID SOMEONE LEAVE THE WINDOWS OPEN? IT FEELS A LITTLE DRAFTY IN HERE.
ARE YOU HOPING I'LL CATCH COLD?
KICKING OVER THE BARRIER, THE KING SUMMONS A PILE OF SMALL ROCKS FROM THE GROUND.
EEEE...
SLAMMING DOWN, HE SENDS THE ROCK PILE HURTLING TOWARDS HIS OPPONENT.
KERUMP!!

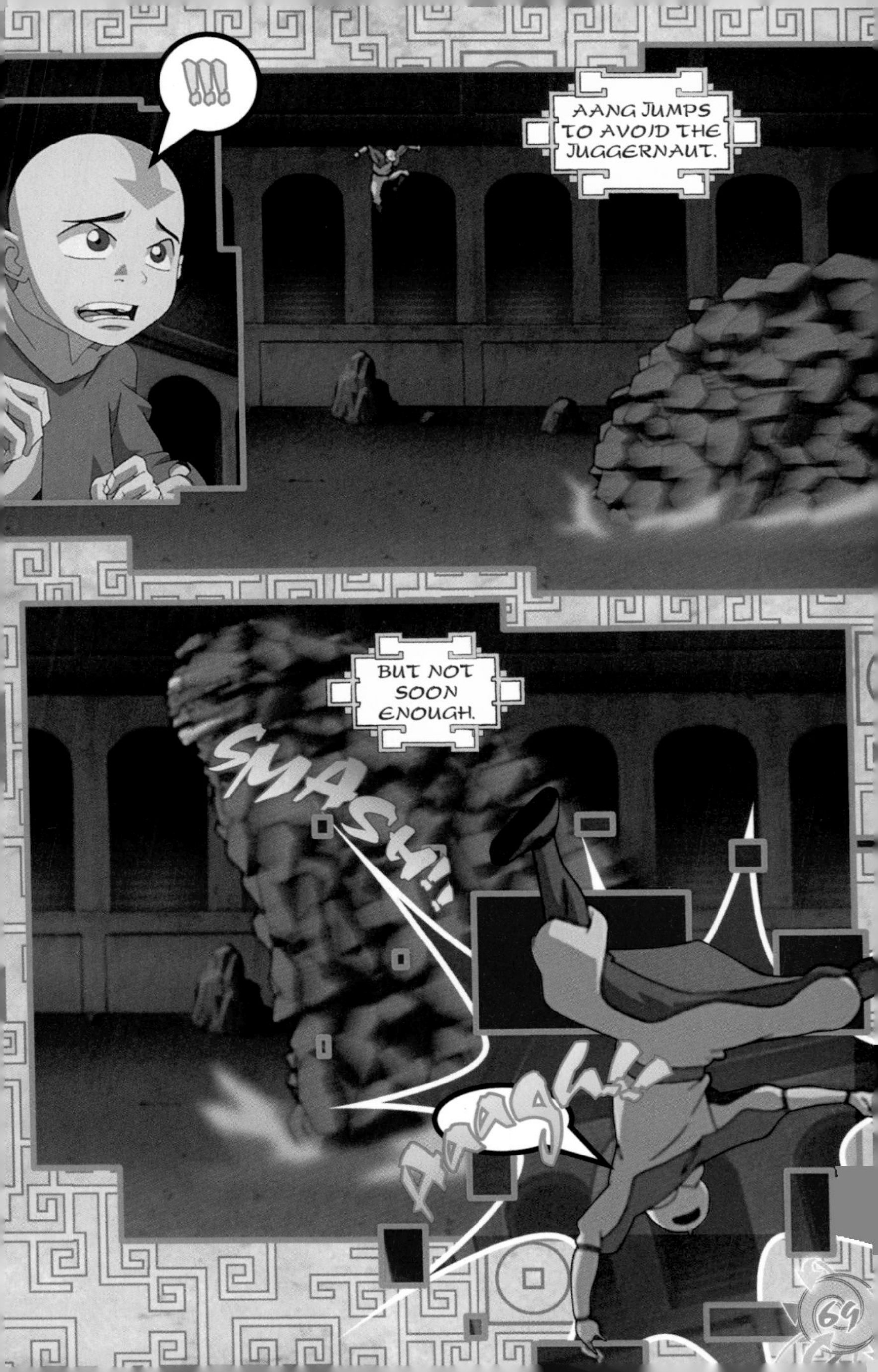
!!!
AANG JUMPS TO AVOID THE JUGGERNAUT.
BUT NOT SOON ENOUGH.
SMASH!!
AAAGH!!

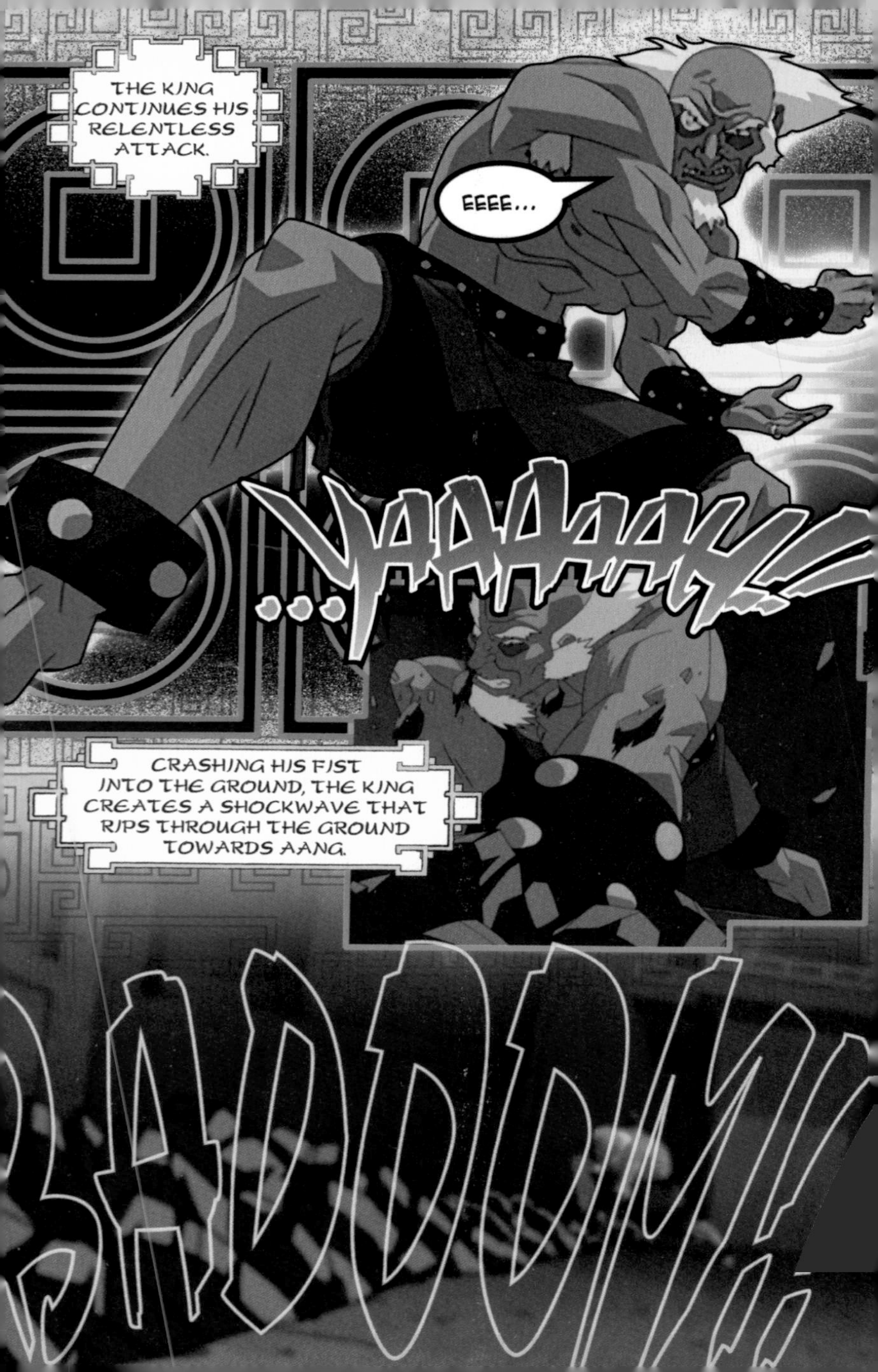
THE KING CONTINUES HIS RELENTLESS ATTACK.
EEEE...
...YAAAAAAH!!
CRASHING HIS FIST INTO THE GROUND, THE KING CREATES A SHOCKWAVE THAT RIPS THROUGH THE GROUND TOWARDS AANG.
BADOOM!

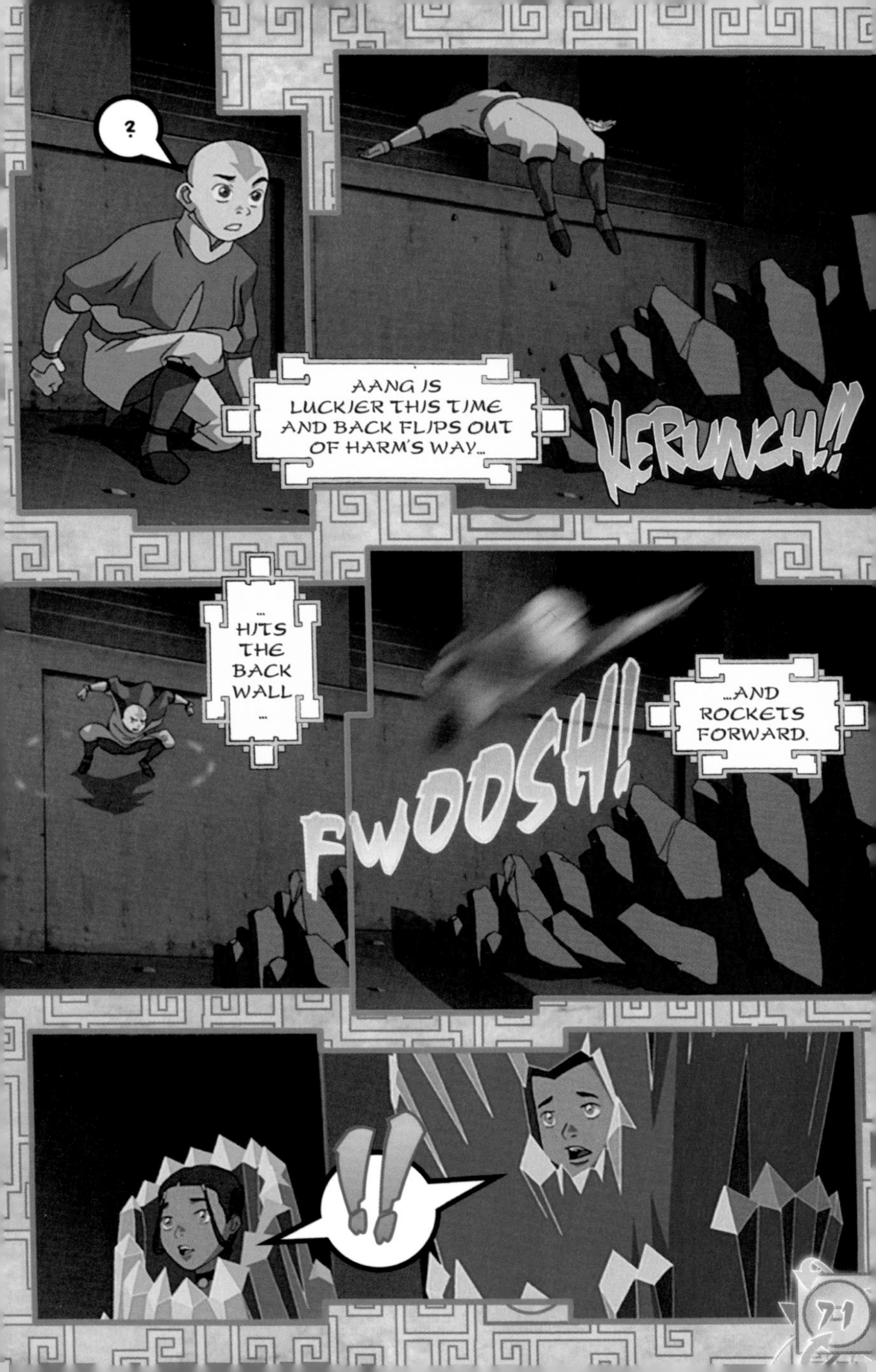
?
AANG IS LUCKIER THIS TIME AND BACK FLIPS OUT OF HARM'S WAY...
KERUNCH!!
... HITS THE BACK WALL ...
FWOOSH!
...AND ROCKETS FORWARD.
!!

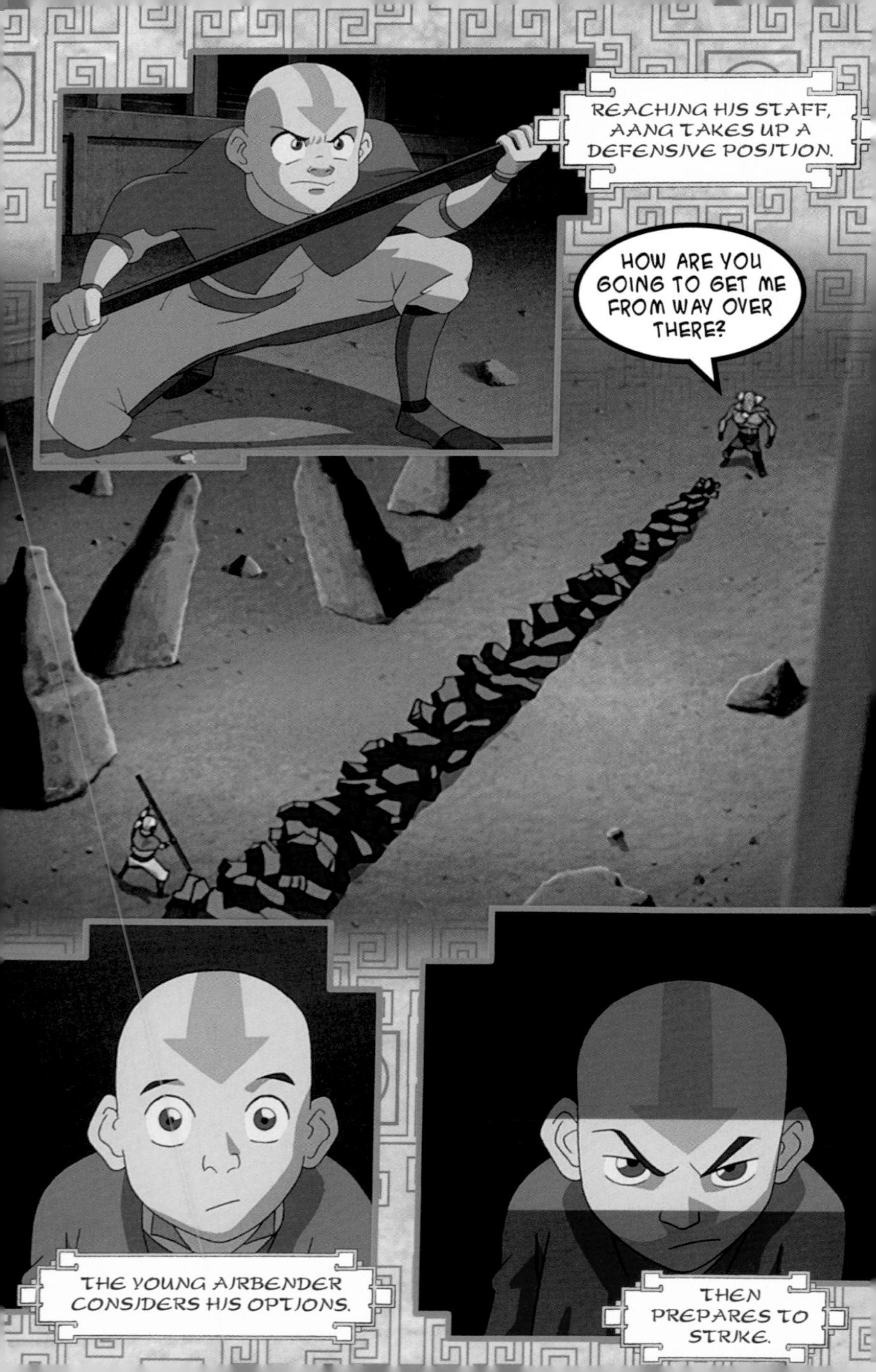
REACHING HIS STAFF, AANG TAKES UP A DEFENSIVE POSITION.
HOW ARE YOU GOING TO GET ME FROM WAY OVER THERE?
THE YOUNG AIRBENDER CONSIDERS HIS OPTIONS.
THEN PREPARES TO STRIKE.

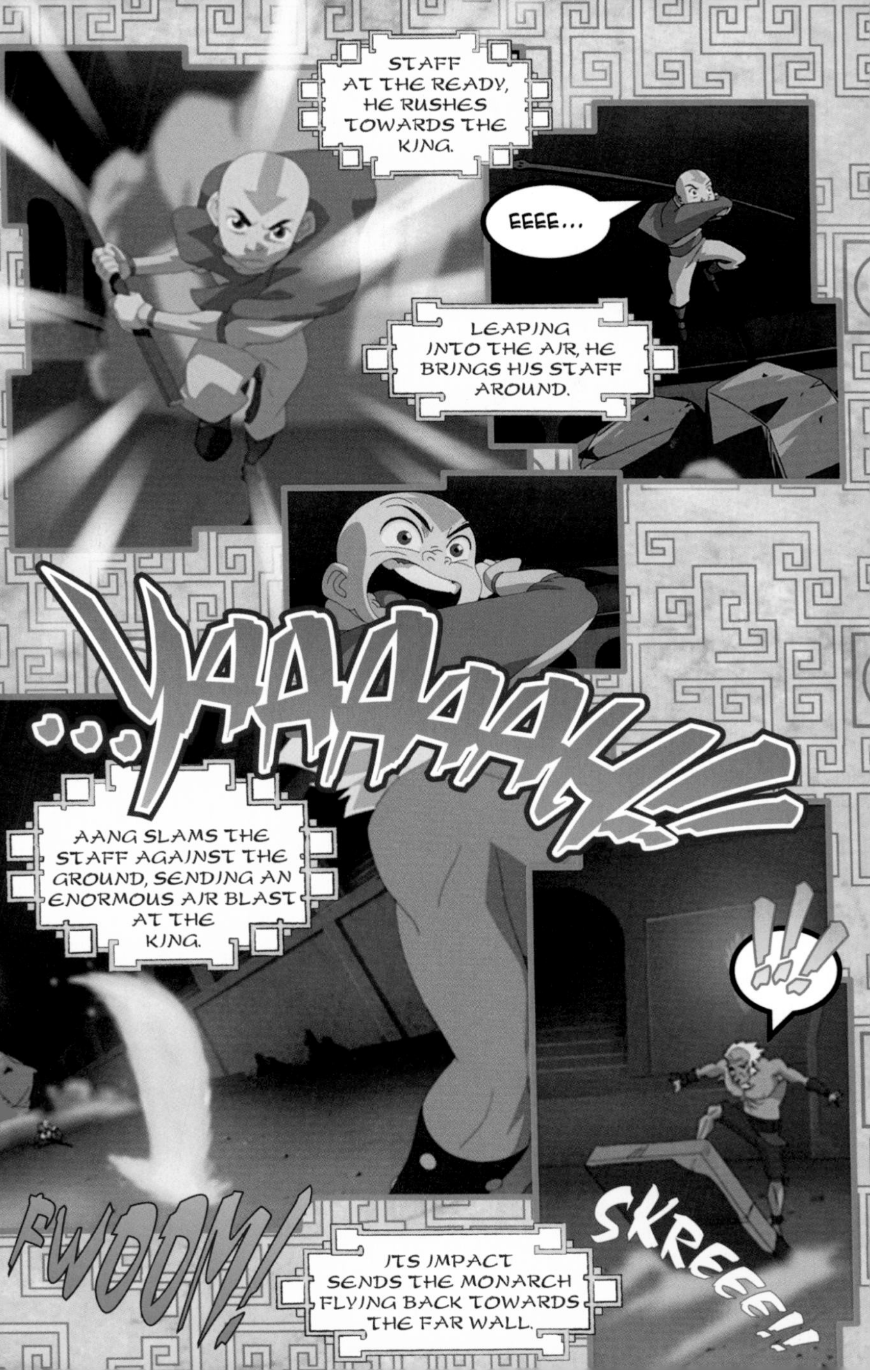
STAFF AT THE READY, HE RUSHES TOWARDS THE KING.
EEEE...
LEAPING INTO THE AIR, HE BRINGS HIS STAFF AROUND.
...YAAAAAH!!
AANG SLAMS THE STAFF AGAINST THE GROUND, SENDING AN ENORMOUS AIR BLAST AT THE KING.
!!
FWOOM!
ITS IMPACT SENDS THE MONARCH FLYING BACK TOWARDS THE FAR WALL.
SKREEE!!

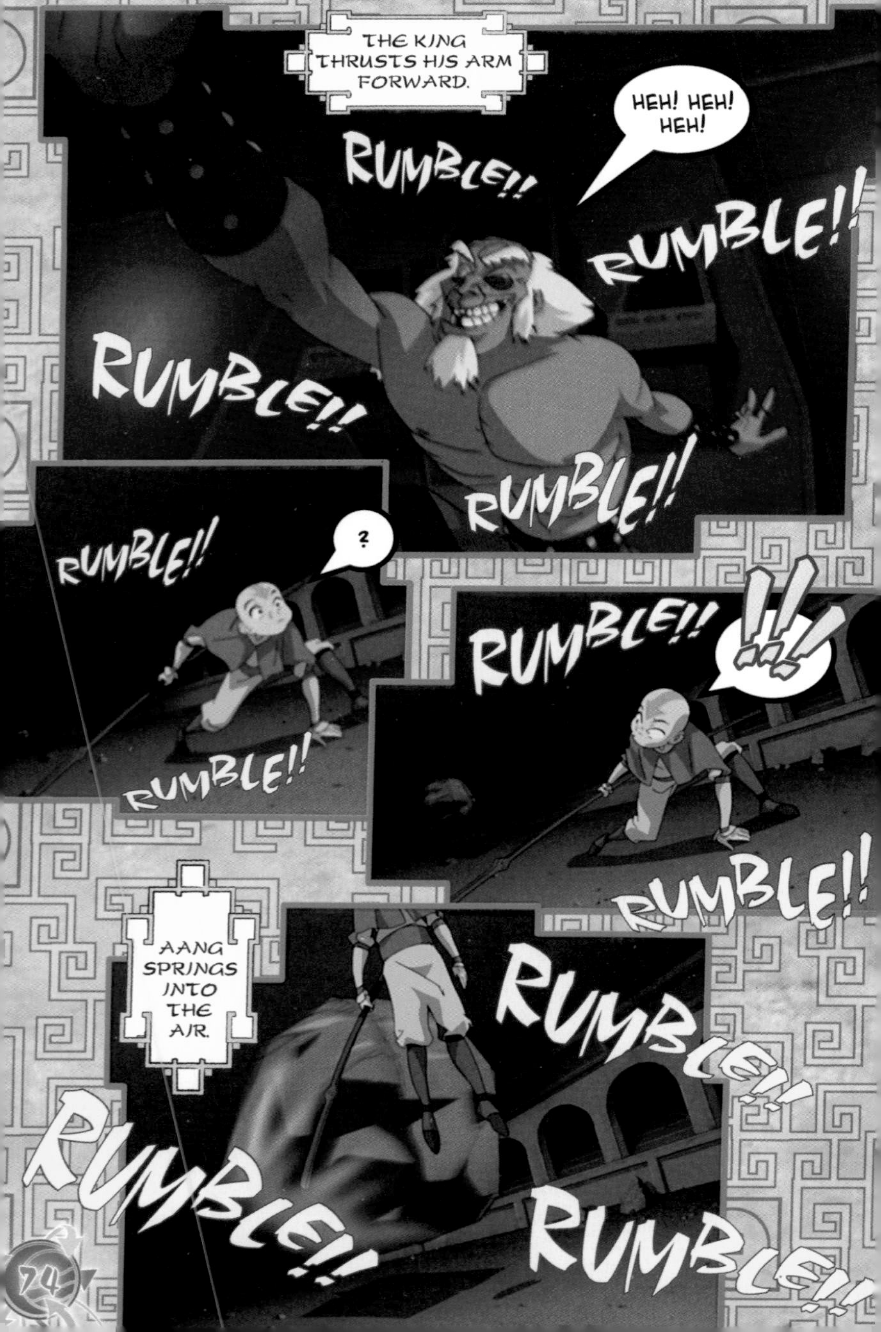
THE KING THRUSTS HIS ARM FORWARD.
HEH! HEH! HEH!
RUMBLE!!
RUMBLE!!
RUMBLE!!
RUMBLE!!
RUMBLE!!
?
RUMBLE!!
RUMBLE!!
!!!
RUMBLE!!
AANG SPRINGS INTO THE AIR.
RUMBLE!!
RUMBLE!!
RUMBLE!!

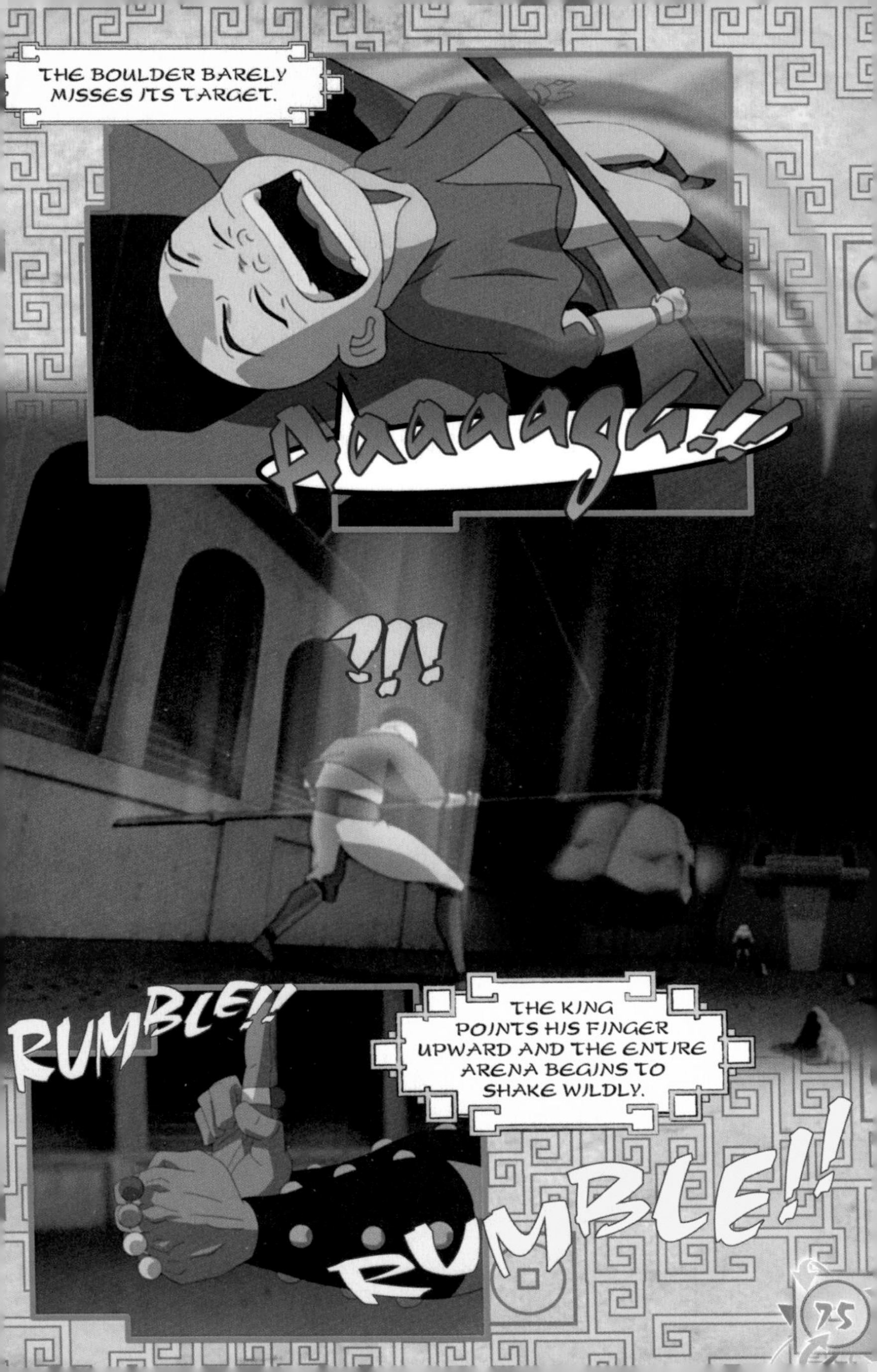
THE BOULDER BARELY MISSES ITS TARGET.
Aaaaagh!!
?!!
RUMBLE!!
THE KING POINTS HIS FINGER UPWARD AND THE ENTIRE ARENA BEGINS TO SHAKE WILDLY.
RUMBLE!!

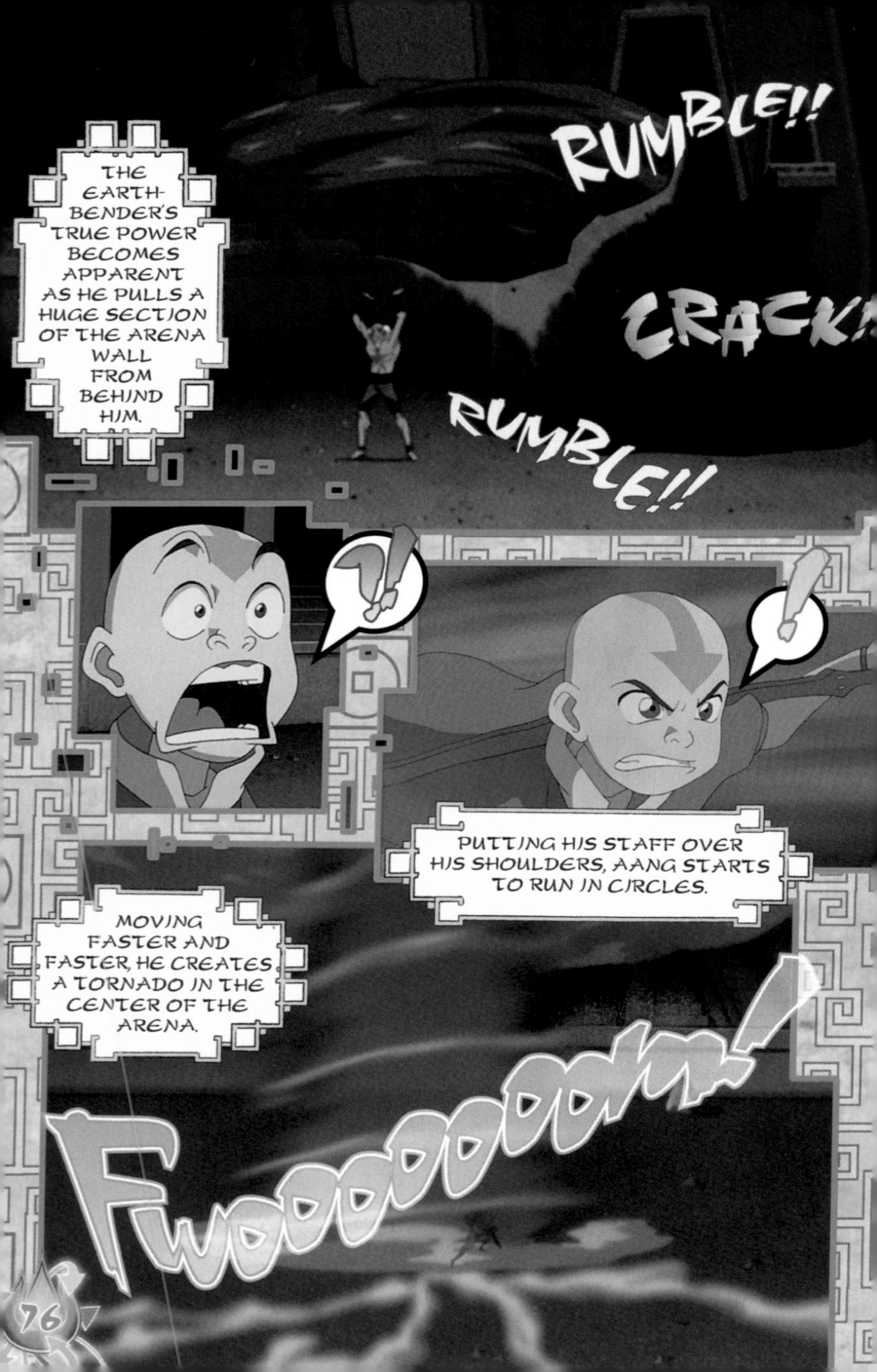
THE EARTHBENDER'S TRUE POWER BECOMES APPARENT AS HE PULLS A HUGE SECTION OF THE ARENA WALL FROM BEHIND HIM.
RUMBLE!!
CRACK!
RUMBLE!!
!
!
PUTTING HIS STAFF OVER HIS SHOULDERS, AANG STARTS TO RUN IN CIRCLES.
MOVING FASTER AND FASTER, HE CREATES A TORNADO IN THE CENTER OF THE ARENA.
FWOOOOOOOM!

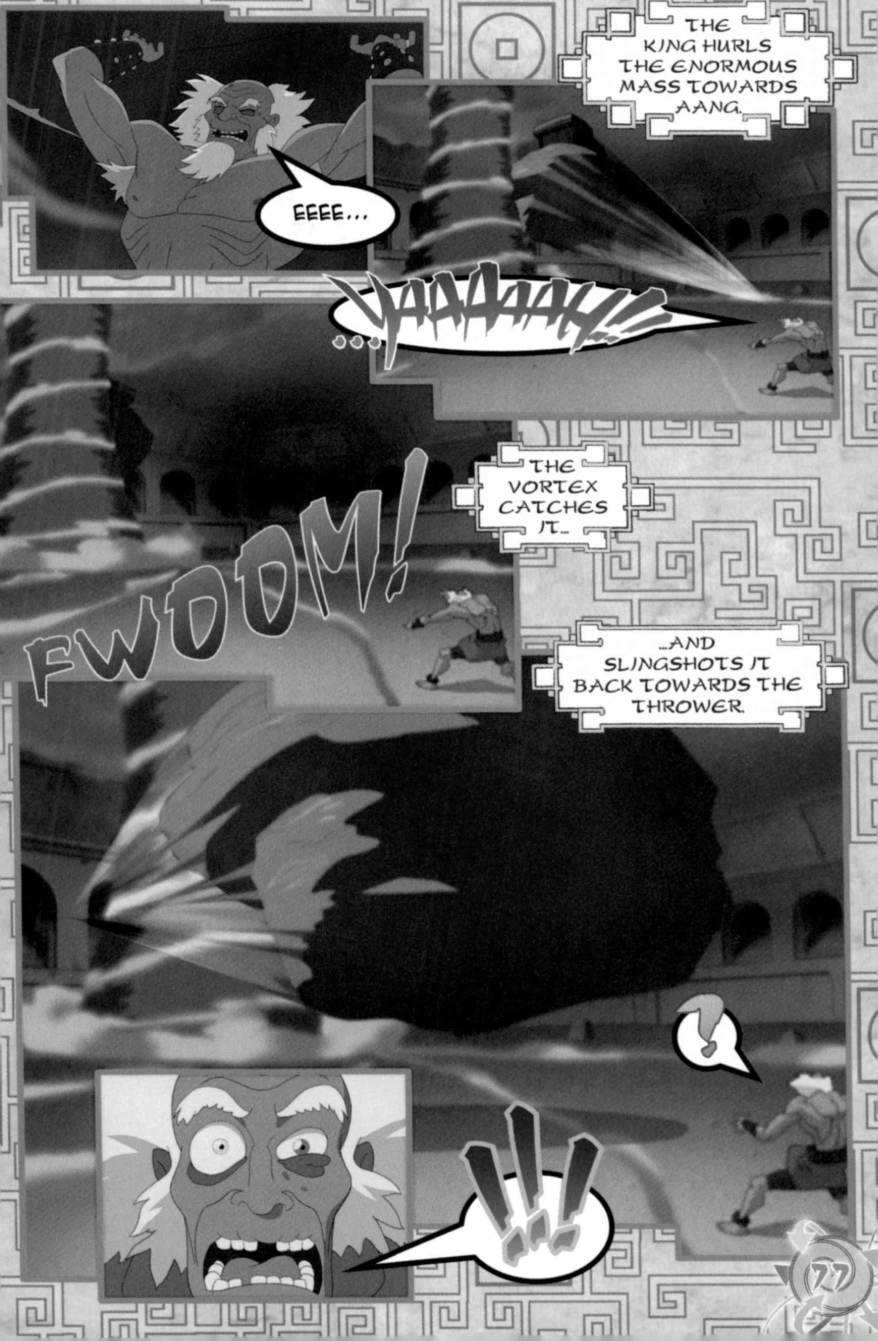
EEEE...
THE KING HURLS THE ENORMOUS MASS TOWARDS AANG.
...YAAAAAH!!
THE VORTEX CATCHES IT...
FWOOM!
...AND SLINGSHOTS IT BACK TOWARDS THE THROWER.
!!!

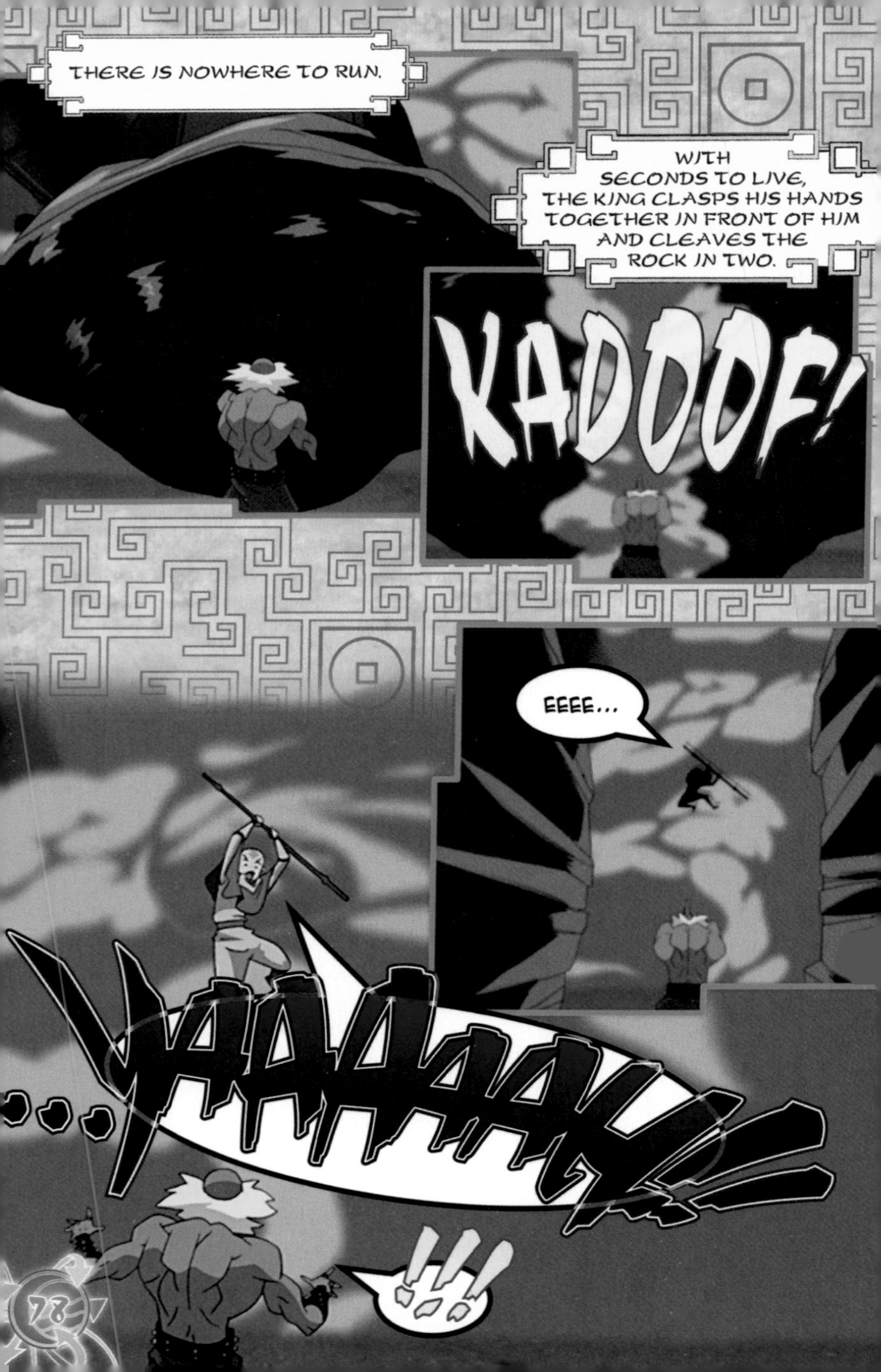
THERE IS NOWHERE TO RUN.
WITH SECONDS TO LIVE, THE KING CLASPS HIS HANDS TOGETHER IN FRONT OF HIM AND CLEAVES THE ROCK IN TWO.
KADOOF!
EEEE...
...YAAAAAH!!
!!!

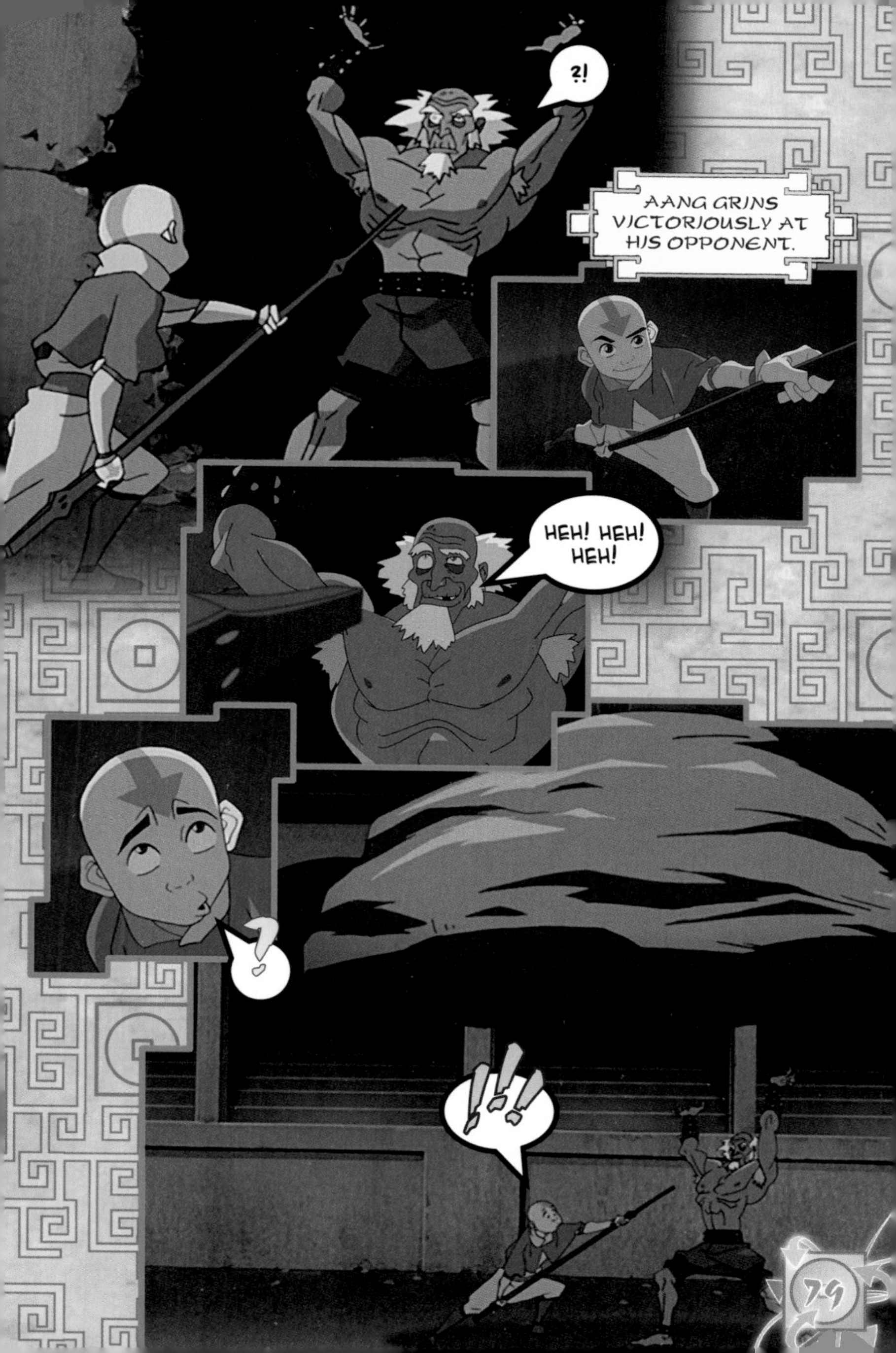
?!
AANG GRINS VICTORIOUSLY AT HIS OPPONENT.
HEH! HEH! HEH!

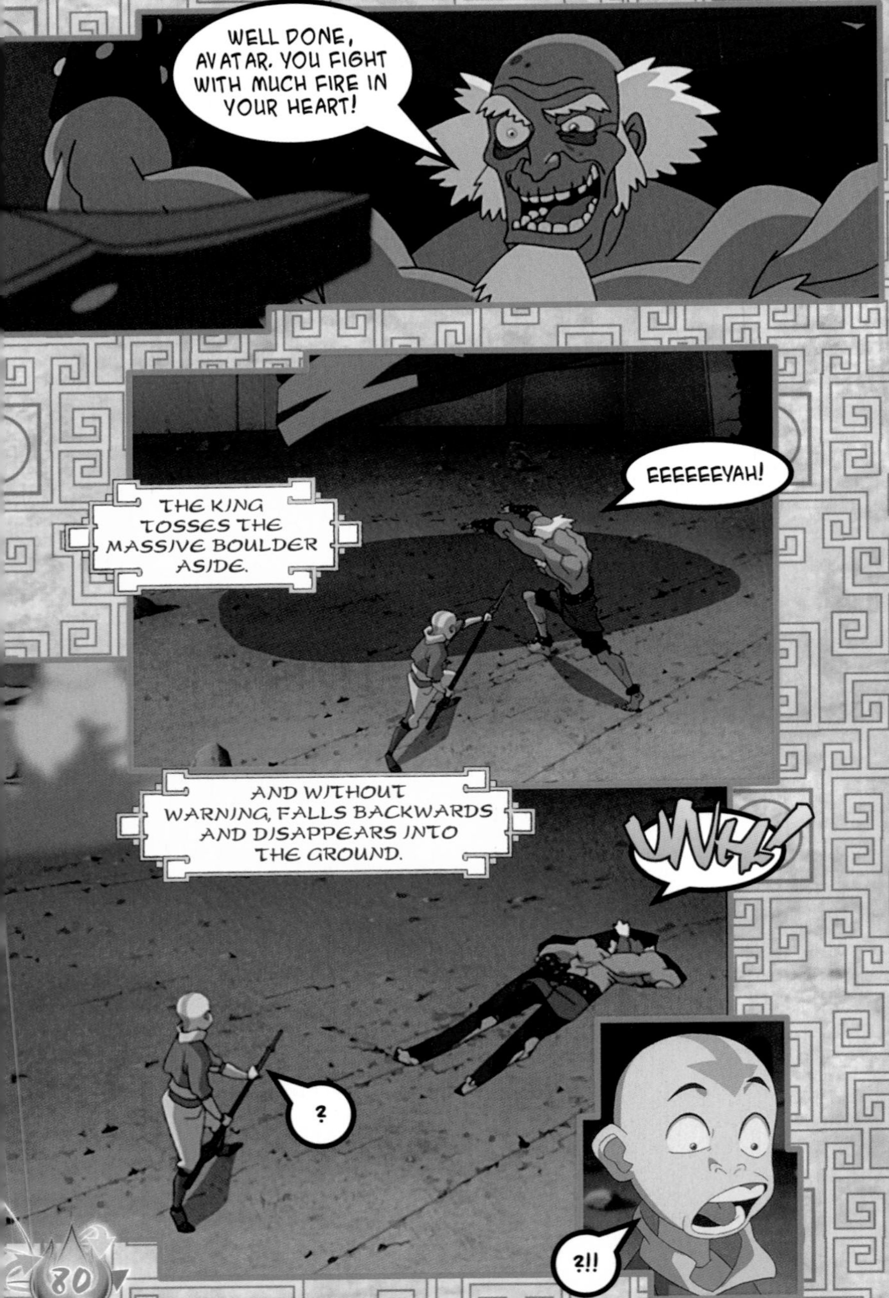
WELL DONE, AVATAR. YOU FIGHT WITH MUCH FIRE IN YOUR HEART!
THE KING TOSSES THE MASSIVE BOULDER ASIDE.
EEEEEEYAH!
AND WITHOUT WARNING, FALLS BACKWARDS AND DISAPPEARS INTO THE GROUND.
UNH!
?
?!!

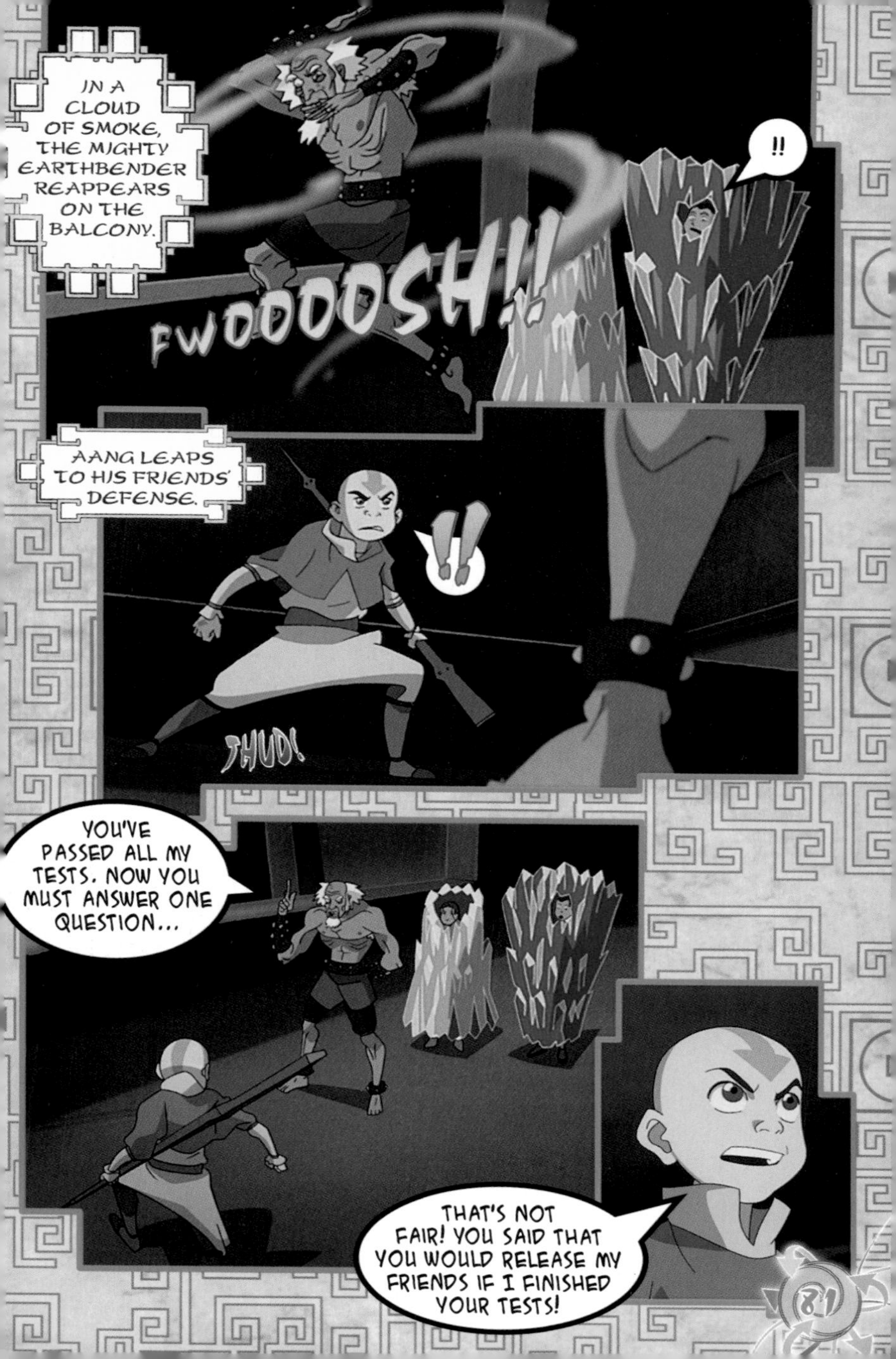
IN A CLOUD OF SMOKE, THE MIGHTY EARTHBENDER REAPPEARS ON THE BALCONY.
!!
FWOOOOSH!!
AANG LEAPS TO HIS FRIENDS' DEFENSE.
!!
THUD!
YOU'VE PASSED ALL MY TESTS. NOW YOU MUST ANSWER ONE QUESTION...
THAT'S NOT FAIR! YOU SAID THAT YOU WOULD RELEASE MY FRIENDS IF I FINISHED YOUR TESTS!

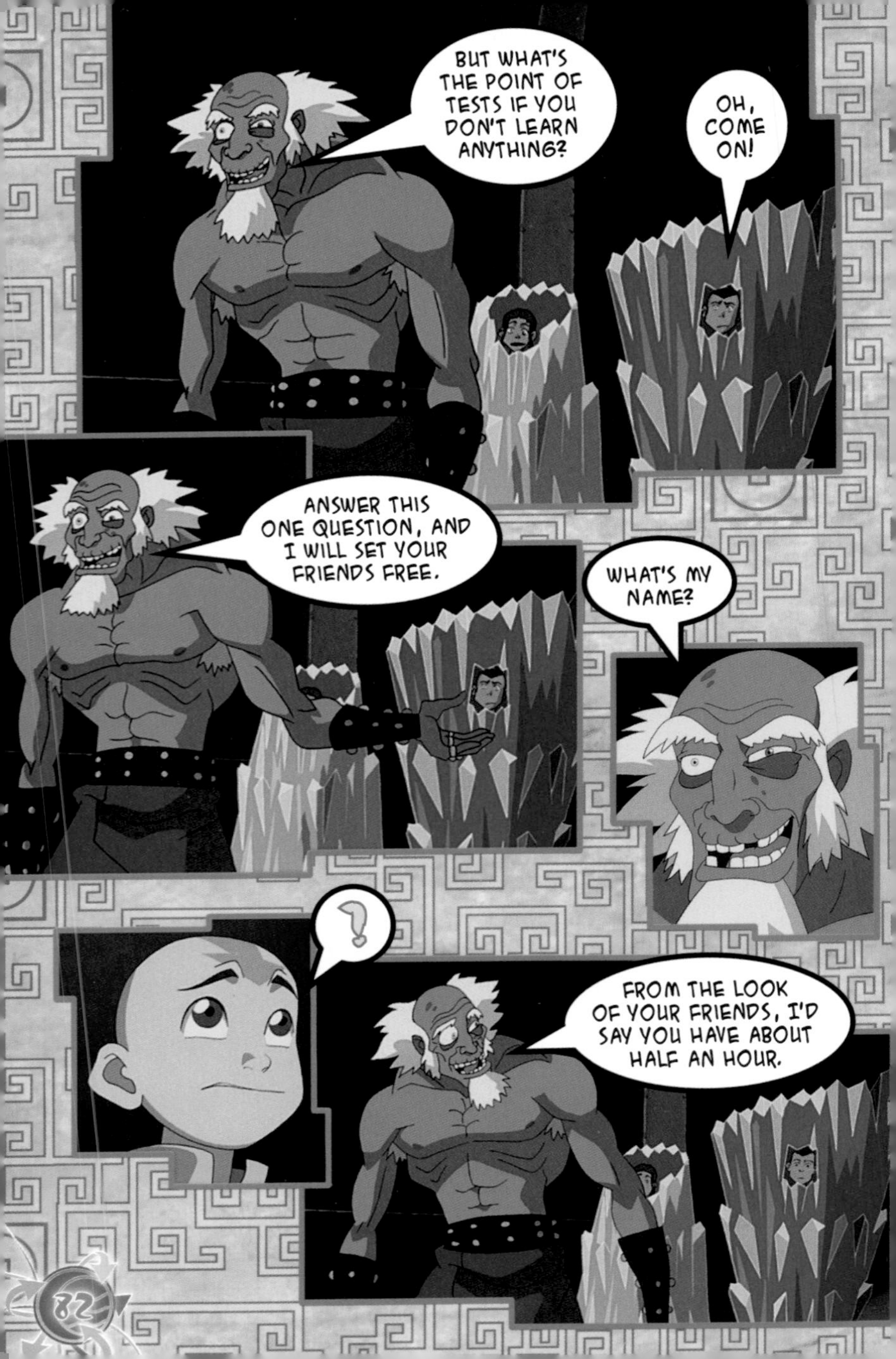
BUT WHAT'S THE POINT OF TESTS IF YOU DON'T LEARN ANYTHING?
OH, COME ON!
ANSWER THIS ONE QUESTION, AND I WILL SET YOUR FRIENDS FREE.
WHAT'S MY NAME?
?!
FROM THE LOOK OF YOUR FRIENDS, I'D SAY YOU HAVE ABOUT HALF AN HOUR.

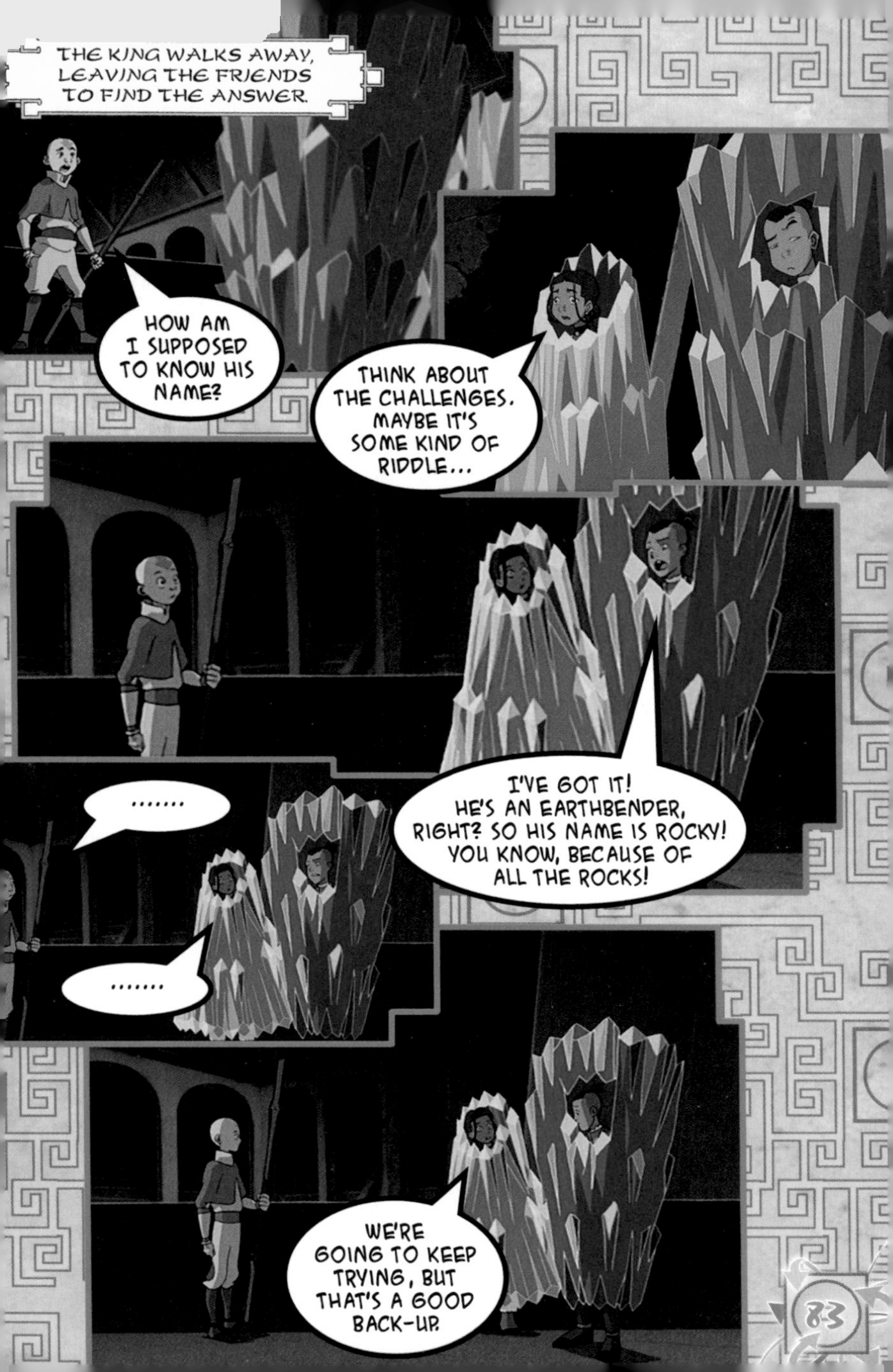

THE KING WALKS AWAY, LEAVING THE FRIENDS TO FIND THE ANSWER.
HOW AM I SUPPOSED TO KNOW HIS NAME?
THINK ABOUT THE CHALLENGES. MAYBE IT'S SOME KIND OF RIDDLE...
I'VE GOT IT! HE'S AN EARTHBENDER, RIGHT? SO HIS NAME IS ROCKY! YOU KNOW, BECAUSE OF ALL THE ROCKS!
....
....
WE'RE GOING TO KEEP TRYING, BUT THAT'S A GOOD BACK-UP.

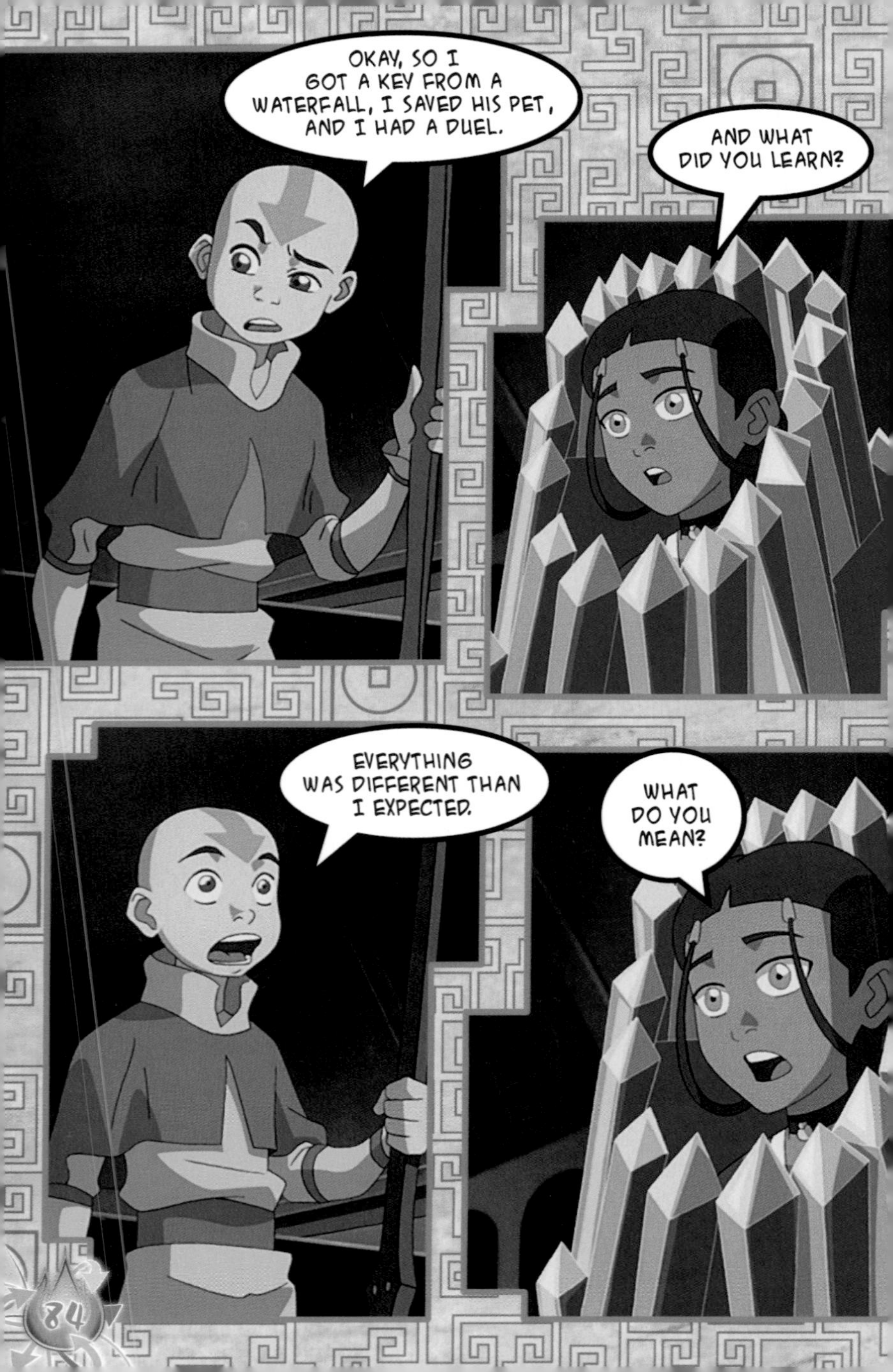
OKAY, SO I GOT A KEY FROM A WATERFALL, I SAVED HIS PET, AND I HAD A DUEL.
AND WHAT DID YOU LEARN?
EVERYTHING WAS DIFFERENT THAN I EXPECTED.
WHAT DO YOU MEAN?

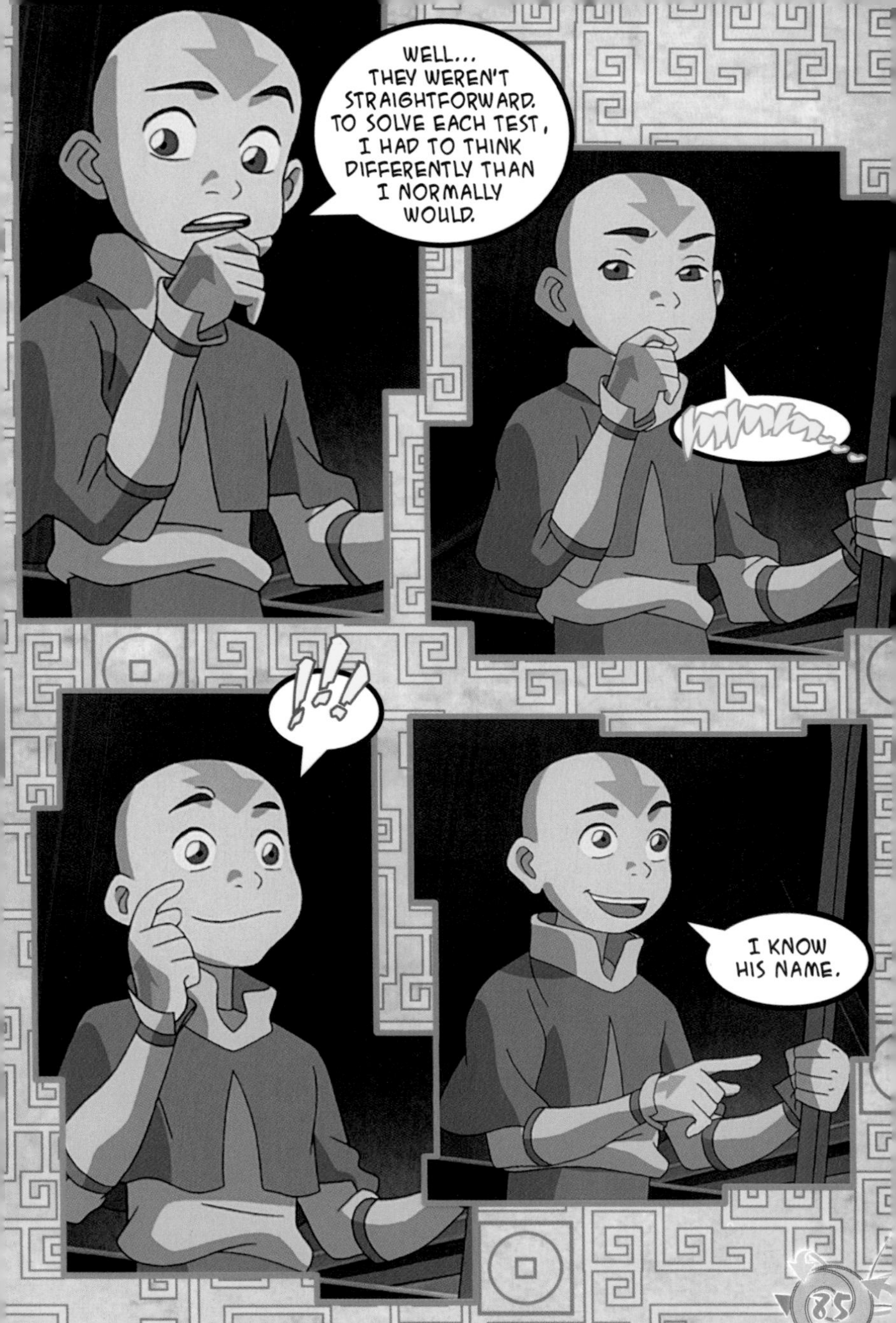
WELL... THEY WEREN'T STRAIGHTFORWARD. TO SOLVE EACH TEST, I HAD TO THINK DIFFERENTLY THAN I NORMALLY WOULD.
Mmmm...
!!!
I KNOW HIS NAME.

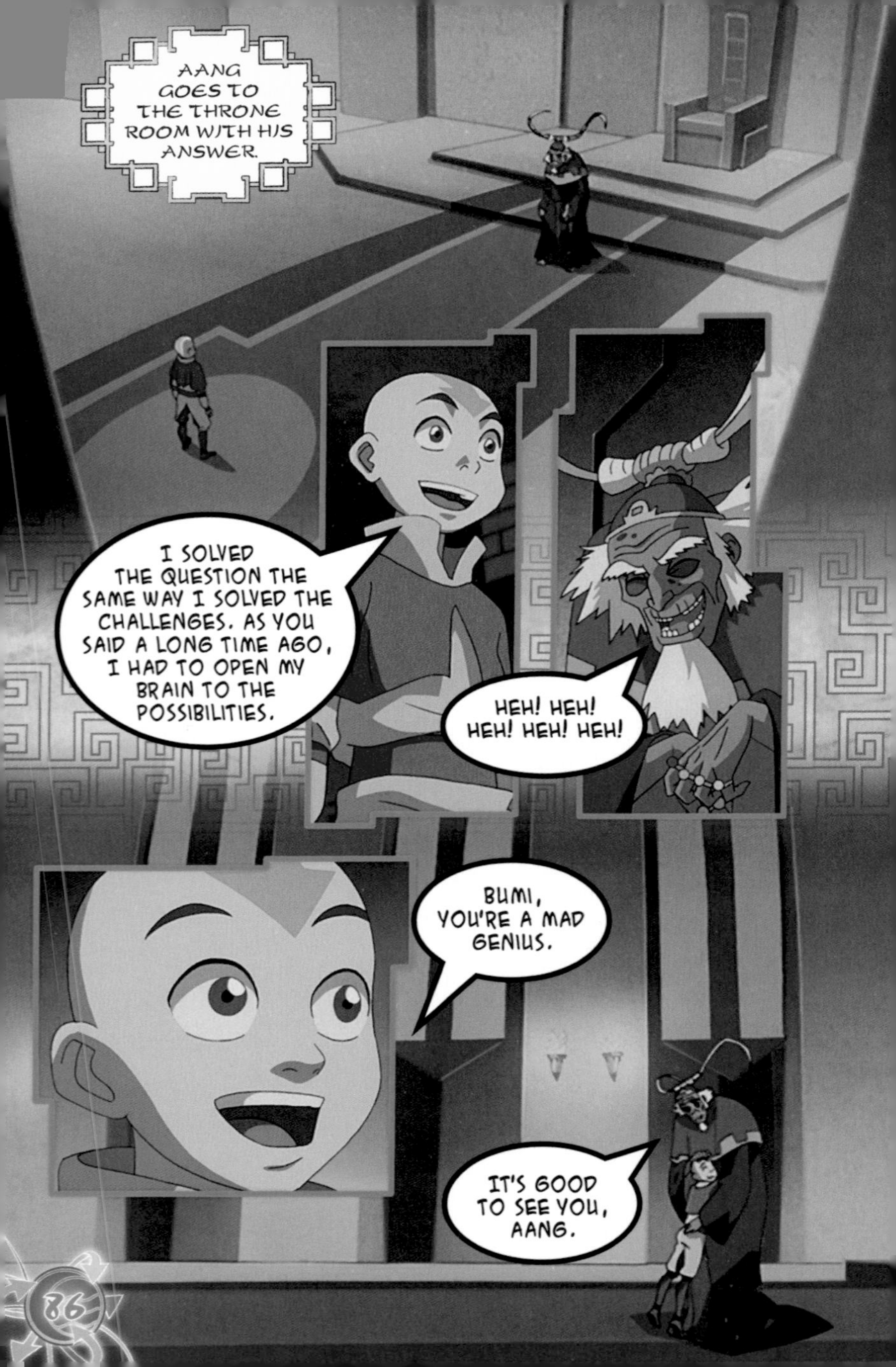
AANG GOES TO THE THRONE ROOM WITH HIS ANSWER.
I SOLVED THE QUESTION THE SAME WAY I SOLVED THE CHALLENGES. AS YOU SAID A LONG TIME AGO, I HAD TO OPEN MY BRAIN TO THE POSSIBILITIES.
HEH! HEH! HEH! HEH! HEH!
BUMI, YOU'RE A MAD GENIUS.
IT'S GOOD TO SEE YOU, AANG.

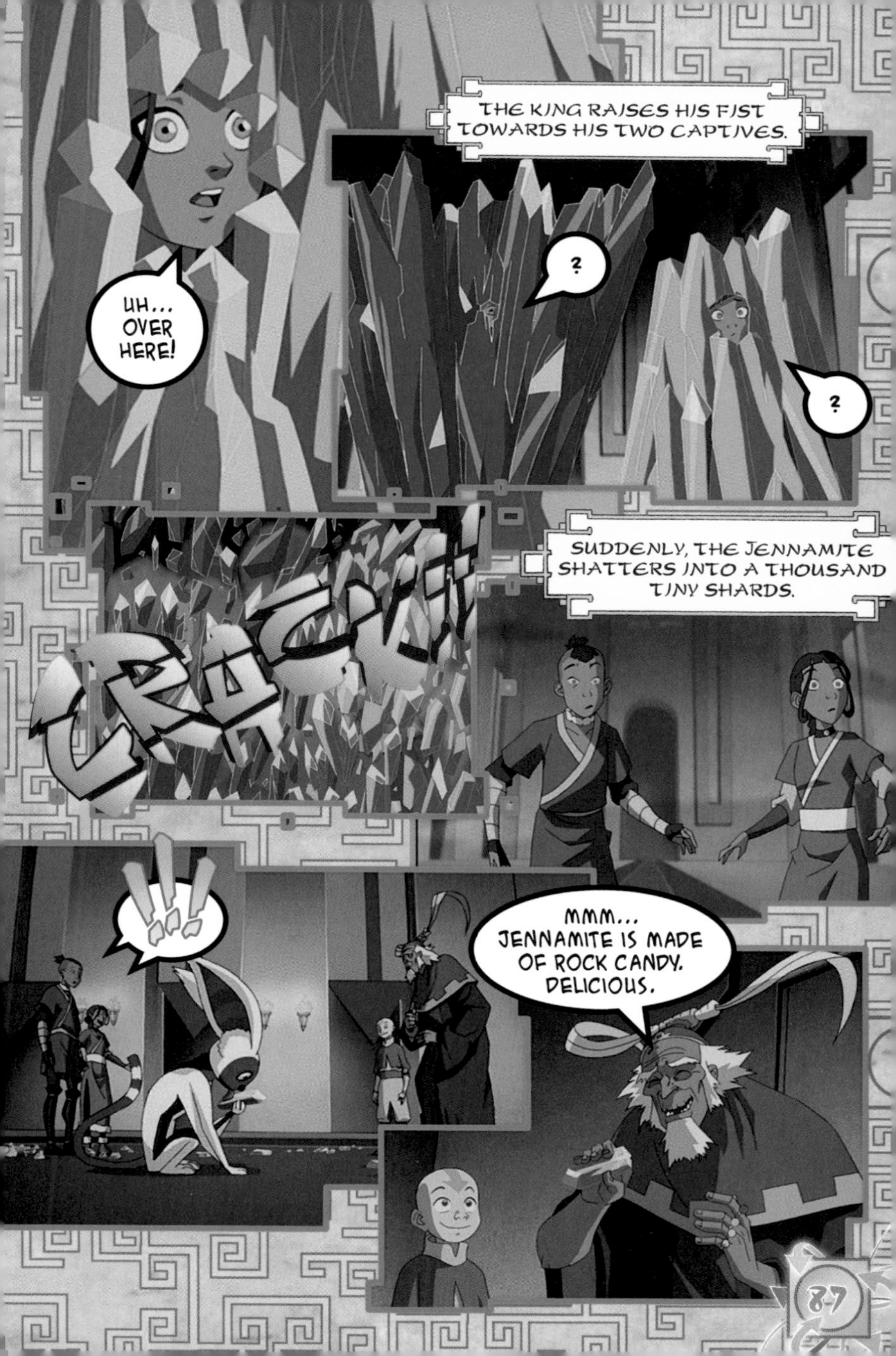
UH... OVER HERE!
THE KING RAISES HIS FIST TOWARDS HIS TWO CAPTIVES.
?
?
CRACK!
SUDDENLY, THE JENNAMITE SHATTERS INTO A THOUSAND TINY SHARDS.
!!!
MMM... JENNAMITE IS MADE OF ROCK CANDY. DELICIOUS.
87

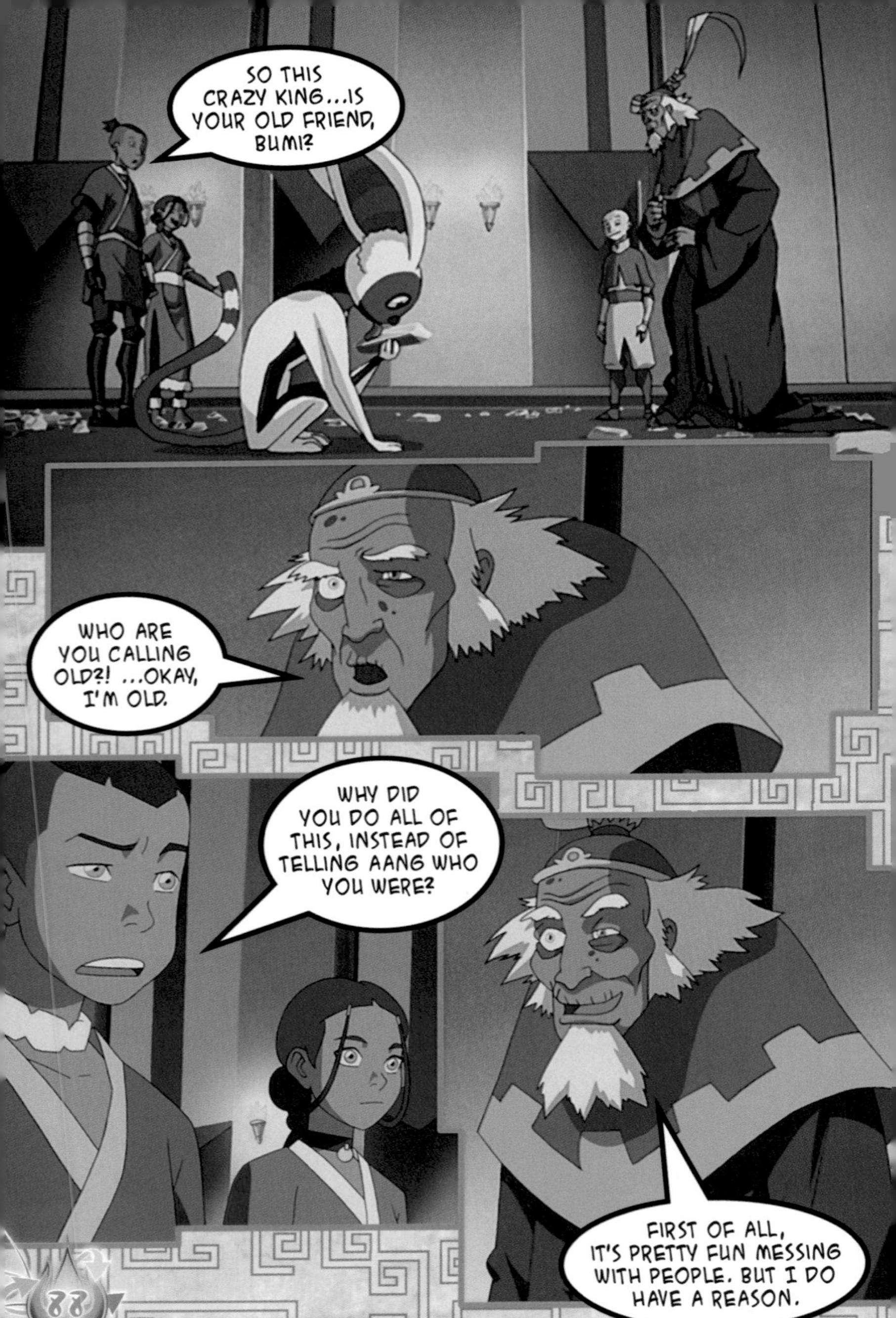
SO THIS CRAZY KING...IS YOUR OLD FRIEND, BUMI?
WHO ARE YOU CALLING OLD?! ...OKAY, I'M OLD.
WHY DID YOU DO ALL OF THIS, INSTEAD OF TELLING AANG WHO YOU WERE?
FIRST OF ALL, IT'S PRETTY FUN MESSING WITH PEOPLE. BUT I DO HAVE A REASON.

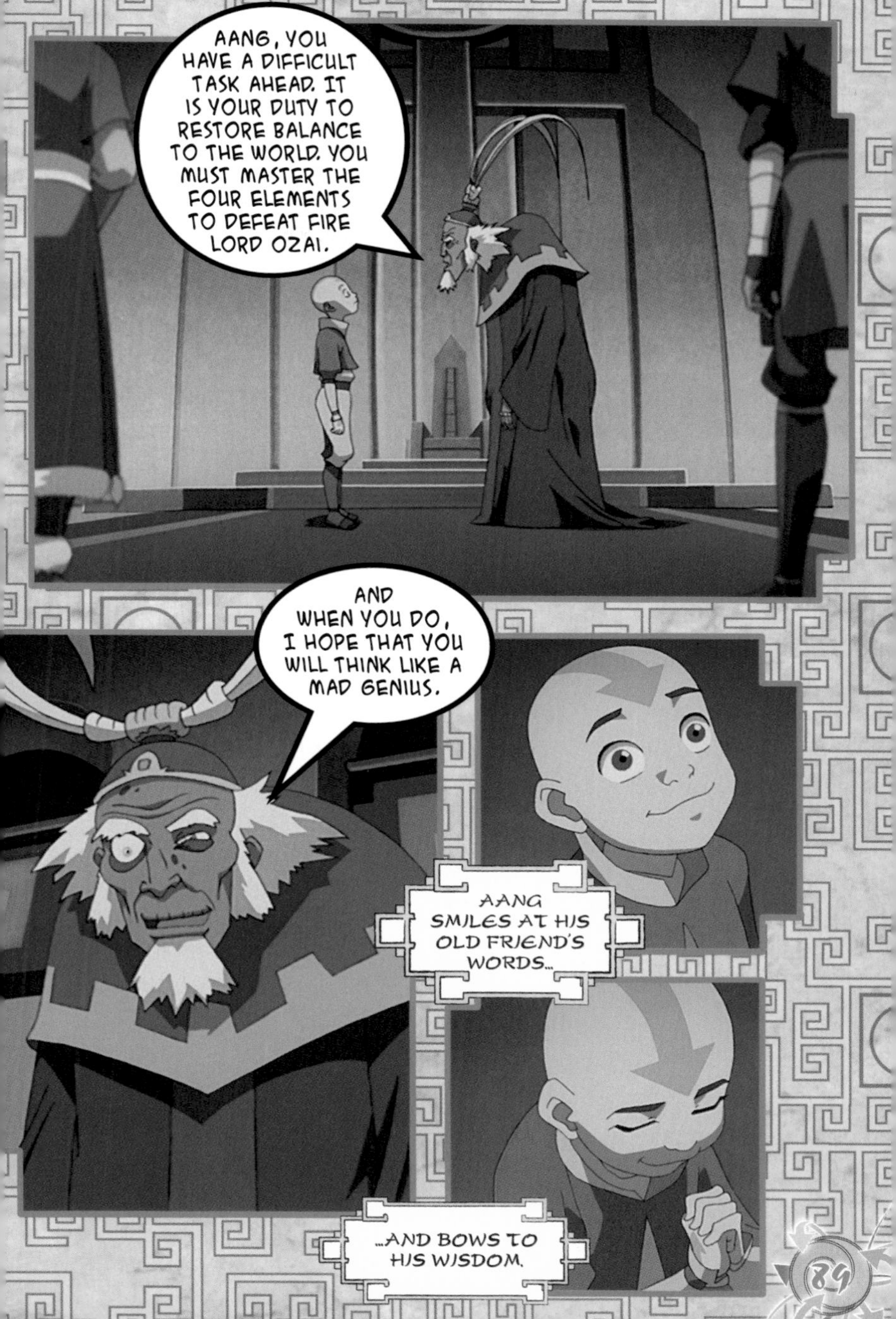
AANG, YOU HAVE A DIFFICULT TASK AHEAD. IT IS YOUR DUTY TO RESTORE BALANCE TO THE WORLD. YOU MUST MASTER THE FOUR ELEMENTS TO DEFEAT FIRE LORD OZAI.
AND WHEN YOU DO, I HOPE THAT YOU WILL THINK LIKE A MAD GENIUS.
AANG SMILES AT HIS OLD FRIEND'S WORDS...
...AND BOWS TO HIS WISDOM.

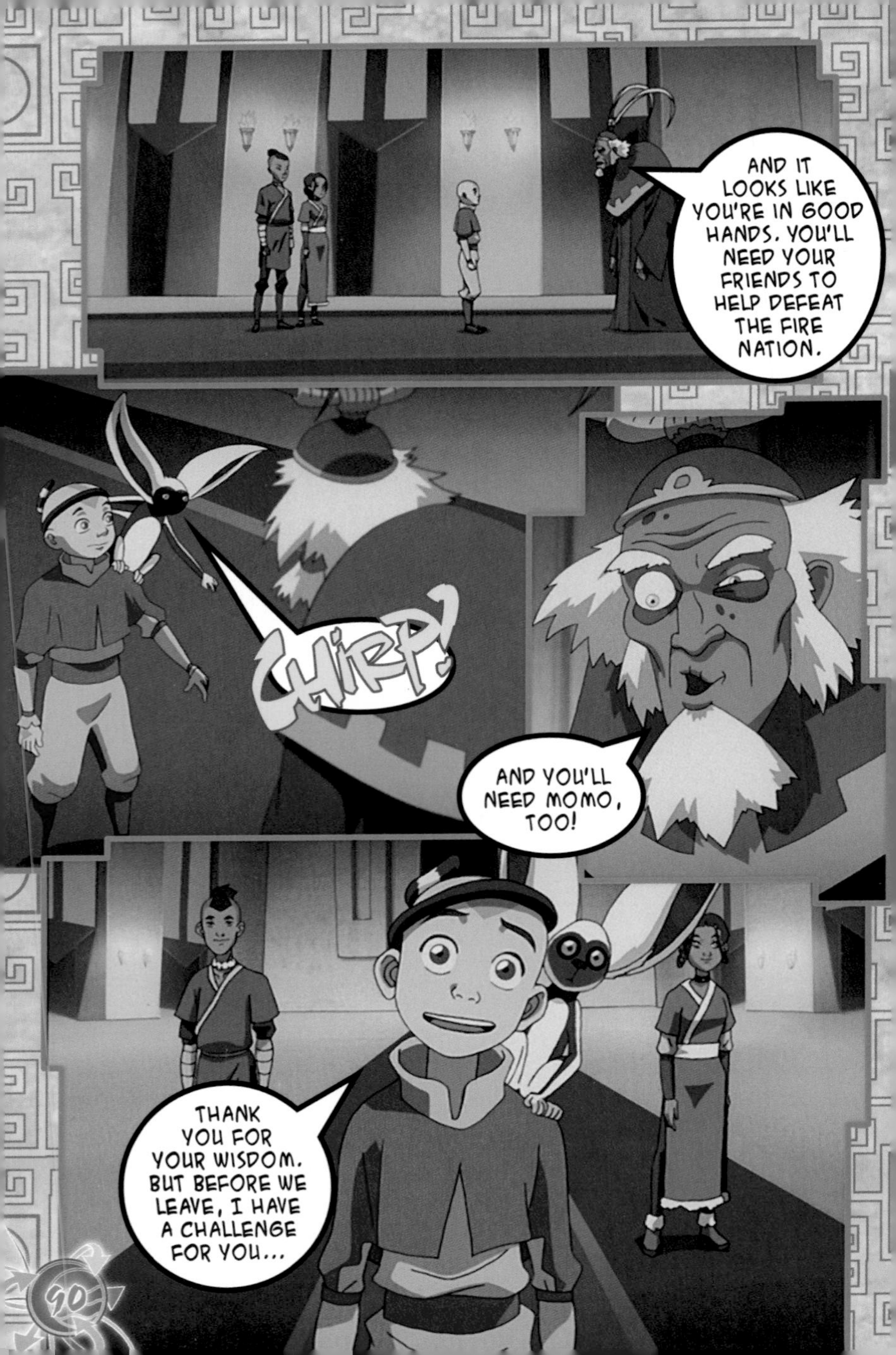
AND IT LOOKS LIKE YOU'RE IN GOOD HANDS. YOU'LL NEED YOUR FRIENDS TO HELP DEFEAT THE FIRE NATION.
CHIRP!
AND YOU'LL NEED MOMO, TOO!
THANK YOU FOR YOUR WISDOM. BUT BEFORE WE LEAVE, I HAVE A CHALLENGE FOR YOU...

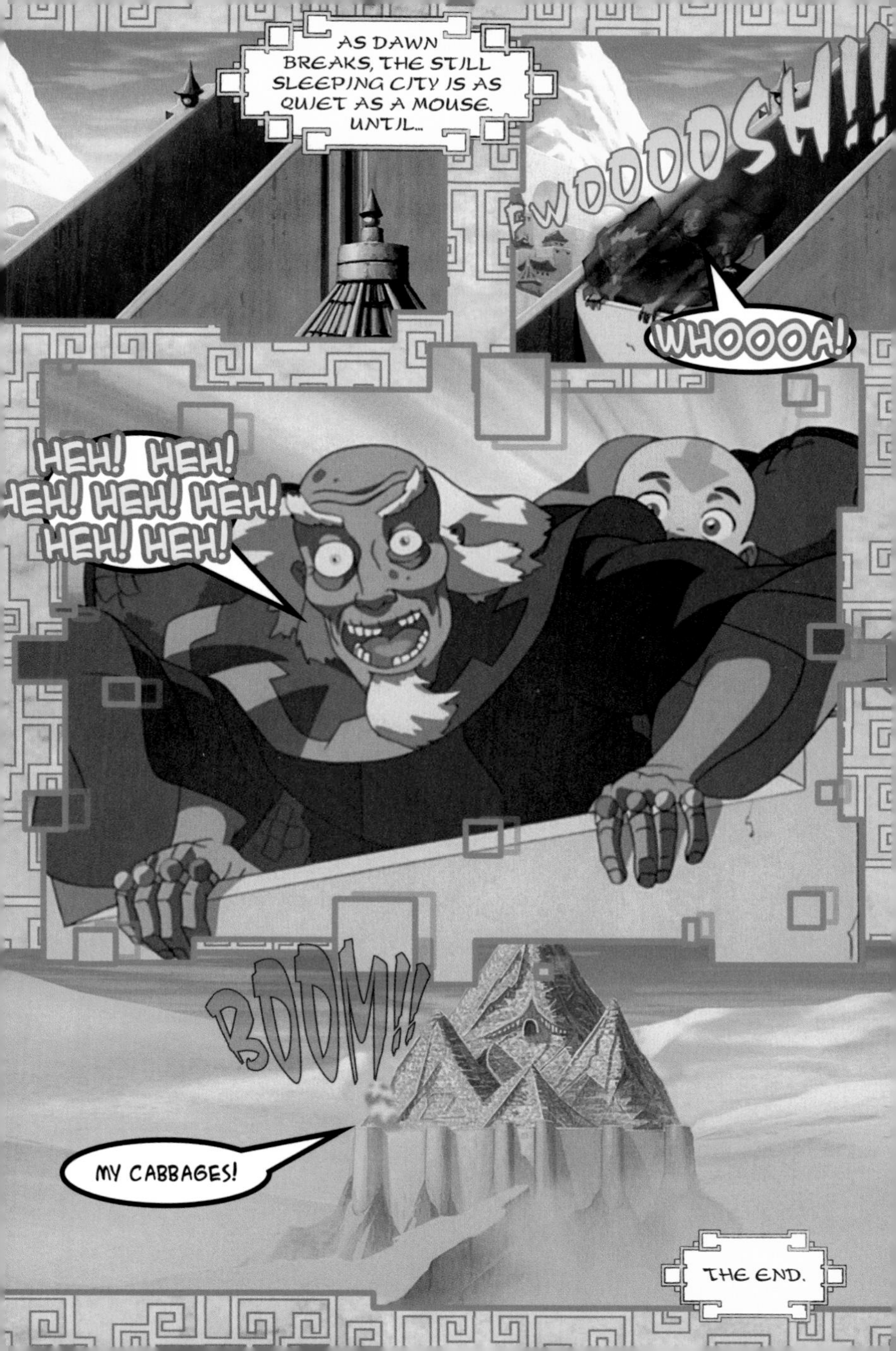
AS DAWN BREAKS, THE STILL SLEEPING CITY IS AS QUIET AS A MOUSE. UNTIL...
FWOOOOOSH!!!
WHOOOOA!
HEH! HEH! HEH! HEH! HEH! HEH! HEH!
BOOM!!
MY CABBAGES!
THE END.

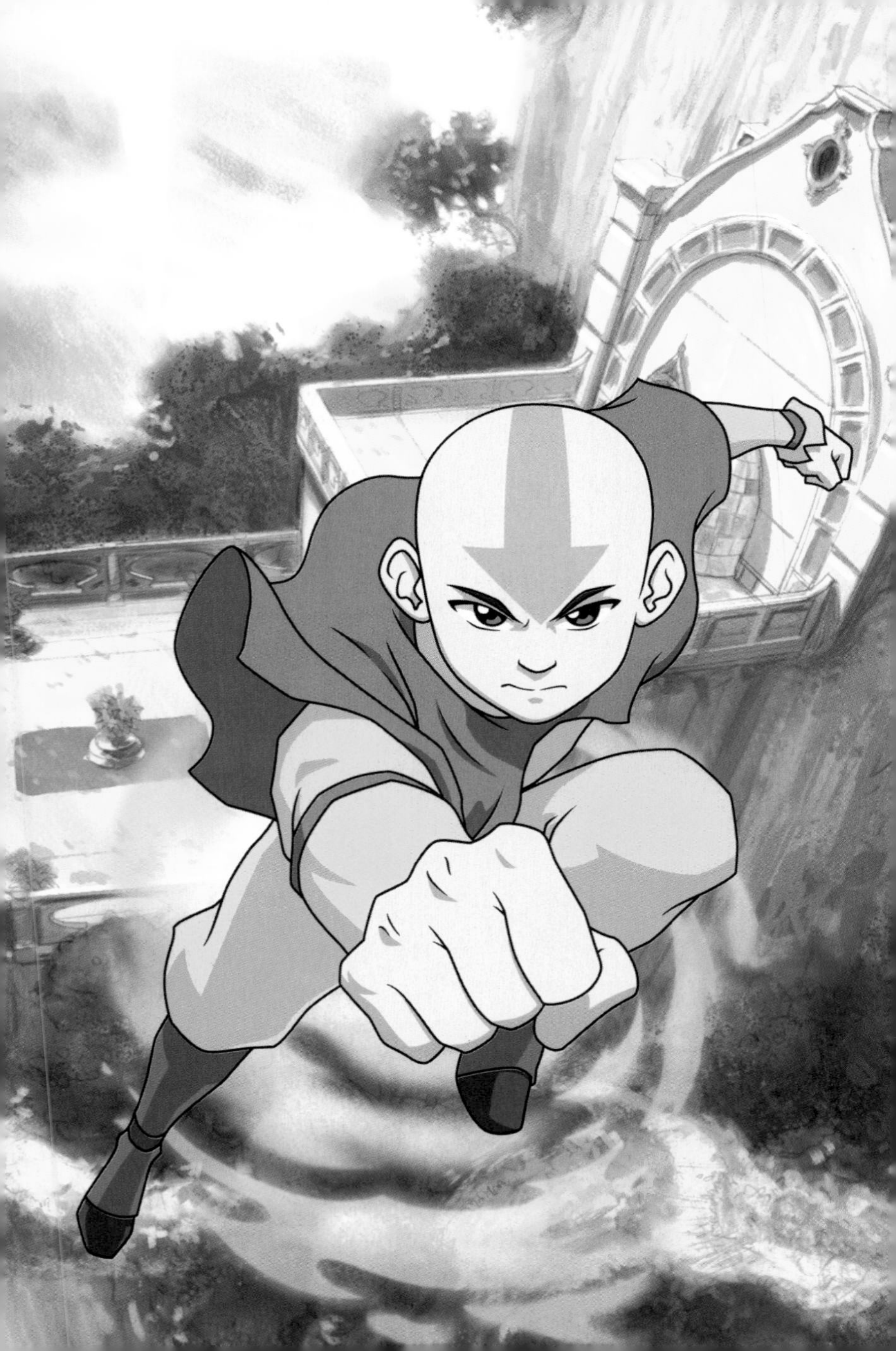

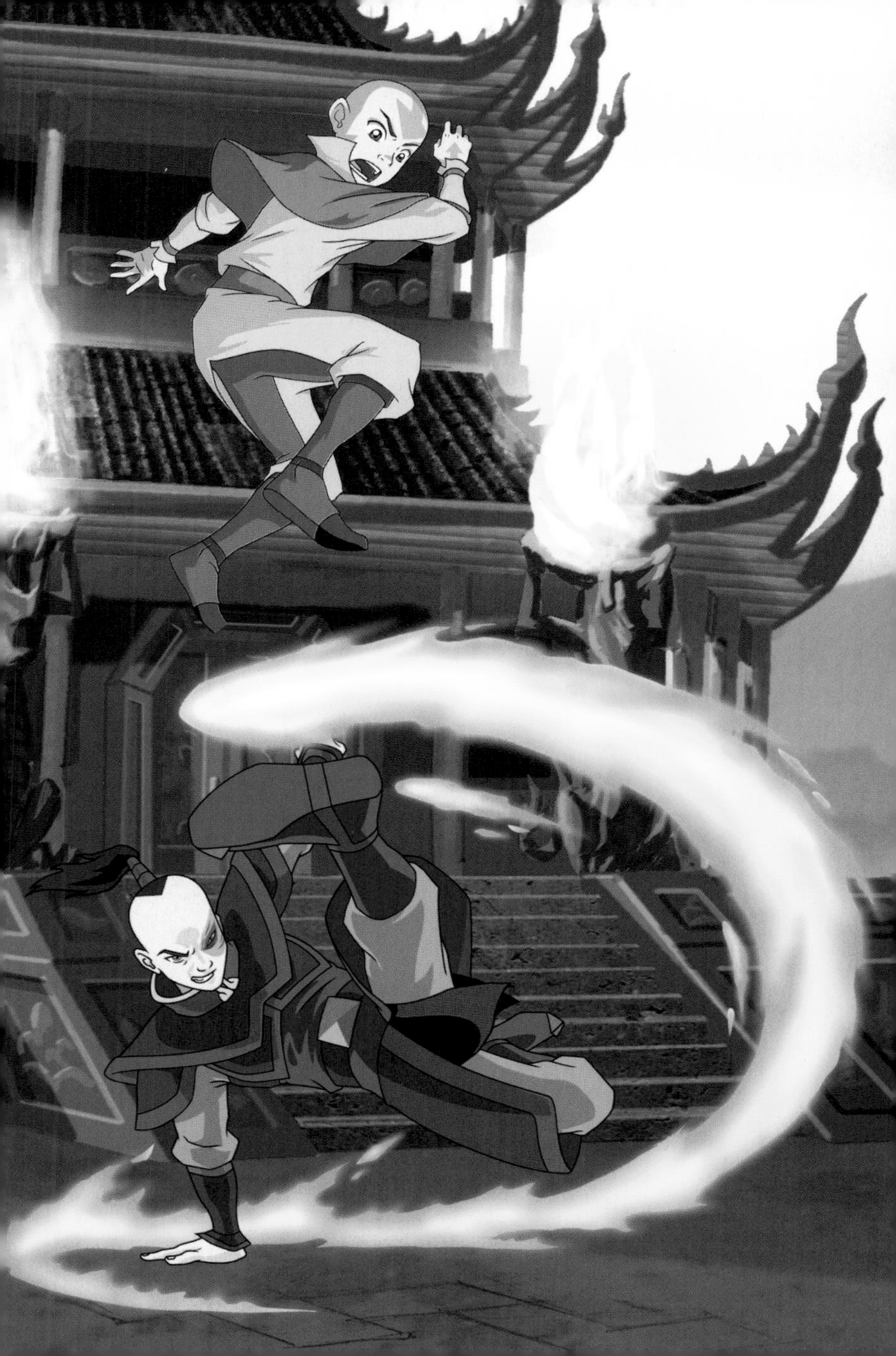

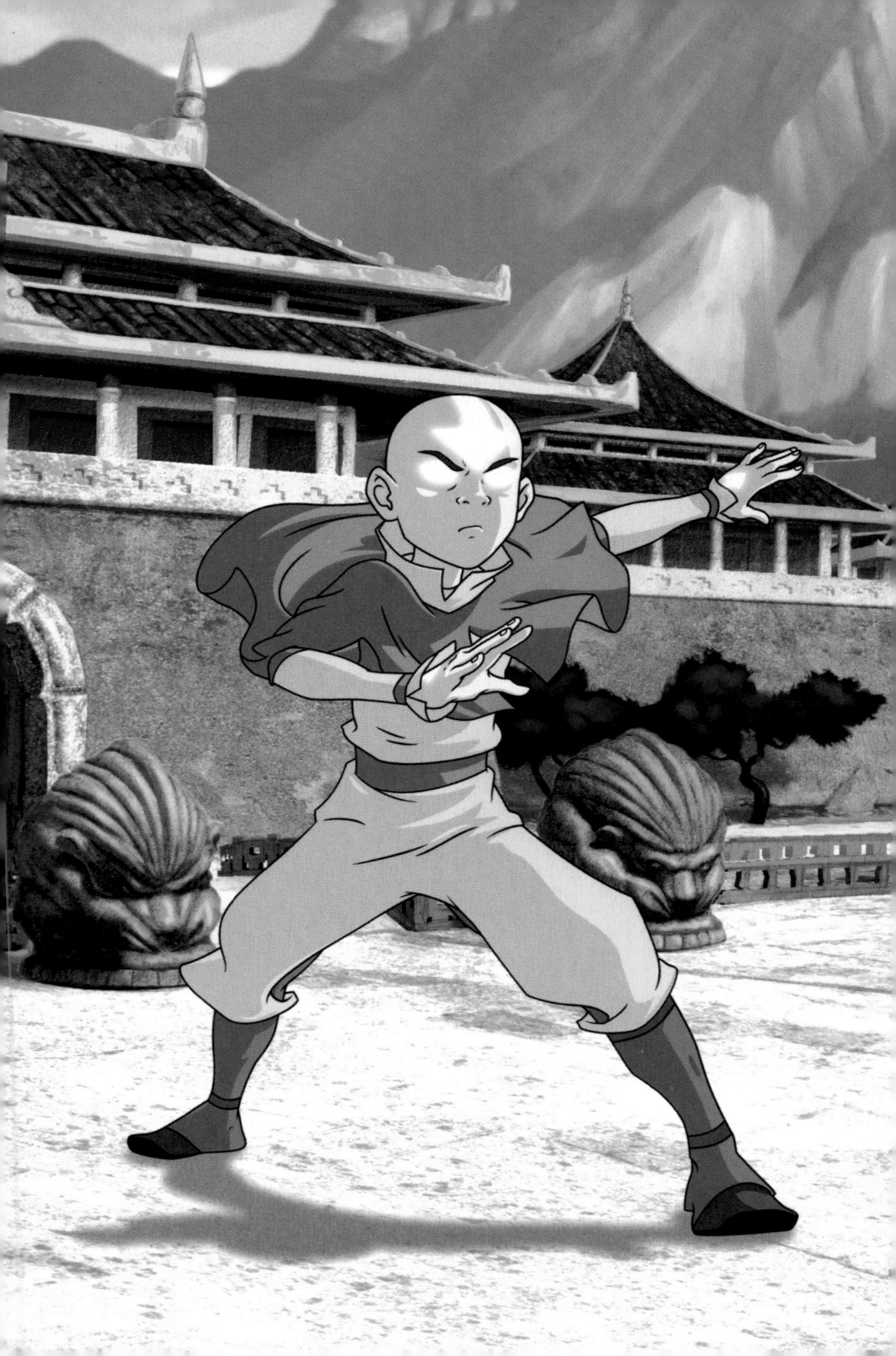

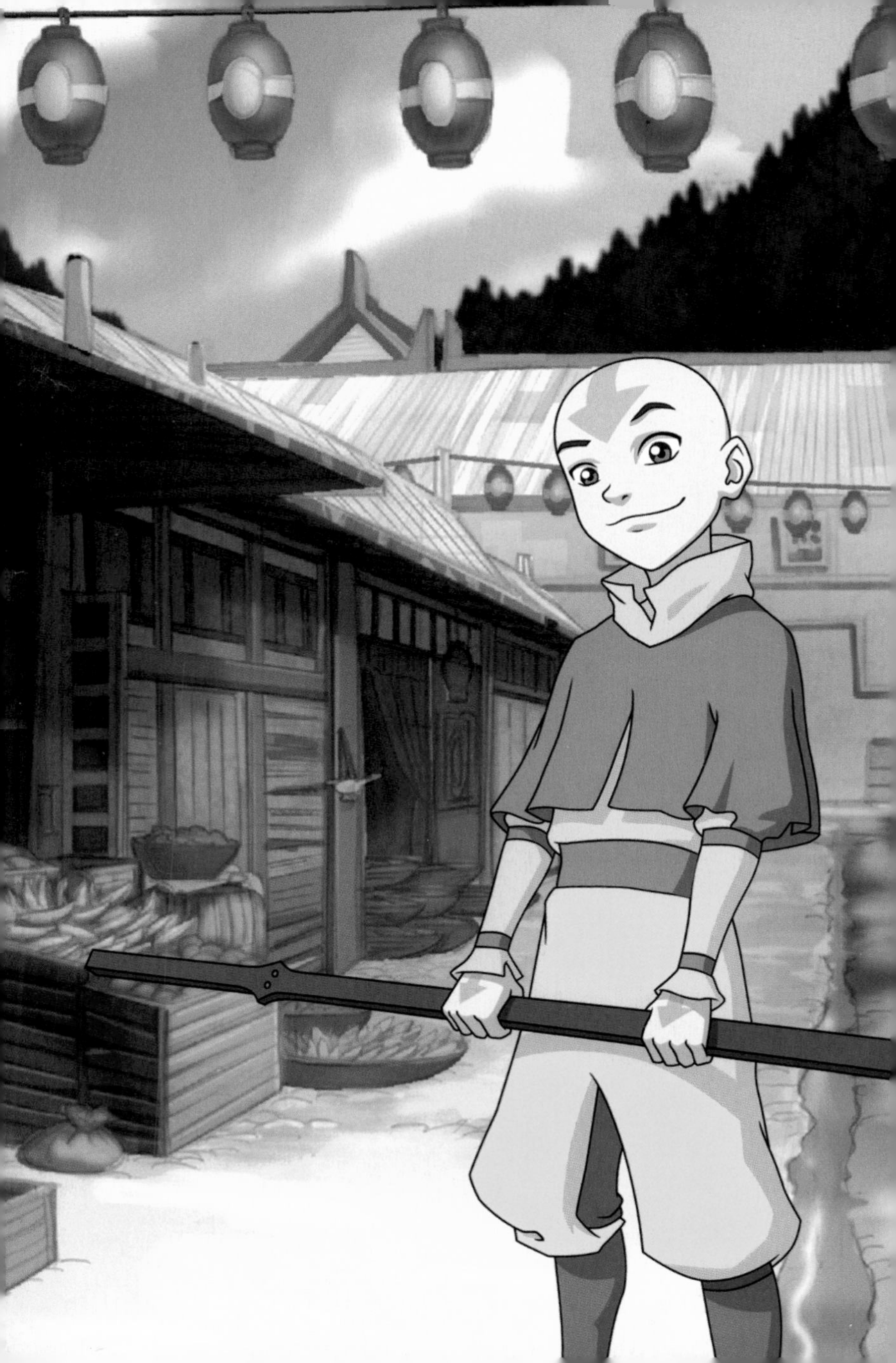

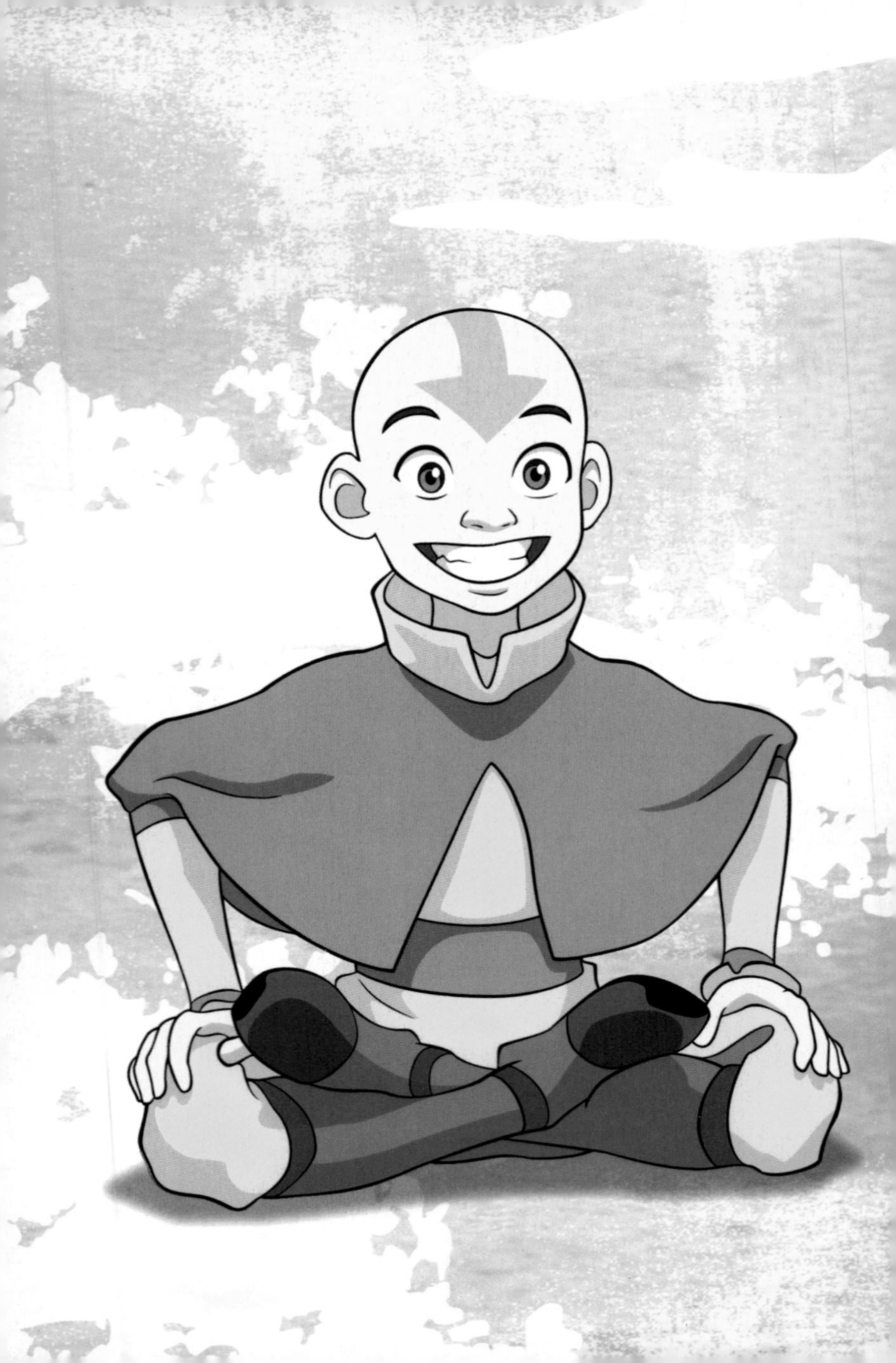

NICKELODEON™

降去神通 AVATAR

THE LAST AIRBENDER™

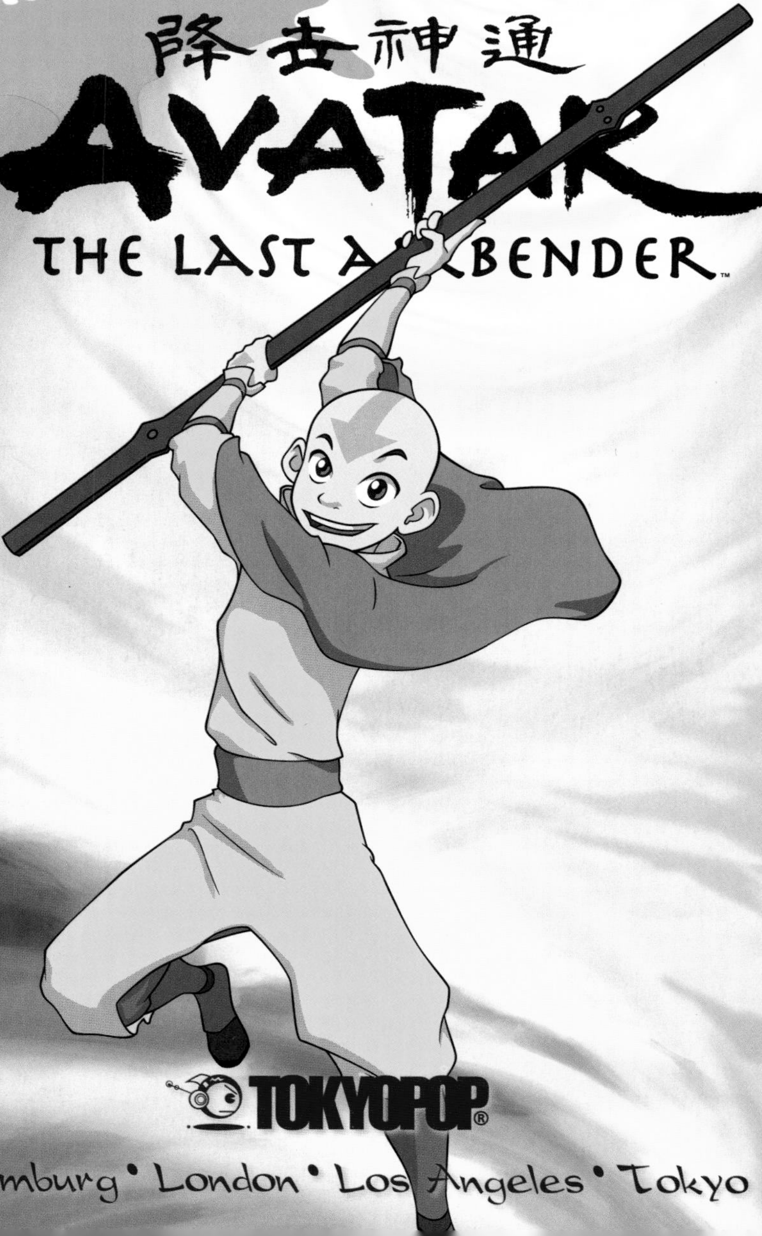

TOKYOPOP®

Hamburg • London • Los Angeles • Tokyo

Contributing Editor - Robert Langhorn
Associate Editor - Katherine Schilling
Cover Designer - Monalisa J. de Asis
Graphic Designer, Letterer - Tomás Montalvo-Lagos

Digital Imaging Manager - Chris Buford
Production Managers - Elisabeth Brizzi
Senior Designer - Christian Lownds
Senior Editor - Julie Taylor
Managing Editor - Vy Nguyen
Editor in Chief - Rob Tokar
VP of Production - Ron Klamert
Publisher - Mike Kiley
President & C.O.O. - John Parker
C.E.O. & Chief Creative Officer - Stuart Levy

E-mail: info@TOKYOPOP.com
Come visit us online at www.TOKYOPOP.com

A **TOKYOPOP** Cine-Manga® Book
TOKYOPOP Inc.
5900 Wilshire Blvd., Suite 2000
Los Angeles, CA 90036

Avatar: The Last Airbender Chapter 5

ISBN: 978-1-4278-0779-3

First TOKYOPOP® printing: June 2007

10 9 8 7 6 5 4 3 2 1

Printed in the USA